CHARLATAN

CATHERINE JINKS

CHARLATAN

THE DISHONEST LIFE AND DISHONOURED LOVES OF THOMAS GUTHRIE CARR, STAGE MESMERIST

VINTAGE BOOKS
Australia

A Vintage book
Published by Penguin Random House Australia Pty Ltd
Level 3, 100 Pacific Highway, North Sydney NSW 2060
www.penguin.com.au

Penguin Random House Australia

First published by Vintage in 2017

Addresses for the Penguin Random House group of companies can be found at global.penguinrandomhouse.com/offices.

Jinks, Catherine, 1963–
Charlatan/Catherine Jinks.

ISBN: 978 0 14378 554 5

Carr, Thomas Guthrie – Trials, litigation, etc.
Gray, Eliza.
Trials (Rape) – Australia – 19th century.
Examination of witnesses – Australia.
Australia – Social life and customs – 19th century.

Cover images: man's face © Illustrated London News, 1885;
clock © Empire City Watch Co.
Cover design by Blue Cork
Typeset in Bembo by Midland Typesetters, Australia
Printed in Australia by Griffin Press, an accredited ISO AS/NZS 14001:2004 Environmental Management System printer

Penguin Random House Australia uses papers that are natural, renewable and recyclable products and made from wood grown in sustainable forests. The logging and manufacturing processes are expected to conform to the environmental regulations of the country of origin.

To Peter Dockrill

PREFACE

Long ago in Moodus, Connecticut, a businessman named Frank Chester Fowler concocted a patent medicine called 'Dr Rudolphe's Specific Remedy'. He claimed that it cured 'the effects of youthful errors, seminal weakness, spermatorrhea, lost manhood, nervous debility, early decay, loss of memory, impotence, gonorrhoea, gleet and premature old age'. By 1894 Fowler was calling himself Professor F C Fowler. By 1896 he had published a book.

The book was entitled *Life: How to Enjoy It and How to Prolong It*. A photograph on the first page showed a round-headed man with a luxuriant moustache and a very slight cast in one eye. This was supposed to be a portrait of Professor F C Fowler, aged forty-one, 'taken many years ago'.

At the time of publication Fowler was just thirty-seven years old.

A large portion of his work was devoted to the evils of masturbation, which, he wrote, would turn young men into eunuchs. But Fowler also castigated the plague of swindlers who, in flooding the country with pamphlets and circulars, were 'prompted by a benevolent desire to warn young men of the terrible consequences of self abuse etc. and *get their money*'. Fowler's stated purpose in writing his manual was to protect the public from such unprincipled quacks. Measured by its contents, he added, the book was cheap at five dollars. And Fowler himself could always be consulted (in perfect confidence) by anyone suffering from those complaints that 'gnaw and prey upon the mind, body etc., of the person so afflicted'.

His book covered a lot of ground, from Manhood to Psychology. Fowler even explored the subject of animal magnetism. All well-sexed men and women, he said, were possessed of great magnetic power – which would diminish with any loss of sexual power. As an example he cited the case of Walter Montgomery, the actor, who lost his ability to control others when deprived of his mojo and subsequently shot himself.

Then Fowler mentioned Thomas Guthrie Carr:

> *Dr. Carr, who recently died, as it is supposed, from an overdose of morphia at Glen Innes, Australia, was an example of a man with tremendous sexual power. Few men or women could withstand his magnetic influence; but as his sexual power failed he lost his power as a mesmerist . . .*

By the time this was written, Carr had been dead for nearly ten years. Yet his name had surfaced half a world away, in an obscure tract by a self-proclaimed 'physiognomist' who had never set foot outside the United States. Clearly, Carr possessed a singular reputation. Twenty years earlier, a New Zealand clergyman had brought a libel action against a journalist named Richard Sherrin, largely because Sherrin had likened him to Thomas Guthrie Carr. In a letter to the *Waitangi Tribune*, Sherrin had accused both men of being birds of prey. He had described Carr as a charlatan, and had made reference to the mesmerist's unfortunate sexual history. Dismissing with ponderous sarcasm the notion that Carr might be a womaniser, Sherrin had protested, 'Woman is his divinity and to her shrine he constantly does homage . . . he cares not for these things.'

It could be argued that Carr's bad name stemmed from a single court case that occurred way back in 1868. But close study betrays hints of a fairly tumultuous personal life. As for his occupation, *that* can't have helped matters. Mesmerists had been regarded with suspicion ever since Franz Mesmer had published his findings on 'animal magnetism' towards the end of the eighteenth century. Mesmer was supposed to have unlocked the secret of a magnetic power that allowed him to cure or even stupefy his patients. He'd said he could do this by passing his hands over a patient's body, manipulating its magnetic field in a way that would make his subject insensible to pain. From the very first, however, his new 'science' had become the focus of enormous controversy. Some people had tried to prove that it was fraudulent, some that it was dangerous. Many of the operators who practised it were out-and-out charlatans, as were their subjects; the whole pursuit soon acquired a seedy, permissive aura.

So it's not surprising that mesmerism should have found a niche in frontier colonies like Australia and New Zealand. Between 1851 and 1871, the gold rush caused Australia's population to triple – and among a generous number of rebellious, unprincipled, shiftless, inadequate and frankly disturbed immigrants attracted by the 'wild west' air of the place was a host of struggling entertainers: actors, singers, acrobats, magicians, spirit mediums, preachers, impersonators. Thomas Guthrie Carr was just one of many stage mesmerists who invaded the Antipodes during Queen Victoria's reign. But he made more of an impression than most, thanks to his tireless self-promotion, his endless court cases, and his renowned licentiousness. The question is: was he really as bad as everyone made out? His salacious reputation stemmed from one alleged rape for which he was never convicted – an incident that damaged the cause of mesmerism as much as it damaged him, in the eyes of the public. And the committal hearing that resulted was inconclusive.

Not that there can be any doubt about Thomas Guthrie Carr's character. He was a short-tempered, hypocritical, bombastic, touchy, conceited man. He was a liar and a cheat. He enjoyed humiliating people. He was irrefutably violent.

It's possible, however, that he wasn't a rapist. Because if he *was* a rapist, then he couldn't have been a fraud.

PART I

THE INCIDENT

I

In 1867, a journalist named Frederick Wilson published an account of his visit to Sydney's Central Police Court, on George Street.

At the time, George Street was the main artery of the city, an endless succession of well-lit and well-supplied shops. The police court stood between Druitt, George and York streets. On one side of it lay Sydney's covered markets; on the other, the churchyard of St Andrew's cathedral. Topped by a modest dome, the courthouse abutted the police station, which crouched behind a high, stone wall. To reach the entrance, Wilson had to pass between two solid gateposts set into an iron fence, then cross a small courtyard and duck under a portico.

He discovered that this portico was plastered with 'tragical posters', each of which 'started off with the word "MURDER!" in four-inch capitals, and subsided at once into very small type – as if they were engaged in a subject they didn't like to speak about.' He related how a desolate troop of prisoners shuffled across the yard from the watch-house into a courtroom that smelled like a night-licensed public bar. Finally, he described the courtroom itself: its bare walls, its notched, hacked, time-stained seats and its boxes full of ragged, uncombed heads. In one corner, he wrote, a constable was examining a piece of paper that had the appearance of 'an immense butcher's bill'. Nearby were a couple of magistrates, and in front of them, two or three attorneys were 'making a second-hand bookstall of the middle table' while they flung mysterious commands at a clutch of busy little clerks carrying large blue bags.

On Monday 14 September 1868, this middle table was occupied by William Roberts and Julian Salomons. Roberts was a former member of the New South Wales Legislative Assembly; among his past clients were bushrangers Ben Hall and Frank Gardiner. A dark and sternly handsome man, he had a big family and an office on York Street. Salomons, aged thirty-three, was slightly more unusual. Short and cross-eyed, with a squeaky voice and a reputation for breaking down mentally after periods of intense work, he had already represented one notorious murderer and would defend several more. But on this occasion his client wasn't accused of murder. Twenty-nine-year-old stage mesmerist Thomas Guthrie Carr had been charged with felonious assault.

It was claimed that he had mesmerised Mrs Eliza Jane Gray of Botany Road, Chippendale, and raped her while she was under his influence.

During his arrest the previous Saturday, Carr had insisted that Gray was trying to extort money from him.

Then he'd been given bail of two hundred pounds – a rather large sum that Carr appears to have raised without too much trouble. But now he was back in the prisoner's dock, at the mercy of Police Magistrate Captain David Scott and an array of other gentlemen (including Anthony Hordern, of the well-known retailing dynasty) whose job it was to weigh the evidence against him. If they decided in Gray's favour, Carr would be committed for trial at the Central Criminal Court. There he would face a possible death penalty, because in New South Wales rape was still a capital offence. In this, as in practically everything else, the colony lagged behind Britain.

Carr's 'prosecutrix', Eliza Gray, was thirty years old, Irish-born and the mother of eight children, one of whom she had already buried. Her husband, William, was away from home a lot; he was a fireman aboard the steamship *Lady Young*, which regularly plied a route from Sydney to the far-flung, northerly towns of Queensland: Brisbane, Maryborough, even Rockhampton. Presenting her testimony to the court, Gray declared that she worked as a forewoman at the Cohen Brothers' Monster Clothing Hall. How she managed to hold down any kind of job is hard to fathom; possibly her thirteen-year-old daughter lent a hand with the younger kids.

Gray's employers, the Cohens, prided themselves on manufacturing 'the best and most varied stock of Ready-Made Clothing in the Colonies'. They loudly advertised the 'painstaking labour' that went into their dress and frock coats, their walking coats, their waistcoats, their tweed and 'angola' trousers. Eliza Gray was one of the many women responsible for assembling 'suits to order, well shrunk, at 8 hours' notice'. She did this, not at the showroom on

George Street, but at a Pitt Street workroom not far from the Sydney Mechanics' School of Arts – where Thomas Guthrie Carr had at one point occupied a private office. So it isn't surprising that when she first saw Carr he had dropped in to order some clothes.

According to Gray he simply came into the workroom, looked at all the girls hunched over their machines, then went away again. But she would have noticed him at once because of his height. Carr was very tall. Years later, in New Zealand, a journalist would describe him as standing 'above 7 feet in his stocking feet'. This may have been an exaggeration; the tone of the entire article was facetious. But the New South Wales *Police Gazette* gave Carr's alias as Long Tom – and one Sydney columnist, writing in 1899, remembered Carr as a tall, big man of 'coarse and sensual, but not unprepossessing' features.

In New Zealand, especially, the height of the 'giant doctor' was often remarked upon. During an assault trial in Wellington, one witness declared that he would not like his nose to be in Carr's great hand. Another, upon describing how Carr had threatened him, turned to the defendant and said, 'I'd have given you more than you bargained for, big as you are.' Long after Carr's death, an itinerant mesmerist making the rounds in New Zealand was all but commiserated because he wasn't a big man, as Dr Carr had been.

Carr's personality was almost as memorable as his height. While some commentators praised his 'fine voice and pleasing address', declaring that he possessed the art of saying just enough and no more, others seemed overwhelmed. 'As a lecturer, he is perhaps too voluble and demonstrative in his gesticulations,' one observer remarked, though another complimented Carr on 'his familiar off-hand style, his nonchalant air, and his fluent disquisitions'. Certainly his delivery must have been unique. In 1872, at a benefit concert in New Zealand, an impersonator gave an impression of Carr that delighted the whole audience. Apparently the mesmerist was a very fast talker – or perhaps it was his vocabulary that set him apart. 'He is never at a loss for a subject upon which to discourse,' Wellington's *Evening Post* observed, 'and has a greater flow of language, and uses a larger number of extraordinary and almost impossible-to-understand words and phrases, than any person in the colony.'

There's also evidence that Carr's pronunciation was unusual. One Melbourne commentator remarked that 'a person who pretends to lecture on "Science and the Bible" and pronounces Thales like Wales, and Seneca with the accent on the second syllable, and Caligula with the accent on the penultimate . . . must surely be undertaking a task for which his education at all events has not fitted him.' Another infuriated columnist made a list of Carr's errors: 'Dante' became 'Dant', 'Barnabas' became 'Banabas', 'indelible' became 'indeli*a*'ble', 'sol'ace' became 'so'lace' and 'envel'op' became 'env*o*l'op'. The same correspondent was also in a frenzy of irritation about Carr's gestures, which were likened to the sails of a windmill, or the jerking of a pump-handle: 'His gesticulations, on several occasions, wore all the appearance of an enraged ourang-outang.'

Carr was loud in every sense. One detractor described him as a charlatan with 'a bold front and a long tongue', who had 'plenty of wind to blow his own trumpet'. He liked to talk. He had 'the gift of the gab'. And when Eliza Gray saw him for the second time, just a day after her first glimpse, he subjected her to the full force of his persuasive powers.

She testified that she was called down to the shop, where Carr was waiting. He told her that she would make a good subject for one of his séances. Gray retorted that she didn't want to be mesmerised.

'Why not?' he asked, taking her hand. Before she could answer, he reeled off a list of the people he'd worked with, though she couldn't (when pressed) remember their names. Possibly some of them were female and he was trying to convince her that any number of respectable women had survived mesmerism unscathed. But even this argument didn't change her mind. Finally, he begged her to attend one of his shows. If this invitation included a card of admittance, Gray didn't mention it – though she was careful to report that he gave her one at a later meeting. So it's possible that when she did go to his first séance, she paid for her own ticket.

A shilling seat at an evening performance can't have been easy to justify for a working-class mother of seven. Carr must have made quite an impression on Eliza Gray.

His opening night was scheduled for Wednesday 1 March 1868, at the Sydney Mechanics' School of Arts. It had already been widely advertised as the first in a series of 'phreno-mesmeric, electro-biological and electro-psychological seances', in which volunteers from the audience would either be mesmerised or have the shapes of their heads assessed. (Electro-biology, electro-psychology, animal magnetism and mesmerism were interchangeable terms at the time – but they certainly sounded more impressive when they were all piled into one sentence.) 'SENSATIONAL CLASSIC TABLEAUX' were promised, 'exhibiting startling statuesque effects, with wonderful manifestations of the varied passions and emotions of the human soul'. There would also be music from a 'first-class artiste'. Doors would open at 7.30 pm, for an eight o'clock start. Tickets were one shilling for the gallery, two for the body of the hall and three for reserved seats.

In addition to running newspaper advertisements, Carr had probably distributed coloured posters and handbills, as was his habit. Some of his posters would surely have been hung around the entrance to the School of Arts – a dignified, sandstone-faced building wedged in among a variety of shopfronts on Pitt Street. While many of the 'splendid establishments' occupying this thoroughfare had been favourably compared to those in Liverpool, Pitt Street was not lined with such fashionably uniform facades. Instead, the occasional four- or five-storeyed structure towered over a patchy array of neat little inns and fruitshops. 'It is not what an architect would call a fine or imposing style of street architecture,' travel writer John Askew confessed, though he hastened to add that the contrast was pleasantly free from 'monotony'.

The School of Arts was one of Pitt Street's more impressive additions, erected as part of the mechanics' institute movement, which was founded to create a scientifically educated artisan class. The building contained a variety of rooms, including a chapel, a reading room and a lecture theatre. When Eliza Gray visited Carr there, shortly before his first show began, she was ushered into his private office and introduced to a young woman named Brooks. According to Carr, this woman had agreed to be mesmerised. She may very well have been the same 'young lady somnambulist' who later appeared in the Newcastle shows of one R Rupert Ewen. 'Somnambulist' was a term often used to describe a mesmeric subject, because such people were cast into a kind of waking sleep; Ewen's female somnambulist was supposed to have performed at Carr's séances in Sydney for at least a month before her trip to Newcastle, so she must have been regularly mesmerised by Carr, and probably had the run of his rooms – just like Miss Brooks.

Whoever Brooks was, however, she failed to convince Eliza Gray to join her on stage. Gray remained in the audience that night.

But Carr wasn't lacking in subjects. When describing his first séance, the *Sydney Morning Herald* noted that, towards the end of the show, 'a dozen young men from the audience, having placed themselves under his influence . . . proceeded to . . . perform the most ridiculous actions, believe the most absurd things, and so on.' The greater portion of the evening, however, was devoted to a lecture on the 'science' of phrenology. Phrenology was a diagnostic system based on the notion that a skull's shape was determined by the kind of brain it enclosed – so Carr invited two women and about eight or ten men up onto the stage, where he examined their heads to ascertain their most prominent characteristics. He also compared the various human skulls in his collection, demonstrating how some had fully developed 'intellectual and moral faculties', while others did not. 'The audience appeared to be deeply interested in the remarks of the lecturer, who is evidently well up on the subject,' the *Herald* reported.

The most amusing part of the show, however, featured Carr's mesmeric experiments. One account of a later

Sydney performance described in detail what people were made to do when Carr mesmerised them. Some were forced to sing, some to dance, some to recite, some to march in a funeral procession. Two of them declaimed over the motionless form of an Aboriginal boy, who was playing the part of their dead comrade. 'If any proof were wanting of the power which Dr Carr possesses over those who were on the platform,' the *Herald* enthused, 'it would be found in the tender caresses bestowed by both young men and young ladies upon the aforesaid black boy, who was made to act the part of a delicate young lady.'

Even the *Herald*, however, was in two minds about the rest of the entertainment. Steel needles were apparently thrust into the cheeks and arms of Carr's subjects, demonstrating that they would feel no pain during subsequent surgical operations. 'The cutting out of a tumour . . . is no fit experiment to be performed in the presence of a mixed auditory,' the *Herald* complained. 'Such experiments ought to at least be confined to the drawing of a tooth . . .'

Fault was also found with Carr's rather cavalier attitude towards his subjects. One man was chased by a mesmerised woman 'bent upon putting a long needle in his arm'. Other subjects, under the impression that they were mesmerists, caused 'considerable annoyance' to people in the front seats after Carr himself had left the hall (apparently without restoring his victims to their senses).

If his first séance was anything like this one, Eliza Gray must have felt grateful that she'd declined to take part.

But later, when he accosted her in the street, she agreed to visit him at home. He wanted to see if he could mesmerise her, he said. Some might argue that she was already mesmerised; why else accept such a dubious invitation?

Luckily, she had the wit to take someone with her. On her first trip to Carr's lodgings, she was accompanied by nineteen-year-old Elizabeth Hook – another Cohen Brothers' employee. At the time, Carr was living in Elizabeth Street, the most 'comfortable' address in the city outside of Wynyard Square. The two women, however, stayed for only a few minutes. 'Let me see if you are good subjects for mesmerism,' he said to them. Then he laid his fingers on their eyes and announced that they were, indeed, good subjects.

They left soon afterwards, with his cards of admittance in their hands.

But Hook's account of the evening differed slightly from Gray's. As far as Hook could recall, Carr had said that she *wasn't* a good subject, because she laughed too much. He had also said that he couldn't mesmerise her against her will. And he had written something on a card that he'd given to Gray, asking her to call on him again at the School of Arts.

From Carr's house, Gray and Hook had then gone to the older woman's lodgings at 74 Liverpool Street, just a few minutes' walk away. They had eaten supper together at about nine o'clock. After forty-five minutes or so, Hook had left – though there was some confusion about this, too. 'I swear I did not go back to Dr Carr's after leaving Miss Hook,' Gray insisted, after questions were raised about Hook's original version of the same evening. When cross-examined, Hook declared, 'I accompanied Mrs Gray from Dr Carr's to her house, and left her at her own door. I am quite positive of this. I had supper with her afterwards. I went home and came back after tea, and we went around the town . . . I did say I did not see her again that night, because I did not remember it. I was confused the other day.' Later in her deposition, Hook calculated that she had gone home for her tea between six and seven o'clock.

She agreed that this had all happened 'on the day the Duke was shot.'

II

Queen Victoria's second son, Alfred Ernest Albert, became Australia's first royal visitor at the age of twenty-three. After charming the citizens of Hobart, Melbourne and Adelaide, he spent several months in Sydney, where he dominated public life. There were balls in his honour. There were concerts. There were two special souvenir supplements in the *Illustrated Sydney News*. The prince's name was used, not only to advertise the Great Australasian Circus ('under the patronage of H.R.H. the Duke of Edinburgh'), but also Madame Sohier's Waxworks, Professor Parker's Grand Assault of Arms, and the Cohen Brothers' Monster Clothing Hall. Beneath a bold heading that announced 'THE DUKE'S VISIT', the Cohens went on to provide a list of their usual stock, all of it 'stamped with originality and high art'.

Above their advertisement on 8 February 1868, just a little closer to the *Herald*'s masthead, was a notice proclaiming the Sailors' Home Picnic. This charitable event was to be attended by the prince, the governor and the Countess of Belmore. Tickets would cost one pound for gentlemen and ten shillings for ladies. The location was given as Balmoral, but the festivities finally took place at Clontarf, on Sydney's Middle Harbour. Here, on

12 March, hundreds of people gathered along the beach to watch the Prince eat his lunch.

Among them was Emily Thorne, the seventeen-year-old daughter of a local businessman. Emily and her family had to endure a lot of discomfort for the privilege of a 'good long look at H.R.H.' The official picnic tent was so crowded they were forced to squeeze their way in, and when at last they did find a place to sit 'the only thing to be seen on the table were empty dishes dirty plates & bones.' After sharing two dusty plates, a tumbler, a champagne glass, a knife, a carving fork and a small fork between the four of them, they left via the prince's table. 'I heard him say "And I had to go to them you know",' Emily was delighted to report. 'He has such a nice voice.'

Afterwards, the Thorne girls drifted over to some trees near the beach. Here they had a good view of the prince as he emerged from the picnic tent and moved towards them, with Sir William Manning at his side. Manning, a local dignitary who became attorney-general later that year, was also president of the Sydney Sailors' Home. According to Emily:

> *As soon as they were about sixty yards from us Annie said, "We had better walk on a little as it seems so rude to stand staring at him here" & I was just going to say something to her when we heard a sharp noise like a chinese cracker & looking towards the place from which the sound came I just saw the Prince fall. Then the whole flashed across our minds in a moment and we all exclaimed "The Prince is shot".*

William Vial, a coachmaker, saw the entire incident at close quarters. In a deposition before a special court convened the next day, he explained that he was about twenty feet away from the royal party when a man came up and levelled his pistol at Prince Alfred. Then he fired.

'The Duke fell on his hands, and rather on his right side, exclaiming, "My back is broken," or something to that effect,' Vial said. At that moment Sir William Manning turned to face the shooter, who cried, 'Stand back!' and fired again. Manning ducked.

Vial jumped on the would-be assassin.

Even with his arms pinioned, this man was able to turn his weapon on Vial. '"You bloody bugger," I think were the words he used,' Vial recalled. But the coachmaker was lucky; his captive didn't have a clear shot, and soon realised it. Instead of shooting Vial, he aimed his pistol at the prince once more. Vial promptly knocked it aside, 'diverting the direction of the ball to the ground'.

In fact, the ball was diverted in the direction of Emily's father's foot. She saw him limping out of the crowd and heard him saying, 'I'm shot, I'm shot.' By this time, a lynch mob had descended on the culprit – and poor William Vial didn't get out of the way fast enough. 'I was caught by the hair of the head,' he reported, 'and treated unmercifully for a time, being thrown down, kicked and beaten in the hurry of the people to get hold of him.' Seized by the beard, punched in the mouth and nose, Vial finally dragged himself clear of the melee.

But he didn't suffer as badly as the shooter. Henry James O'Farrell was nearly torn limb from limb; a rope was thrown over a tree to hang him. He was only saved by the efforts of the police, the chief justice, and members of a ship's band that had been playing under the trees. By the time he arrived back in Sydney, his clothes were in ribbons, his eyes were black, his nose was swollen and his lips were 'puffed out'.

It took a while for the news to spread. When it did, Sydney was thrown into a state of near hysteria. The streets were thronged; according to the *Herald*, 'it was evident that some gigantic calamity, affecting all classes of the people, had taken place'. O'Farrell's fate had been sealed from the moment he pulled the trigger, though he was later found to be a confirmed alcoholic with a history of mental illness. When Colonial Secretary Sir Henry Parkes visited him in prison to ask why he had committed so heinous a crime, the prisoner answered, 'Come, come, it is not fair to ask me such a question – the Prince is all right – the Prince will live, you need not fear about him – it's only a side wound – I shall be hanged, but the Prince will live.'

He was right. The prince did live and O'Farrell was eventually hanged. But before that happened, Thomas Guthrie Carr used the disaster to his own advantage.

On the evening of 12 March, after meeting with Eliza Gray, he announced to his audience at the School of Arts that he was cancelling his show. It would be unseemly for such an entertainment to take place, he said – and no one disagreed. However, despite referring to the attempted assassination as a 'calamity', Carr wasn't too squeamish to pursue the person responsible. Within weeks he was sitting in O'Farrell's cell, chatting with someone he later described as 'a man of extraordinary impulses . . . sensitive to the least annoyance, captious, satirical, and severe in his censure'. The two men discussed death, Melbourne, and literary topics. Carr then read O'Farrell's bumps.

Exactly how he got in to see the prisoner became a subject of much debate. On 21 April, just a few hours after

O'Farrell was hanged, Carr's name was bandied around the New South Wales Legislative Assembly. 'Did the Colonial Secretary, on Friday last, or on any other day of last week, address a communication to the prisoner O'Farrell?' the Member for Hastings, William Forster, asked Sir Henry Parkes in parliament that afternoon. Forster then went on to inquire if this communication had somehow referred to 'a proposed visit to the prisoner by one Dr. Carr, a lecturer on mesmerism in this city'.

Parkes replied that he'd sent no communication to O'Farrell at any time. But Forster pressed him further. 'Did Dr. Carr, in pursuance of an order from the Colonial Secretary, visit the prisoner O'Farrell, have a conversation with him, and ask him his opinion upon the theory of the immortality of the soul?' Forster demanded.

Parkes, in response, claimed that on 18 April Carr had applied to him for an order to see O'Farrell. Following protocol, Parkes had then given Carr a note for the principal gaoler. If O'Farrell had no objection, the note read, Carr should be admitted to his cell.

But this may not have been the whole story. Parkes had already received a letter from one Edward Johnson, urging that O'Farrell be mesmerised. 'We have amongst us a clever mesmerist,' Johnson wrote, referring to Thomas Guthrie Carr, 'and I venture to say that if he were placed in the prisoner's cell he could extract information from him that may tend to bring his accomplices to justice.' The accomplices to which Johnson referred were members of the Fenian Brotherhood, an Irish republican organisation. In a letter that O'Farrell wrote before he died, he admitted that although he had formerly claimed to be 'one of many', he had, in fact, 'no foundation for stating that there was a Fenian organisation in New South Wales.' But by the time this letter reached him the colonial secretary had already warned his counterparts in Melbourne and Brisbane about disloyal organisations corrupting the colony.

Parkes had always been a firm believer in the Fenian threat.

By allowing Carr access to the prisoner, he had perhaps been hoping that the mesmerist might ferret out some of O'Farrell's secrets. If so, he was doomed to disappointment – and his decision soon got him into trouble. He was forced to defend himself again and again in parliament, where Thomas Garrett, Member for Shoalhaven, was utterly scathing. Garrett regretted that the mesmerist had been allowed to see O'Farrell. Referring to Carr, Garrett claimed that there had been 'enough excitement about the man already without trying to increase it', adding that they would probably soon see a rash of placards all over town, advertising a lecture on O'Farrell's phrenological development.

After reading these remarks in the *Herald*, Carr was quick to retaliate. He insisted that he had never asked for O'Farrell's opinion on the immortality of the soul. The subject had never been mentioned. Nor had he alluded to O'Farrell's impending doom, the nature of his crime, or his motives for committing it. Carr's only question to O'Farrell had been 'What is your theory of Death?', at which the warder, John Carroll, had remarked, 'Doctor, I hope you will not discuss questions of religion, as the priest has left strict instructions that he is not to be interfered with in any way.'

'Oh no, this is not a religious but a metaphysical argument,' O'Farrell had exclaimed. And Carr had supported him. 'Religion has nothing to do with it,' he'd said. 'We are discussing questions of philosophy, not of religion.'

According to Carr, O'Farrell had received him in a courteous and humorous manner. The prisoner had heard him lecture in Ballarat, and had once lived near him in Melbourne. Though there's no indication that they were ever properly acquainted, it seems that O'Farrell remembered very clearly his previous encounter with Carr onstage. 'When I asked permission to examine his head,' Carr wrote of their gaolhouse meeting, 'he said "With pleasure; it is not the first time you have done so"; and then asked if it would not look better if it was "graced with a chignon".'

Carr finished by insisting that his visit had been one of scientific inquiry. 'All those interested in the progress of mental science,' he argued, 'will accord to Mr Parkes their sincere thanks, and be amazed that men shambling after notoriety should keep a body of intelligent representatives one hour and a half in the discussion of a point which . . . does not violate the principle of their Constitution.'

It's hard to say how much truth there was in Carr's account. William Forster was adamant that during Carr's visit, warder John Carroll had remonstrated with the mesmerist, before reporting his behaviour to the superintendent of Darlinghurst gaol. 'There was proof that this unhappy man [O'Farrell] would have preferred not to have been visited by Dr. Carr,' Forster declared. Ten months later, when a parliamentary committee was formed to investigate the O'Farrell affair, John Carroll himself insisted that the prisoner had been willing to talk to Carr only until the mesmerist mentioned 'matters connected with the next world'. Then the warder had prevented Carr from pressing the point, since O'Farrell had seemed unwilling to pursue it.

Yet despite William Forster's claim that the prisoner had been persecuted by people 'from whom the Government ought to have protected him', even Forster could do nothing to prevent Carr from witnessing O'Farrell's execution.

Somehow, on 21 April, Carr managed to wangle his way into the grounds of Darlingurst gaol, alongside such dignitaries as the mayor of Sydney, the police superintendent, and the sheriff of New South Wales. Hangings were no longer performed in public and Sir Henry Parkes had been besieged by applicants – all of whom were promptly referred to the sheriff. In the end, it was a select group of about one hundred souls that gathered behind a barricade in the prison's north-west quadrangle to watch O'Farrell die. The fact that Carr was among them can perhaps be attributed to his 'magnetic influence'.

We have no record of his reactions to the event. If he was expecting to hear any last words from the prisoner, his hopes were dashed. O'Farrell met his end in utter silence, though he did shake hands with his attending priest. 'No sign of tremor or trepidation was visible in the prisoner,' the *Empire* reported. O'Farrell's final statement became the embarrassing letter that was read before parliament two days later, in which he denied ever having encountered a Fenian organisation. This letter contained only one, small insight:

> *From continually thinking and talking of what I may still be allowed to call the wrongs of Ireland, I became excited, and filled with enthusiasm on the subject, and it was when*

under the influence of those feelings that I attempted to perpetrate the deed for which I am now justly called upon to suffer.

O'Farrell's remarks were soon broadcast all over Australia and New Zealand, eventually finding their way to the rest of the world. But Carr still had enough private material to start peddling his assessment of O'Farrell's character – just as Thomas Garrett had predicted he would. Within days, Carr's interview with O'Farrell had become a part of his show. The mesmerist claimed to have drawn up a phrenological report, which was to have been submitted to its subject a few hours before his death. But the catholic archbishop of Sydney, John Polding, had intervened on O'Farrell's behalf, begging Carr not to disturb the prisoner's peace of mind. And Carr, apparently, had deferred to him.

So it was to a paying audience that Carr finally delivered his last judgement. After reading O'Farrell's bumps, Carr had concluded that the prisoner's 'wonder' organ was not highly developed, and that his 'destructiveness' bump was of only moderate size. 'Wit' was very large, 'calculation' very small. 'His brain, while it showed a mind capable of good intellectual parts, was not well balanced,' Carr's analysis ran. 'The selfish sentiments preponderated. The domestic sentiments were ill-expressed.' It would have been hard for anyone to disagree with his claim that O'Farrell's propensities required 'a self-government that he seldom exerted'. There must have been nods all round when Carr diagnosed 'a person subject to extreme reactions, to periods of deep melancholy – faith struggling with despair'. According to the *Empire*, Carr was applauded vigorously at the conclusion of his speech. Then his audience settled back to watch him stab more people with steel pins.

Months later, out in the country, Carr was still dissecting O'Farrell on stage. In one advertisement, he promised to give particulars of his interview with the condemned man and explain 'the nature of the objections' made by the Legislative Assembly. No doubt he was keen to defend himself against public attacks on his reputation. But by that time, he was facing an even darker threat.

By that time, he must have been worried about Eliza Gray.

III

Armed with their cards of admittance, Elizabeth Hook and Eliza Gray attended another of Carr's séances together. Hook couldn't remember the exact date of this show, though she knew it occurred after 12 March. Before joining his audience, she and Gray stopped by Carr's private rooms – and Gray went in without Hook. When she emerged again, she informed her friend that she had been introduced to Miss Brooks.

Gray herself wasn't sure, 'on reflection', when she had met this lady. Initially she'd testified that they had been introduced to each other on the night of Carr's first performance. After Hook's deposition, however, she admitted that it might have been a day or two afterwards. She just couldn't recall.

But she was certain that, shortly after the incident at Clontarf, she was passing the School of Arts one lunchtime when Carr accosted her again. Shaking her hand, he invited her inside for five minutes, because he wanted to speak to her. Then he asked her to buy a yard of elastic, and mend his necktie. This request wasn't as outlandish as it sounds. In later testimony, a saddler and harness maker called Robert Lucas confessed to visiting Gray three or four times because she was a 'tailoress, working machines'. He and other men 'went there for clothes', he said, and he also employed her to sew carriage cloths and trimmers' braid. If Carr had needed new elastic in his necktie, Gray would have been the obvious person to provide it.

So that afternoon she bought the elastic and returned to the School of Arts. Elizabeth Hook went with her – though once again, Hook did not accompany her into Carr's rooms. 'He had three rooms there, one leading to the other,' Gray explained. She added that Carr took her through the second room and into the third, where she mended his necktie. It was the only time she saw him alone before Wednesday 18 March, she claimed.

On that day, Sydney was still reeling from the shock of recent events. The *Herald* was packed with reports of (and invitations to) 'meetings of indignation' held all over the colony. Notice was given that a Grand Temperance Demonstration would have to be postponed, 'in consequence of the attempt upon the life of H.R.H. Prince Alfred'. Philip McCarroll, a butcher on Pitt Street, included the following doggerel in his advertisement for mutton, beef and black pudding:

What makes each face look pale, and wan, and sad?
Where lately all was festive, gay and glad;
Alas! Where comes the gloom throughout the land?

> *A vile assassin has upraised his hand,*
> *To take the life of that dear Royal one,*
> *Alfred beloved, our own Victoria's son . . .*

Oddly enough, Carr's advertisement of the same day didn't try to cash in on popular feeling. No mention was made of the royal sufferer. 'DR CARR . . . induces nightly on delicately organised ladies, as well as on strong men, PHYSICAL INSENSIBILITY TO PAIN', it read, adding that, for all nervous afflictions, Carr could be consulted daily at the School of Arts. His offices there were actually consulting rooms where he provided phrenological delineations of character and painless tooth extractions for ten shillings and sixpence a pop. According to Eliza Gray, he had promised to read her bumps as payment for the mended necktie. That was why she went to his rooms on the 18th, though (once again) she was vague about the exact time. It could have been between one or two, or between two and four – she gave different estimates on different occasions. Elizabeth Hook later calculated that she had left Gray at the School of Arts between two and three in the afternoon.

Carr greeted Gray in his first room, then escorted her into the third. Here her testimony becomes muddled. It seems that he left her there for about twenty minutes, and that while she was waiting she began to feel sick and giddy. When she rose to go, however, Carr met her at the door. 'Stop, I will be with you in a moment,' he said. So Gray returned to the chair and sat down.

But what happened then?

In her first deposition during the committal hearing in September, she claimed that the next thing she remembered was lying on the sofa as Carr patted the left side of her head. It wasn't until later in the hearing that she contradicted this statement. 'Dr Carr touched me on my face while I was seated on the chair, and said I had a very benevolent face,' she recounted. 'He had a paper before him, which he said was for delineation of character, and which he promised to give me. He was moving a handkerchief about from one hand to the other. He then threw it on the table before me, and I don't remember any more.'

She explained that Carr had taken her own handkerchief from her so he could wipe his face. 'If I had known he was going to mesmerise me, I would not have allowed him to do so,' she said. 'I believe I was mesmerised. I was insensible. I became powerless.' She couldn't judge how long she was in the room; it was certainly more than a quarter of an hour. When she came to her senses she felt as if she had woken from a heavy sleep. 'I felt very faintish, weak, and sleepy while in the room, and felt very sick afterwards,' she told the court. She was also aware of a 'sickly, close kind of smell'. But she suspected nothing until she saw Carr putting a belt around his trousers.

That was when she accused him of rape. 'Taking advantage' were the words she used.

'Human nature is wicked,' he replied. Then he pointed out that no one would ever know, if she kept her mouth shut. 'I told him . . . that I would never come there again,' she attested. 'He said he would mesmerise me and bring me there.' He was warning Gray that he could mesmerise her whether she liked it or not – directly contradicting the statement he'd made to Elizabeth Hook at his lodgings.

After this exchange, Carr led Gray out of his rooms to the stage in the lecture hall. Here she walked about for a while until she felt better. Some people came in, but Gray didn't speak to them. Instead, after parting with the mesmerist, she went back to the Cohens' workroom, arriving at about four o'clock.

It was a half-holiday, but Gray and Elizabeth Hook had promised to stay back and 'tack for the machines'. Hook was still there, waiting. Gray had earlier told her friend that Carr was going to read her bumps; now Hook had to escort the tottering forewoman home to Liverpool Street, because Gray felt too ill to continue working. 'Mrs Gray went and laid down on the sofa directly she got in,' Hook related. 'She appeared to be very ill. I went to get her a glass of water. I asked her what was the matter. She said, "Oh Good God, Lizzie, I've been mesmerised".' Hook stayed with her friend for ninety minutes and Gray was ill the whole time. Under cross-examination, Hook said that she had known Gray since February, but had not once seen her faint.

In later testimony, Gray was adamant that, before 18 March, she had never slept with Carr nor with any man other than her husband. Moreover, Carr had previously given her no cause for concern. 'He had not taken any liberties with me up to that time, nor had any familiarities passed between us,' she said of the mesmerist. She also dismissed the suggestion that she had ever been alone with him at his lodgings. Mrs Burns, Carr's landlady, hadn't once complained about 'improper conduct' on Gray's part; on the contrary, she had asked Gray to drop in again. Nor had Carr visited Gray's house before 18 March. Gray defended her reputation with enormous energy. The occurrence in Carr's rooms, she maintained, could not have happened 'unless Dr Carr had mesmerised her'.

When she finished her first deposition, Carr was remanded for a week. Bail was allowed as before. The magistrate then turned his attention to other matters: a breach of the peace, an illegally detained goat, a deserted wife, some unlawfully felled trees, and several cases of common assault.

Two days later, a letter appeared in the *Herald* from the Cohen Brothers. They had noted that Eliza Gray was claiming to be in their employ. 'This statement is entirely untrue, as it is now nearly five months since she left our establishment,' they pointed out. In fact, she had resigned in April, owing to ill-health.

A day after this letter was published, Carr performed at the City Hall, Newcastle. 'It may be thought by some, perhaps, that, owing to an unpleasant circumstance in Sydney, he will not appear in Newcastle tonight,' the *Newcastle Chronicle* remarked. 'His agent assures us that the annoying occurrence to which we allude will not allow Dr Carr to disappoint the people of Newcastle . . .'

He was back in Sydney again by 21 March, for the next stage of his committal hearing.

PART II

BEFORE THE INCIDENT

I

Sometime in 1839, somewhere in Newcastle-on-Tyne, Thomas Guthrie Carr was born to John Carr – a coal merchant – and Mary Guthrie. Twenty-five years later, in 1864, he was still in town when the Davenport Brothers arrived there. We know this because he took exception to them.

Ira Erastus and William Henry Davenport were famous American spirit mediums. They claimed that, even when they were tied up and shut inside a special three-door cabinet, all kinds of supernatural activity would take place – most of it involving musical instruments that flew around the room. They were a controversial pair who were greeted by riots in Liverpool and challenged by some of the leading magicians of the day.

Among their detractors was the author of a work entitled *Modern Spiritualism an Imposture; or the Davenport Fraternity*

Unmasked. This pamphlet contained a lecture delivered in Newcastle on 18 November 1864. It was written by Thomas Carr, Esquire.

'In company with the Brothers Davenport, the spirits again have visited our town,' Carr declared in his attack, 'and by their freaks have thrown the timid into a strange excitement. Having enriched themselves with our gold, they have left the victims they have gulled to bless them with their unreserved contempt.'

There followed a detailed, eyewitness account of a Davenport séance that the author himself had attended. Carr described how he and several other customers were confronted, in a darkened hotel room, by a seven-foot-high cabinet containing a violin, guitar, tambourine and trumpet. He painted a vivid picture of the four men who greeted them at the door and instructed them to take a seat:

> *Dr Ferguson . . . is very eccentric, and a little slovenly in his style. Mr Fay is a pleasant, jolly-looking youth with twinkling eyes and with a free and easy manner. The Brothers Davenport are short and thin, have neat little hands and feet, and have dark restless eyes, which, I thought, betrayed considerable anxiety.*

The proceedings began with a speech from Dr Jesse Babcock Ferguson – an American spiritualist preacher – who insisted that the Davenports were merely passive agents of forces beyond their control. After the brothers had entered their cabinet, they were bound hand and foot by selected members of the audience. The doors of the cabinet were shut. The lights were dimmed.

The fun began.

Strange noises sounded from within the cabinet. A hand became briefly visible in the diamond-shaped window above one of its doors. There was an 'attempt at music'. Then the doors opened, revealing that the brothers were still bound. Once more the doors were closed. The musical instruments immediately jangled 'in the most dreadful discord', as the doors opened and shut, showing the brothers tied, untied, tied again . . .

The next trick involved a member of the audience, one Captain Hanson. He was placed between the two brothers and bound to each. Inside the sealed cabinet, there were spasmodic attempts at music. The captain felt hands touching his face. When finally exposed to the public gaze, he was wearing a tambourine on his head – and the brothers were still tied up.

At this point they were untied by their assistants and a table was placed in the middle of the room. Every instrument was moved to the table. Mr Fay was fastened to a chair. One of the Davenports was similarly tethered, while everyone else had to hold hands and form a semicircle. 'Our honour as gentlemen was appealed to,' Carr wrote, 'and, much against our wish, we became a staff of policemen, watching the movements of each other.'

Then the last light in the room was extinguished. In utter darkness, the trumpet and tambourine began 'to frolic on the floor'. There was a dreadful noise, 'as if some huge pre-adamantine monster was attempting to play the guitar'. Someone gave a shout as he was rapped on the head. One of the Davenports, who was holding Carr's hand, asked, 'Would you like to be touched?'

When Carr said he would, the same Davenport advised him to, 'Ask them.'

'Ask who?' Carr inquired.

'Ask either of them,' the brother answered.

So Carr addressed the other Davenport. Almost immediately, he felt something tap his brow and flick his hair forward. During all this, instruments were being whisked around the room 'as though they were attached to an elastic band'. Carr heard the sound of ropes being undone and felt the same ropes zipping past his legs. When a light flared again, the two bound men were untied and instruments were scattered around the room.

Finally, after another brief spell of total darkness, the brothers were shown to be tied up yet again, with different knots. Their cords were then sealed with wax, and sheets of white paper placed under their feet. The lights were snuffed out. Someone called for Mr Fay's coat to be removed. At last Mr Fay cried, 'It's off!' More light was provided.

Mr Fay had lost his coat.

Another gentleman kindly offered his, which was laid on the table. But it didn't stay there long. As soon as darkness descended, Mr Fay exclaimed, 'It's on!' Carr had to concede that it was, indeed, on. 'Not very gracefully on, certainly, yet the light showed the coat upon his back,' he said.

By now the spirits seemed to be growing weary. Once darkness had been restored for the last time, they began to untie the brothers. Suddenly Carr felt something flung around his neck. 'Of course I could not see in the dark,' he wrote, 'and my hands were safe in custody, and so I was obliged to submit to this indignity.' Meanwhile, one of the Davenports began to recite the alphabet. Every time he paused, the table gave two knocks. 'The spirits thus spelt the word of parting,' Carr concluded, 'and vanished as abruptly as they came.'

Having described his experience, Carr went on to analyse and debunk the Davenports' methods. He started by pointing out that the brothers were of low moral character because they had been convicted of swindling. He then argued that the rope used to bind them was 'of the finest and softest kind that could be secured for the purpose' and that it was cut into short lengths, making it easier to manipulate. More importantly, he said, the Davenports had refused to be tied with any rope except their own.

Then there was the matter of the so-called 'spirit hand'. It had clearly belonged, not to a female or an infant, but to a full-grown man. 'Part of the coat-sleeve and wristband was distinctly visible', Carr scoffed. As for the Davenports, they had emerged from their cabinet looking exhausted, their breathing irregular and their hearts galloping. In the dark, their voices had been strained, like that of a man 'swimming and talking at the same time'. According to Carr, this alone disproved their claim to physical passivity.

But the most suspicious element of all had been the darkness. 'We are told to investigate the causes of certain phenomena,' he said. 'We are told that "we have eyes but see not;" "that we are sceptics;" "that we should hear before we strike." And when we go to witness the phenomena and investigate into its causes, we are surrounded by darkness dense as the tomb!'

The rest of Carr's lecture was a long and rambling discourse on matter, intelligence, God, metaphysics, Indian jugglers, Professor Houdini and John Henry Anderson, the

'Wizard of the North' who had reproduced the Davenport's illusion on stage. Carr had received a letter from Anderson, which he quoted in full. The London-based magician explained that he was performing nightly, in 'the full blaze of gas-light', the same set-pieces that the Davenports had always performed in the dark. 'That these manifestations are the results of trickery and confederacy, no sane man can for an instant doubt,' Anderson declared – and Carr enthusiastically agreed with him. Spiritualism, Carr concluded, was a demon that had afflicted the world with a hell-born curse. Only 'screaming idiots' would mourn its demise.

Years later, Thomas Guthrie Carr laid claim to this waspish little essay. In a letter to the *Otago Daily Times* he recalled that when the Davenport Brothers visited Newcastle, he had attended their private séance and lectured in the Nelson Street Hall against their spiritual claims. On another occasion, he remembered taking part in *three* of the Davenports' séances. Spiritualism seemed to be a pet topic of Carr's; he would regularly rail against it as being contrary to the laws of nature.

But however much he abused the Davenports, it's likely that their success – and perhaps even their manipulative methods – had some influence on the course of his own life. Though he accused them of being 'impious imposters and low-bred charlatans', he ended up in a very similar line of work himself. How exactly this came about is difficult to determine, because Carr was a practised liar. More than once he claimed to be past president of London's East End Phrenological Society – an organisation that hasn't left any trace of itself behind. He also said that he'd authored several books. But neither *Modern Spiritualism and the Crucible*, nor *The History of Modern Spiritualism*, nor *The Phreno-Mesmeric Students' Manual* seems to exist anymore. He even maintained that he'd worked at Guy's Hospital in London, though he didn't appear to have a medical degree.

There's a very small chance that he might have had some medical training. The chairman of his Davenport lecture was William Murray, who taught physiology at Newcastle's College of Medicine. Murray had qualified as a doctor in 1859, when he was twenty years old. He later helped to found the local Hospital for Sick Children. The fact that he accepted Carr's invitation might have meant that the two young men were acquainted, either because Carr happened to be a medical student himself, or because they were both on the same lecture circuit. (Apparently, Murray liked to spend his lunchtimes giving religious talks to factory workers.) On the other hand, Carr later got into the habit of using volunteers from the audience when he was appointing chairmen, so he and Murray may not have known each other at all.

One thing, however, is certain. If Carr had possessed a medical degree in 1864, he would have referred to it in print. He made so much of Murray's that his own wouldn't have escaped notice. And though he did, eventually, start using the honorific 'Dr', he shouldn't have. In New Zealand he once described himself, under oath, as a professional mesmerist and lecturer, adding shiftily, 'I decline to answer whether I am a physician or surgeon, or whether I am registered as a qualified medical practitioner.' In Sydney, he seemed unable to supply prescriptions to his patients; instead he had to apply to one Dr Charles Eichler, of Bridge Street. When questioned by William Roberts, who 'wanted to know whether [the] prisoner was a doctor of medicine or of laws or what', Eichler could only say vaguely, 'I don't know what the prisoner's qualifications are. He is, I believe, a professor of mesmerism.'

At the time, the regulation of medical practice was still in its infancy. Qualified doctors were often viewed with as much suspicion as full-blown quacks, and almost nowhere in the colonies was it illegal to perform surgical procedures without a licence. Nevertheless, wherever he went, Carr was accused of being a fraud and a humbug. Less than a year after his arrival in Australia, a committee of Adelaide worthies was considering whether to inquire into 'Carr's right to the title assumed by him'. Two years later, in New Zealand, Carr's bona fides were publicly questioned by John Rutherford Ryley, a highly qualified member of the New Zealand medical establishment, who had studied under Joseph Lister and pioneered the use of carbolic acid as a sterilisation agent. Ryley poured scorn on Carr's medical pretensions. 'Pshaw! Mountebank!' Ryley wrote savagely, urging Carr to 'roll up your greasy carpet and move on to the next street!'

Ryley vehemently rejected the claim that Carr had ever worked at Guy's Hospital, or as a demonstrator of anatomy at Durham University. Carr's other claim – that mesmerism was 'universally recognised' by the medical profession – also infuriated Ryley, who declared that most mesmerists' demonstrations were the result of collusion between the operator and his subjects. Finally, Ryley laid into Carr's associate, Dr James Grant. Grant, Ryley scoffed, had first declared himself to be a member of the Royal College of Surgeons, Edinburgh; then to be a member of the Royal College of Dentists, Edinburgh (which didn't exist); then to be a licentiate in dental surgery of the Royal College of Surgeons, London; then to be a member of the Royal College of Dentists, London; and then to be a licentiate of the Royal College of Dentists, Edinburgh, all in the space of a few weeks. 'As regards the medical practice of Dr Carr, and his colleague, Dr Grant,' Ryley said, '. . . I may have occasion soon to speak from my professional experience.'

Carr's response was swift and vigorous. He attacked Ryley's record, pointing out that after sixteen weeks of Ryley's treatment, a certain patient had grown worse instead of better – but was 'now nearly well' under Carr's regimen. As for Mrs King of Stafford Town, her blindness had not been cured by two of Ryley's operations, whereas Carr had 'restored her sight completely'.

This wasn't true. The dispenser at the local hospital wrote a letter to the local paper saying as much. The only patient named King treated at the hospital, he pointed out, had not suffered from an eye disease at all. As for Mrs King, her husband soon brought an action against Carr for improper medical treatment of his wife. 'DR CARR AGAIN,' the *Sydney Morning Herald* declared when reporting the case, adding, 'The mesmerist seems never to be out of trouble.'

Carr obviously did end up with a medical practice of some kind. At one point, rumours even circulated that he might have been a ship's surgeon. A witness at his 1868 committal hearing for rape, when asked if Carr had been the surgeon on board a ship called the *Palm Tree*, simply said he didn't know. In fact, the *Palm Tree*'s surgeon was called John James Hill; no doubt Hill's conviction and brief imprisonment for immoral conduct on board the ship (namely, drinking and fornication) might have caused

Eliza Gray's lawyer to conflate the two doctors. A man named William Maddison, who claimed in a published letter to have sailed to Melbourne with Carr, strongly denied that Carr had served as either a surgeon or a chaplain on board the *Palm Tree*. He did, however, all but concede that Carr had been a passenger on the same ship. According to Maddison, both he and Carr had arrived in Melbourne on 25 July 1866 – and the *Palm Tree* was the only ship from England to dock that day.

The *Palm Tree* itself became notorious, not only for the behaviour of its crew but for the mistreatment of its passengers. Whether Carr played any part in the on-board shenanigans is hard to say. As Maddison pointed out, the mesmerist's name was never once mentioned in official reports on the matter.

Then again, Maddison spent some time as Carr's secretary, so he wasn't exactly a neutral witness.

One thing Maddison didn't refer to was Carr's medical status. It was a subject that he passed over – probably with good reason. Because if Carr had a genuine medical degree on his arrival in Melbourne, then why didn't he make use of it? Why, on first surfacing in the local press, did he advertise himself as the *Reverend* Thomas Guthrie Carr?

II

In 1868, an English newspaper called the *Newcastle Weekly Chronicle* noted that an old friend had popped up in the Antipodes. 'In Newcastle he was more noted for his assurance than his scientific knowledge,' the paper observed, 'although he did lecture on spiritualism, and often "held forth" as a local preacher.' It went on to remind its readers that 'Dr' Carr had suddenly disappeared from Newcastle-on-Tyne just as he was about to lead a young lady to the altar, only to turn up as a 'full-blown doctor' on the other side of the world. 'Where he gained his diploma it is difficult to say,' the article concluded, 'but his doings in Australia have amused some Newcastle people.'

It's clear from contemporary reports that before arriving in Australia, Carr was struggling to make a name for himself in Newcastle. One account of his talk about the Davenports describes its attendance as 'not very numerous'. The next day, however, Carr was at it again. During a concert being held to help a blind man buy a clothes mangle, Carr 'very kindly took it upon himself to be the medium of conversation between the blind performers and the audience'. He was a natural-born showman, irresistibly drawn to the spotlight. But in Britain he was sharing this spotlight with the cream of the empire's entertainers. He might have thought his prospects would improve in the colonies.

'When the Newcastle doctor came to Melbourne,' wrote journalist Richard Sherrin, 'and had expended the whole of his funds, and had exhausted his credit, he adopted the charlatan business, and went in for mesmerism and lecturing.' Though by no means a friend to Carr, Sherrin seems to have accepted that the mesmerist was properly qualified. But if Carr *did* begin his colonial career as a doctor, it wasn't widely known. One of his good friends, John Huxtable, testified at the 1868 committal hearing that he had first gone to hear Carr speak after seeing him referred to as a 'lecturer on Christianity'. Carr's earliest advertisements don't describe him as 'Dr Carr', or even as the 'Reverend Dr Carr'. Nor do they mention phrenology or mesmerism. Instead, his first public talks were on the kind of religious topics that he had almost certainly tackled as a local preacher in Newcastle: 'Modern Spiritualism', 'the Apocalyptic Gospel', 'St John the Mystic' and 'Baxter in the Crucible, or the Coming Battle'.

Michael Baxter, the subject of this last speech, was a self-proclaimed English prophet. In 1866 he published a controversial book entitled *Louis Napoleon, the Destined Monarch of the World . . . subsequently to become completely supreme over England and most of America, and all Christendom, and to cause a great persecution of Christians during the latter half of the seven years, until he finally perishes at the descent of Christ, at the end of the War of Armageddon, about or soon after 1874.* Carr wasn't the only preacher to attack this work. The Reverend H Higginson tore it to shreds in a speech called 'Modern Prophecies of the Approaching End of the World based on fallacious principles', which he delivered at Melbourne's Unitarian Christian Church about a month before Carr himself tackled the subject. Carr's own lecture took place in September 1866, at St George's Hall. His proceedings 'commenced with the singing of the doxology and closed with a benediction.' According to the *Age* and the *Argus*, Carr argued for two solid hours against Baxter's prophecy – especially his analysis of mystic numbers.

Apparently, attendance was moderate.

This may have been because of a scathing public attack on his first 'Apocalyptic lecture', which took place in late August. During the speech, Carr went out of his way to sneer at the scholasticism of English universities, then promptly committed 'vile murders' upon the English language with his atrocious pronunciation. 'Blundering like this on the part of any public speaker is disgraceful: in a clergyman it is intolerable,' a reviewer complained, before going on to describe how several people had walked out, disgusted at Carr's manner of delivery:

> *By way of demonstrating [Saint] John's eagerness to obey his master's behest, "Follow me!", Mr. Carr, amongst other things, said "John didn't hesitate for a moment – he didn't say, "I'll go and ask my mother!" – no, – he went at once." The way this was uttered may have befitted the acting of a player, but on the lips of a minister of the Gospel we thought it sadly out of place. The same remarks apply to the phrases "none of that damnable cant", "the eternal squall of the little children" and "A good, true, Masonic brother was John." Levities like these are very unbecoming . . .*

This wasn't the last time someone questioned Carr's level of education. A South Australian correspondent, after examining the degrees that Carr claimed to possess, asked what 'DPS' and 'MPAL' were actually supposed to *mean*. Carr's mispronunciations suggested that he was an autodidact; they certainly undermined his insistence that he'd studied at Guy's Hospital. In Beechworth, Victoria, a local newspaper once totted up all the mistakes he'd made during a lecture. The pyramids of Egypt, it was pointed out, didn't lie on the Libyan range, unless they had been moved. Robert Owen was not the name of an eminent comparative anatomist, but of the socialist writer. Giordano Bruno was not the pupil of Galileo, but was burnt to death long before Galileo published his heretical discoveries.

The same article described Carr's words thundering down like a wave of mortar shells, though the mesmerist himself had seemed 'more concerned about the sound than the sense of his grand periods'. Another critic once described Carr's style as pompous, affected, overbearing, unrefined and arrogant, and his voice as harsh, rude and unmusical. 'Yet still there is a grand array of fine rounded periods, well set and condensed ideas,' this detractor had to admit, adding that, 'he never flounders, has a great copiousness of language, and always finishes off with a great thunder clap.'

Carr was obviously more of a showman than a preacher, so it isn't surprising that he suddenly changed tack. In October 1866, though still calling himself the Reverend T Guthrie Carr, he started lecturing on phrenology. He also dabbled in juicy topics like 'Love, Courtship and Matrimony' for 'the Married and Marriageable'. He played music. He used mesmerism. He borrowed an array of busts and skulls from Philemon Sohier and his wife, the proprietors of Madame Sohier's Waxworks. The Sohiers' notorious collection included wax portraits of royalty and criminals, as well as live 'freaks' like nine-year-old Esau the Bearded Boy. Clearly, Carr had learned his lesson. Two-hour religious lectures weren't going to fill seats.

An account of Carr's show on 13 October 1866 demonstrates how quickly he had refined his skills. After speaking for about an hour on phrenology, Carr called for silence. Then, while a piano softly tinkled, he performed 'the various passes and motions employed by mesmerists to bring their subjects under control'. A lady up the back of the hall soon became visibly affected. A Maori spectator down the front staggered from his seat, rushed up onto the stage and seized Carr by the hair, brandishing a walking stick. Carr motioned for the man to drop his weapon. The man did so. Carr next made him pray, sing, dance and weep by manipulating his phrenological 'organs'.

The affected lady from the rear seats was also summoned to the platform, where she promptly fell asleep.

By the beginning of November, Carr was advertising private phrenological consultations at St George's Hall. He was even promoting the fact that he'd hired an 'efficient amanuensis' to help him handle the press of customers on his doorstep. Soon he was lecturing on 'Mesmerism, Electro-biology, Fascination and Phrenology' to packed houses. The mayor of Melbourne had agreed to chair his show. On at least one occasion, Carr read aloud his phrenological analysis of Robert Closky, alias Burke, a bushranger who was hanged on 29 November. Carr claimed that this analysis had been done at the public's request, and that Closky himself had declared it to be 'perfect and just' the very night before his hanging. The governor of Melbourne Gaol, said Carr, could bear witness to that.

Oddly enough, Carr's name was not on the list of people who watched Closky's execution. The only 'practical phrenologist' present was Professor James H Hume, who once publicly condemned Carr as somebody who had 'brought indelible disgrace upon the profession'. Hume's specialty seemed to be career counselling. 'A General Difficulty with Parents,' his advertisements ran. 'What is this young man best adapted for?' Long after Carr had left Melbourne, Hume was still doggedly reading bumps. In 1878 he published a booklet called *Phrenologist Hume Reads Characters Correctly*, describing how he could direct his patients towards 'the most suitable occupations'.

By that time, Carr had long since left Melbourne – though not without a lot of fanfare. During his time in the city, he had built up an impressive network of friends. Chief among them was the slightly shadowy dentist Andrew MacLean, who published in the *Argus* a gushing letter in praise of Carr:

> *We, the undersigned, warm friends and ardent admirers of you, both in your public capacity as a delineator of one of the most abstruse yet beautiful of sciences, and in your private capacity on account of the courtesy and gentleman-like manner in which you have treated us . . . cannot permit you to depart upon your proposed tour without carrying with you some slight mark of our esteem and the high appreciation in which we hold your talents . . .*

This letter urged Carr to give another course of lectures: six on phrenology and six on mesmerism. It was signed by more than thirty men, including MacLean himself, John Huxtable, Lord Mayor William Williams, MP Stephen George Henty, a couple of upholsters, a jeweller called Leopold Burmeister, and a publican called Joseph Cleal. According to MacLean, seventy-two other people who also signed the letter didn't have their names published.

In response, Carr promised a dozen more lectures, which were duly delivered. No doubt that outcome had been his plan all along. (MacLean, after all, was about to become his secretary.) How many of the signatories were genuine friends, and how many were imposed upon, is something we'll never know. Though Carr was a blatant operator, he also had a knack for ingratiating himself.

On 23 November 1866, he gave his final lecture. Then

he packed up and left for Ballarat. With him went Andrew MacLean and a certain Maori assistant whose services had become indispensable. It's likely that John Huxtable also accompanied Carr, because Huxtable had business interests in Ballarat. The forty-year-old entrepreneur had opened a restaurant and reading room there, as well as a music warehouse and 'general repository'. His contacts in town would have been very useful to Carr – who gave his first lecture in Ballarat on 17 January 1867.

A few weeks later, the *Age* noted that a far less illustrious publication had made sly reference to the mesmerist's departure. 'The Reverend Thomas Guthrie Carr, phrenological lecturer at St George's Hall, has suddenly left Melbourne, to the disgust of many anxious gentlemen who have not had settlement of their little bills,' the *Woods Point Times and Mountaineer* had reported. The *Age* confessed that it had been unable to confirm this statement, but had published the item anyway.

Carr's response was scorching.

'There is not, to my knowledge, nor the knowledge of my secretary, a "little bill", nor yet a large one, due by me to any gentleman or tradesman, commercial firm or private speculator, of any kind whatever, in the whole of Melbourne,' he trumpeted, going on to call the charge 'an unscrupulous libel'. He also pointed out that rather than leaving suddenly, he had announced his plans every night for nearly a week, in front of large crowds, at St George's Hall. What's more, he had promoted his imminent arrival in Ballarat with five hundred posters and numerous advertisements.

'It is a strange anomaly that a gentleman who could afford to pay £104 to public charities within a few days after his departure, could not have a sum adequate to pay a few anxious gentlemen their "little bills",' Carr finished, giving his address as the Mechanics' Institute, Smythesdale, Ballarat.

Despite his protests, Carr may very well have left unpaid bills in Melbourne. He was reduced to bankruptcy more than once in his life – and donating to charity wouldn't have precluded dunning tradesmen. At one point, for example, he gave a show that was supposed to be in aid of the Beechworth Children's Fete. Yet at the same time, he was being chased by the *Ovens and Murray Advertiser* for overdue advertising fees.

The fact is, Carr used public-spirited gestures as part of his pitch. For years he would promise loudly to give a portion of his ticket sales to local charities: to the Alexandra Lodge of Good Templars in New Zealand; to the Organ Fund of Adelaide Town Hall; to the hospital at Copeland, New South Wales. Whether all of these donations were actually made is a question worth asking. Some were, certainly. In 1879, his donation to a Hill End widow was handed over by an independent witness, and in 1867 he was given a life governorship of the Bendigo Benevolent Asylum in recognition of a twenty pound gift. Even his donation to the Anglican church at Sebastopol, near Ballarat, eventually reached its destination – though not without a certain amount of controversy. (A month after it was promised, the thirty-four pounds still hadn't been placed 'to the credit of the building', though this, it transpired, was the fault of church administrators.) In 1871, however, the anonymous author of a letter to the *Oamaru Times* pointed out that Carr had recently told an audience he was about to erect public baths in Dunedin, New Zealand. 'I am glad of it,' wrote the correspondent, 'and hope the Professor will take the first plunge – no man needs it more . . .'

Thirty-five years later, Dunedin's citizens were still discussing their need for public baths.

Though Carr might have had a genuine civic conscience, there's no doubt that his charitable impulses helped ease his passage through towns where he was an unknown quantity. They improved his reputation – at least among some people. But not all of his philanthropic gestures were well received. On one occasion in Adelaide he undertook to give a Sunday lecture for the benefit of another local widow. But she wouldn't cooperate. A few days later he announced huffily that 'his lecture on Sunday evening for the benefit of Mrs Barclay and family would not take place, as the lady objected to receive the proceeds, for reasons which he supposed were quite satisfactory to herself, but he guaranteed that a sum of not less than £50 should have been handed over to her.'

By that time, Carr had abandoned the title 'Reverend' and was calling himself a doctor, plain and simple. This change did not go unnoticed in Melbourne. 'It is less repugnant to the feelings of the religious community that he should dub himself "Doctor",' one Victorian correspondent slyly remarked. Carr had also perfected the techniques that he used again and again to ensure maximum publicity. First he would bombard a particular location with advertising. Then he would move into a prominent hotel and open offices in the nearest town hall or mechanics' institute. Years after his first visit to Bendigo, a witness recalled how, after taking rooms at the Shamrock Hotel, Carr had issued dinner invitations to many of the town's leading citizens. This would have enabled him to study their behaviour, as well as to win their trust. When reading the bumps of local worthies on stage, he would have needed some knowledge of their tastes and habits to produce a successful analysis.

Carr would also gather together a team of less exulted locals – mostly young men – who would perform nightly in his shows and run errands for him. The Bendigo witness mentioned how Carr would send these young men 'to the Shamrock Hotel for soda water and parcels from his room'. Wherever he went the mesmerist would hire a team of agents, some of them ethnically diverse. The 'eccentric aboriginal boy Prince Tommy', who performed in many of Carr's New South Wales shows, ended up replacing the mesmerist's Maori assistant. In Bendigo, this man more than earned his keep; Carr would put him under the influence, then 'show what power he had over him by making him suffer needles and other sharp instruments being thrust into various parts of his body without apparently feeling any pain'.

As Carr became more confident he allowed his shows to spill out onto the street, for maximum exposure. In New Zealand, a mesmerised shoemaker was in a crowd before the supreme court when Carr allegedly made him burst into song. At one show, several young men were told to wait for Carr in front of his hotel the following afternoon. On turning up as requested they were mesmerised and compelled to perform some 'ludicrous antics' in front of several hundred people. The same thing happened to a Maori mailman on another occasion. Then there were the youths sent out one night to deliver a 'gold nugget' to the Bank of New Zealand. 'On our way home we found them quietly but determinedly waiting for admittance,' the show's reviewer reported. 'After a little, Dr Carr came up and told them to make off to Swan's, as there was a policeman after them.' They immediately galloped off and tried to hide in Swan's Hotel.

Sometimes the victim was a young woman. In Sydney, Carr had a female subject who was frequently mesmerised, blindfolded, led away from the hall by a group of Carr's young men and abandoned. According to the *Herald*, she was once led into the rear of a shop in Pitt Street, 'with which she was entirely unacquainted'. Carr then drew her back to the stage by exerting with his mesmeric powers.

It's unlikely that the shop in question belonged to the Cohen Brothers. By that time, Carr and Eliza Gray were not on good terms.

Carr's first séance in Bendigo took place at the Lyceum Theatre on 22 March 1867. From there he moved into South Australia, taking his secretary and his Maori assistant with him. Carr was now a consummate self-promoter. His advertisements had become quite striking:

> *Is coming, Dr Carr, phrenologist*
> *Is coming, Dr Carr, physiologist*
> *Is coming, Dr Carr, anatomist*
> *Is coming, Dr Carr, electropsychologist*
> *Is coming, Dr Carr, mesmerist*
> *Is coming, Dr Thomas Guthrie Carr.*

In the same advertisement, Andrew MacLean promised that Carr would be available to treat tumours, derangement, deafness, stammering, diseases of the eye, sciatica, rheumatism and neuralgia using his powers of animal magnetism.

Publicity like this worked extremely well. On 16 May, when Carr gave his first séance at Adelaide's Town Hall, the spacious building 'was soon filled almost to overflowing'.

A member of parliament named William Townsend presided. Carr began by seating about two dozen young, male volunteers in front of the stage. Then he gave a talk on phrenology, drawing attention to the heads of several spectators, whose characters he delineated in 'a free and sketchy style which the audience seemed to relish greatly'. (That of a well-known restaurateur, the *South Australian Register* noted, was particularly amusing.) The rest of the evening was devoted to displays of mesmerism that caused 'unbounded mirth'. Carr's Maori assistant was involved, as was a certain 'little boy' said to travel with the mesmerist. This lad was made to sing; the Maori was stuck with the usual sharp instruments, before being reduced to a state of complete muscular rigidity. 'His legs stretching over the platform bore the weight of a gentleman of 18 or 20 stone,' the *Register* marvelled, pointing out that most of the other mesmerised subjects lived in Adelaide, so it 'seemed impossible . . . that there could be any collusion between the operator and themselves.'

The show ended with a New Zealand war dance, which Carr's Maori assistant performed at his command. 'His hideous howling and frightful gesticulations,' the *South Australian Weekly Chronicle* observed, '. . . reminding one of the wretched condition of uncivilised man.'

After this roaring success Carr continued to do well for a while, filling the town hall night after night. His second lecture was on 'Purpose and Ambition', his third on 'Modern Mystery and Ancient Scepticism'. His show on 21 May was a riotous affair; the hit of the evening was a display called 'The Soldier's Funeral', in which Carr's mesmerised subjects formed themselves into a military corps, accused the unfortunate Maori of treason, 'executed' him, then carried him around on their shoulders to the tune of the 'Dead March'. 'In pantomime they fired three volleys over his grave, and then knelt down to take a last look at their departed comrade', the *Register* related.

But there was one slight hiccup. When Carr's Maori subject was supporting on his rigid legs a well-known sergeant of police, who weighed at least sixteen stone, a certain Dr Campbell checked the mesmerised man's vital signs. This must have been done at Carr's invitation, since the mesmerist later pressed Campbell for his findings. They were unexpected. Campbell announced that he had noted a 'decided muscular contraction' in the subject's body when the policeman's weight settled onto it.

Carr was rattled. He said that Campbell must have been mistaken – that such a thing had never happened before. The highest medical authorities in Melbourne had testified to the absence of such effects. Carr invited the most sceptical to come up on stage and see for themselves. He staked his reputation on what they would find.

Within a week, he began to suffer setbacks.

His next show passed without incident. Its subject was 'The Qualifications requisite for the Pulpit, the Bar and the Press', and he offered a fifty pound prize for the best essay on phrenology submitted to him. (These essays he proceeded to ignore, according to the *South Australian Weekly Chronicle*.) Then he went off to Port Adelaide for a couple of nights. On the 27th he was back in town, where he spoke about 'Washington the Patriot and Napoleon the Man of the World' – but only for twenty minutes, since he'd learned his lesson and shortened his speeches. His next lecture, again at the town hall, was on 'The Philosophy of

Life'. The Chairman was careful to explain that he'd been present at Carr's séance in Port Adelaide and felt that press reports of the show had been unfair. Owing to the queen's birthday, he insisted, the audience had been in a festive mood and had 'showed symptoms of what was supposed to be disapproval' – not because they were sceptics, but because they were determined to be jolly.

In fact, the audience had hissed at Carr, whose attempts to mesmerise them had failed. No one had succumbed to his powers except for a handful of subjects from his Adelaide show. Perhaps it was a Port Adelaide resident who, a few days later, publicly but anonymously complained about the evils of mesmerism. This attack elicited the usual sharp reply. Carr defended his demonstrations. He insisted that mesmerists were no worse than other people, since their powers were no more open to abuse than those of clergymen, politicians or medical practitioners. In response to the demand that he submit to a public grilling, Carr declared that he had expressed not only his willingness, but his desire to do so – though he drew the line at donning a special suit without pockets. 'The feeble visual organs of "J.H.B.",' Carr wrote, 'fail to observe that if my clothes or pocket handkerchief contains anesthetics [*sic*] of any kind, I, from contact with the same, will be the first to experience the state which I attempt to induce in others.'

Scepticism continued to mount, however. The *Register* noted in its gossip column that there was talk of a committee being formed to meet privately with the mesmerist, so that doctors of high professional standing could assess Carr's claims. Criticism like this may well have reduced his income. He had to cancel his show at Norwood Town Hall because only thirty people turned up.

Perhaps that's why he began to vary his program. On 31 May, after Carr had lectured on 'The Gentleman and the Clown', chairman Andrew MacLean announced that a séance would be held 'for the convenience of schools' that very afternoon. (This was probably some kind of children's show, designed to tap into the educational market.) A week or so later, in White's Assembly Rooms, Carr shared his stage for the first time with two other headline acts: Shakespearean actor-manager William Hoskins and his talented young protégé, Marie St-Denis, who later committed suicide in Melbourne. White's Assembly Rooms were Adelaide's leading entertainment venue; located in King William Street, they consisted of a large, gas-lit auditorium abutting several smaller chambers. Hoskins and St-Denis were said to have appeared there at Carr's request. They sang a few songs and performed scenes from *Macbeth* and *Romeo and Juliet* for a 'numerous and select audience'. Then Carr mesmerised several young men, who were closely scrutinised after Carr had stuck surgical instruments into their hands. No one doubted that the subjects were in a mesmerised state.

The event was such a success that Carr soon decided to join forces again – this time with a recently hired assistant named Edwin Turner Osbaldeston. In his lecture 'Spirit-rapping and Modern Spiritualism', held at White's Assembly Rooms on 28 June, Carr once more attacked the Davenport Brothers (who by this time were world-famous, although they had not yet visited Australia). Then he introduced Osbaldeston as the Davenports' former secretary and had him perform a rope trick. After being tied up by two 'well-known' volunteers from the audience, Osbaldeston freed himself in less than two minutes. It was a classic Davenport move. But what were the odds that Carr should have hired someone who had actually worked for the Davenports?

In 1864, when the brothers first arrived in England from America, Osbaldeston was employed at a Turkish bathhouse on London's Euston Road. By March 1865 he was on a ship to Australia with his wife. During the interim he may very well have become the Davenports' secretary, though this seems highly improbable. At the time they already had a secretary: well-known opera and theatre impresario Henry D Palmer. If Osbaldeston *was* hired, it would have been as an innocent-looking spectator who could be trusted to tie ropes properly. Perhaps he did the kind of work for the Davenports that he did later for Thomas Guthrie Carr. Or perhaps he was making the whole thing up.

A year after reaching Brisbane, Osbaldeston was in Melbourne, advertising a 'Grand Drawing Room Entertainment' by 'Mr Osbaldeston, late agent of the Davenport Brothers'. It involved illuminated photographs, the Davenports' rope-tying trick and a 'talking hand'. In 1867 he was at it again, in Adelaide. According to the *South Australian Register*, he put on a show for schoolboys that involved a piano, a magic lantern and (of course) the famous talking hand:

> *Mr Osbaldeston then gave a brief sketch of the Davenport Brothers' tricks and impostures, after which a person in the audience was secured with rope. Mr Osbaldeston whispered a few words in his ear, and he freed himself from the rope, with some slight assistance from the operator, in about one minute.*

Osbaldeston even went in for mesmerism. Sixty years later, an Adelaide resident recalled how Osbaldeston used to mesmerise his little brother, to treat the boy's deafness. According to the same source, Osbaldeston had come to Adelaide *with* Carr. Evidence suggests otherwise, though it's possible that Carr first met Osbaldeston in Melbourne, where they both lived at around the same time. Osbaldeston was working at the Turkish baths in Lonsdale Street when they burned down one night in December 1866, while he and his family were in residence. He then left town to manage Ballarat's Turkish Baths. But on the opening of a new bathhouse in Adelaide, its lessee, Thomas Bastard, invited Osbaldeston to become his manager – and Osbaldeston moved again.

Apparently, he didn't get along with Mr Bastard. 'The negotiation was suddenly terminated by an altercation,' the *Sydney Morning Herald* reported, '. . . which ended in the latter [Bastard] being soused in the bath.' When Thomas Guthrie Carr finally hired him, Osbaldeston was teaching calisthenics to schoolchildren.

That was just before Carr became the target of an opinionated Methodist minister.

III

James Maughan was born in a village near Newcastle-on-Tyne. After serving as church clerk during his late teens, he was called to the ministry at the age of twenty-one. In 1862 he arrived in Adelaide with his wife and four children. By the time he clashed with Thomas Guthrie Carr he was forty-one years old – a stern-faced man with a broad nose, deep-set eyes and a beard like an electrified sea anemone.

Maughan prided himself on his scientific acumen. He once read a paper about Adelaide's drainage system to the local Philosophical Society. On another occasion, he was approached by a friend who had purchased what he thought to be oxide of manganese, but which had subsequently exploded. According to Maughan's biographer, when Maughan examined the substance, 'it was ascertained to be chlorate of potash, and produced a second explosion which seriously injured Mr Maughan.'

Like Thomas Guthrie Carr, Maughan had loudly decried the 'rashness and folly' of prophet Michael Baxter. 'Louis Napoleon, the coming struggle, and Christ's Second Advent' was a lecture that Maughan delivered at White's Assembly Rooms and later published. Other subjects he addressed publicly included 'The Great Events in England and Europe during 1870', 'Wonders of the World's Great City' and 'Chemistry of Beefsteaks and Apple Dumplings'.

On 18 July 1867, Maughan gave a talk on 'The Swindling Aspects of Mesmerism and the Trickery of Clairvoyance' at his church on Franklin Street. He may have decided to speak out because of recent developments in the push to have Carr's claims assessed by a medical committee. Two weeks earlier, Carr himself had invited a group of doctors to one of his shows. He had mesmerised the 'little boy' in his entourage (whose name was Johnny), and one of the doctors had removed Johnny's fingernail, on stage, before a large audience. The boy hadn't flinched, but when it was suggested that the same operation be performed on a second subject, the audience had baulked. Some spectators had risen to their feet in protest.

So Dr Bayer had proposed that Carr mesmerise one of his own patients, who needed an operation on his foot. After briefly consulting this young man in a nearby 'ante-room', Carr had returned to the stage and announced that the subject didn't want the operation performed in public. It would be done that evening in private, he'd said.

Though robbed of their surgery, the doctors had agreed to pass judgement anyway. Dr Gunson had found Carr's powers convincing, but doubted that they could ever replace chloroform. Dr Clark had agreed with Dr Gunson, though he'd personally defied Carr to mesmerise *him*. Dr Spicer, who had mesmerised several people himself in the past, couldn't have been more enthusiastic:

> *He had rigidly watched and examined the subjects that evening, and his opinion was that they did not feel what they were being subjected to. He described the operation of removing a finger-nail as one of the most excruciating operations which could be performed. He mentioned that he had examined the iris and pupil of the eye of the patients while they were being experimented on. He found there was not the slightest action of the pupil, which remained quite fixed and rigid. He defied any person to put his iris into that condition . . .*

The séance had been a success for Carr. His panel of doctors had certainly endorsed him. But the event had caused quite a stir. 'A poor friendless boy is taken on the stage and tortured by having one of his fingernails cut off,' a furious correspondent had written to the *Advertiser*. '. . . Would any parent have allowed their child to be thus cut about to please Dr Carr and fill his pocket?' As far away as Victoria, the *Hamilton Spectator* had run a story condemning the 'barbarous cruelty' of removing a boy's fingernail on stage. 'That Dr Carr could have this done to a youth under his care has revealed his character as a man, as much as his skill as a mesmerist,' the columnist had declared angrily. 'Poor "Johnny" may now be seen with his arm in a sling; would it were the doctor's.'

As for the sceptics, they hadn't been silenced. James Maughan was one of them. When Maughan's lecture was advertised, Carr took note. In fact, Carr may very well have been the author of an impassioned letter signed 'Justice' that appeared in the *South Australian Advertiser* on 4 July. Its tone was so hot-headed that Nicholas Caire, a local photographer, was moved to intercede. He pointed out that Maughan had not launched an attack on Carr, but on fraud. 'I think . . . it will be found that Dr Carr and "Justice" have taken the rev. gentleman's advertisement in the wrong light,' he wrote soothingly. 'No one has yet tried to disprove the great influence of Dr Carr as a mesmeric agent . . . the advertisement does not refer to him personally at all.'

But Carr wasn't one to back down from a fight. He turned up at Maughan's lecture with Andrew MacLean in tow. As soon as Carr appeared, he was warmly applauded. Then he sat down in the half-empty hall and listened to Maughan's speech without, apparently, uttering one word. Perhaps he was hoping that his large and somewhat formidable presence would be reproof enough.

Maughan began by comparing mesmerism to astrology. He argued against the theory of animal magnetism, using an actual magnet to demonstrate that if he could draw a person from the other side of the room, he would need about fifty tons of magnetism in his body. He then went on to trace the history of mesmerism, describing Joseph Mesmer's 'gross impostures', the spread of his theories throughout Europe and the frequent frauds perpetrated in his name. Next the clergyman tore into clairvoyance. He summoned to the stage a lad called Thomas Waldie, who was blindfolded. When Maughan held up various objects behind Waldie's back, the boy described each one – but Maughan went on to reveal that the whole thing had been 'contrived between himself and his subject beforehand'.

Finally, Maughan theorised that mesmerism was based on mental impression alone. He instructed Waldie to look intently at an object until he had hypnotised himself, then asked the youth to do all manner of ridiculous things. In the audience were doctors Clark and Spicer (both of whom had attended Carr's last séance), and Maughan invited them both up on stage to examine the subject. Dr Spicer tried to bend Waldie's arm, without success. He declared that he was looking at a state identical to that presented by subjects 'recently in White's Rooms and the Town Hall'. But when he and Dr Clark wanted to do a surgical test – or at least apply ammonia to the Waldie's nose – Maughan refused. He said that *he* didn't want to be blamed for exhibitions of that character, as certain other people had been.

The audience applauded.

Dr Clark seemed won over. He announced that he personally believed mesmerism to be self-induced. He praised Maughan for his attempt 'to sift truth from the falsehood' and joined Dr Spicer in thanking the chairman, barrister Samuel Way, who later became Chief Justice of the supreme court. The entertainment closed with a few verses of 'God Save the Queen', sung by the church choir.

Four days later, the *Register* was metaphorically rubbing its hands with glee. 'It now appears pretty certain Dr. Carr and the Rev. Mr. Maughan will break a lance in public on the important matters which have formed the subjects of their lectures,' the newspaper crowed. Thanks to huge public demand (and possibly at the request of local editors, who must have been sick of running letters on the subject), a committee had been established to inquire into the claims of each party. It met on the evening of 29 July 1867, in White's Arbitration Room, and was packed with weighty, respectable names. Charles Todd, who occupied the chair, was head of the Electric Telegraph Department, as well as the official astronomical and meteorological observer. He was responsible for laying the first transcontinental line from Adelaide to Darwin; Alice Springs was named after his wife. Doctors Spicer, Whittall and Gosse were also on the committee – as was George Hamilton, the Commissioner of Police; Police Magistrate Samuel Beddome; supreme court Justice William Wearing; and Samuel Way.

Their first job was to listen as Maughan and Carr gave their views on how things should proceed. The committee then decided 'not to go into matters connected with Dr. Carr's right to the title assumed by him or into his personal character and pretensions' – a clear reference to the question of Carr's medical degree. Next, everyone agreed on the parameters of the investigation, which were that Carr should prove:

> *First. That a man's moral and intellectual character and manifestations are indicated by the size of certain organs or portions of his cranium.*

> *Second. That he (Dr Carr) is able to give a complete analysis and estimate of character, talents and temperament from a person's phrenological development.*
>
> *Third. That he is able to magnetize or communicate some occult influence to water, sticks, or any other form of matter, by which they will obtain certain properties of which they were not before possessed.*
>
> *Fourth. That he is able to magnetize the brains of certain persons, and to communicate himself to them mesmeric or magnetic influence . . .*
>
> *Fifth. That he is able to cure all nervous diseases by means of animal magnetism.*

Carr objected. He had never claimed that he could cure all nervous diseases, he said. In response, Maughan produced one of Carr's charts. There it was, in black and white: the mesmerist had claimed that he could cure all nervous diseases.

A misprint, said Carr. Certain members of the committee grumbled that 'Dr. Carr ought to be held responsible for his own public statements'. At last, however, it was agreed to rephrase the fifth point:

> *Fifth. That the reputed curative influence of mesmerism is unreliable.*

All parties declared themselves satisfied with this framework. But when Carr was called upon to prove his claims, he was shocked. He understood that this was to be a preliminary meeting, he said, to arrange for a public discussion. Maughan then waved one of his letters at Carr. In it, the clergyman had clearly proposed – and Carr had tacitly accepted – that mesmerism should be investigated by the committee *before* being publicly discussed. Why would Carr have any objection to that? Maughan wasn't afraid of the public. He was prepared to set aside four nights to appear on stage. But the committee had been convened to investigate this matter privately.

Carr took a lot of convincing. At last he agreed to present his proof at the next meeting – which eventually took place on 8 August. But when he appeared before the committee again, he refused to cooperate. Instead he announced that he had only ever consented to a *public* discussion.

Maughan had a sense of humour. He offered to increase the committee's membership to one hundred, but Carr wouldn't budge. So the committee had no choice; it passed a resolution to dissolve itself.

'The discussion on mesmerism . . . has all ended in smoke,' the *Geelong Advertiser* glumly reported. The matter didn't end there, however. A week afterwards, Carr advertised his next two lectures – which he described as the public discussion that Maughan had rejected. He promised to prove his own claims, while showing that Maughan's lecture had been unscientific, illogical and absurd. He even used the word 'collusion'.

Appalled, the committee promptly reconvened. It met at Charles Todd's offices, on King William Street, to consider Maughan's written complaint about Carr's latest attack. After some debate, the committee moved that the mesmerist's advertisements were 'calculated to cause misapprehension'. It also resolved that Maughan (unlike Carr) had behaved in a straightforward manner.

Carr went ahead regardless. At his first séance, William Wearing presided as chairman. Though he'd missed the most recent committee meeting, Wearing insisted that he was a neutral party. Then he read aloud a letter from James Maughan. The clergyman had written to explain why he couldn't be present – and why Carr shouldn't be charging an entrance fee. Mr Justice Wearing refused to comment on the 'sufficiency or insufficiency' of Maughan's excuses. Instead he invited Carr to step forward and defend himself.

The mesmerist did so. He explained that he had been denounced as an imposter simply because the powers of magnetism were so rare and obscure. He also pointed out that he didn't believe in clairvoyance, no matter what James Maughan might have said. And he accused Maughan of wanting to approach the whole issue of mesmerism in a 'philosophical and metaphysical way', rather than subjecting it to a series of practical tests.

Suddenly a well-known restaurateur jumped to his feet. He drunkenly demanded to know if the mesmerist was a doctor or a parson. Confusion followed. Some people laughed. The heckler was invited up onto the stage, where he mumbled a few incoherent questions before being led off again. Carr continued. He insisted that he had a right to vindicate himself in public, because Maughan had not defamed him in private. He requested that the audience appoint a new committee of inquiry – which it promptly did. This committee included Attorney-General Richard Andrews, Commissioner of Police George Hamilton (again), Police Magistrate Samuel Beddome (again), a couple of parliamentarians, and the Reverend Denzil John Holt Ibbetson. All of them were in the audience. All of them were invited to watch carefully as Carr magnetised an inanimate object.

Carr then took a glass of water, breathed into it, made a few 'cabalistic passes over it with his hand' and gave it to a pageboy who had volunteered to be mesmerised on a previous occasion. Having drunk from the glass, the pageboy promptly fell into a trance.

At this point the Reverend Ibbetson spoke up. He believed that mesmerism was the result of 'mental impression', he said. Couldn't Carr step behind a screen, and from there produce a result without telling the subject what it would be? Or perhaps Carr could take *two* glasses of water, one magnetised and the other not, and administer them so that the subject didn't know which was which. If that worked, then Ibbetson would wholeheartedly accept Carr's claims.

Oh no, Carr said quickly. A subject always had to know what effect was required, just as a patient had to know what to expect from a medicine. Changing tack, he went on to insist that the boy Thomas Waldie, who had supposedly hypnotised himself at Maughan's lecture, was actually a fraud. Waldie had been mesmerised by Maughan beforehand, in the church. And Carr had proof of it.

He asked William Wearing to read aloud a letter from Waldie, who stated that he'd visited James Maughan's house and had been mesmerised there. 'The night before his lecture on Mesmerism he mesmerized me again in his own church,' Waldie's letter ran, 'and did not awake me from that state properly, so that I felt myself . . . as if mesmerized all the following day and could hardly attend to my employment.' He had been mesmerised again just before Maughan's lecture, though he felt sure that he would have returned to full consciousness when pinched, had it not been for a 'pass' made by Maughan across his forehead. 'I cannot mesmerize myself,' Waldie concluded. 'I have often tried but could not succeed, and I am sure I could not be mesmerized without an operator.'

As it happened, Waldie himself was sitting in the audience. When Carr asked him if his statement was true, the boy replied that it was. Satisfied, Carr launched into his usual round of 'manifestations', closing with a few songs from little Johnny – who had probably shed his sling by this time, since it wasn't mentioned in the press. Johnny sang 'The Bonnie Hills of Scotland' and 'Paddle Your Own Canoe':

I've travelled about a bit in my time
And of troubles I've seen a few,
But I've found it better in every clime
To paddle my own canoe.
My wants are small, I care not at all
If my debts are paid when due;
I drive away strife, in the ocean of life
If I paddle my own canoe.

At the close of the entertainment, which had lasted three-and-a-half hours, the Reverend Ibbetson moved that, in the opinion of the committee, Carr's manifestations were perfectly genuine. This motion was seconded by the commissioner of police.

The next day, Maughan wrote a letter to the *South Australian Advertiser.* He insisted that he had never once mesmerised Waldie. On the contrary, Waldie had mesmerised ('or rather, hypnotised') himself at Maughan's house, a week before Maughan's lecture, in the presence of Samuel Way and two other gentlemen. 'The talk of

Mr. Carr about a "grain" of magnetism, and his confounding magnetic force with magnetic weight, must have been intensely amusing to his audience,' Maughan concluded. 'I hope Mr. Todd was present to enjoy the laugh.' No doubt the clergyman thought that Charles Todd, a bona fide scientist, was well placed to appreciate the sheer idiocy of Carr's so-called 'science'.

Carr hit back, of course. '"A drowning man will grasp at a straw",' he quoted, pointing out that Waldie's letter had been read by a supreme court justice to nearly a thousand people – who had also heard Waldie stand up and testify to its truth. The boy's own father had confirmed his son's statement, to Carr, in the presence of another gentleman. 'I have nothing more to say to one who [has] shrunk from an honest, straightforward public investigation' were the mesmerist's final words.

But Maughan hadn't finished with Carr. In a letter to the *Advertiser*, published the day after, he rejoined:

> *The boy Waldie called on me last night, and wrote down the following remarkable statement: "I never told Dr. Carr that Mr. Maughan mesmerised me on the Thursday evening before his lecture, though he tried hard to bamboozle me and get me to say that he did; but I denied it. Mr Maugham never mesmerised me. I mesmerised myself by looking at a coin. I told Dr. Carr, in answer to his questions, that I had tried to mesmerise myself by making passes over myself, but that I could not do so . . . but I could do it easily with a coin. I did not write that letter Dr. Carr read at the meeting. He wrote it himself. I did not understand . . . that those false statements were in it."*

At the bottom of this letter, the editor added that no further communication on the subject would be published, except as an advertisement. The very next day, the *Register* took up the slack. This paper published two more letters at Carr's request: one was Waldie's original statement, the other a declaration made by John Callow, the gentleman who had witnessed Waldie swear, 'in a clear, distinct, and intelligent manner', that he could not mesmerise himself. Callow claimed to be deeply insulted by Waldie's subsequent retraction, which had impugned Callow's judgement and honour. 'In justice to Dr. Carr as well as to myself,' Callow announced, 'I have considered it my duty to deny so barefaced an untruth.'

Wearily, the editor expressed a hope that the publication of these two documents would end the controversy once and for all.

But it didn't. On 26 August, the paper ran a final letter from Thomas Waldie's father, Walter, who blasted Carr's 'shameful conduct'. According to Walter, Carr had tried to get Thomas to confess that he had been swindling the public; then, when that didn't work, the mesmerist himself had branded the boy a liar. Walter insisted that Carr had 'mystified' Thomas, and put words into his mouth:

> *I consider Dr. Carr has behaved very shamefully to entrap an innocent and unsuspecting boy into making ambiguous statements of which he did not fully understand the meaning, and then trying to impeach his truthfulness because the boy will not allow him to brand Mr Maugham and himself as having been guilty of collusion and fraud.*

Meanwhile, Carr was busily attacking Maughan on another front. Three nights before, he had publicly defended his phrenological skills at a second séance. First he'd read the bumps of several 'well-known colonists', whose faces were covered so that he wouldn't be able to recognise them. Then he'd given his usual demonstrations, during which one of the more distinguished guests had had half his coat pulled off. 'The dexterity and suddenness of the unexpected feat brought the house down – rounds of applause and hearty laughter, which endured for some time, were elicited,' the *Register* remarked. It also noted that, early on in the show, Carr had accused Maughan of hypocrisy – by alluding to a certain essay about the causes of rust in wheat.

By that time everyone in Adelaide was aware of the rumours. Months earlier, the South Australian Agricultural and Horticultural Society had offered a prize for the best essay on diseases in wheat, and Maughan had been one of the entrants. On 3 May he'd been declared the winner. But as soon as his essay was published, it had faced a barrage of criticism. Maughan was charged with copying whole paragraphs (and several diagrams) from another work entitled 'Blights of the Wheat and their Remedies' without acknowledging the fact. One member of the society had even declared that 'the great part of the essay had been compiled out of a sixpenny book purchaseable in Adelaide'.

Maughan vigorously denied that two-thirds of his essay had come from another source. His response was as furious as Carr's might have been. He publicly upbraided his critics – including the judges and the winner of the second prize, William Owen. Maugham claimed that he had never seen the book he was accused of plagiarising:

I beg, with great respect for Mr Owen's veracity, to inform him that when he says that five-sixths of my essay were borrowed from other men's works on 'botany and micology' (sic) he utters what is not true. Had Mr Owen, however, in his essay, given us a little more of other people's sense, and less of his own nonsense, it would have been better for his fame.

The society wasn't impressed. Many of their subsequent meetings revolved around whether action should be taken or not. Meanwhile, Thomas Guthrie Carr was using the affair as ammunition in his fight against Maughan – which quickly spread into neighbouring Victoria. When the *Hamilton Spectator* noted that Carr had had 'anything but an untroubled reception in Adelaide', it received an enraged response. 'Your correspondent,' Carr wrote, 'is either utterly ignorant of the application of the term "charlatan" or he most ungenerously misapplied it.' On visiting Bendigo again, Carr began his first lecture by referring to his recent controversy with Maughan. He insisted that Maughan had come off second best in the encounter, after refusing to engage with the mesmerist in public. A Melbourne correspondent to the *South Australian Weekly Chronicle* pointed out, in November 1867, that Carr had been 'lecturing in the provincial towns since he left Adelaide, and does not fail to make capital out of his alleged triumph over the Rev. Maughan'.

But this tale of triumph did little to improve Carr's fortunes. Shrinking audiences and a growing scepticism began to dog his shows. In Clare, for example, he was boldly challenged at one of his lectures by a certain Dr Bayne, who demanded that Carr answer three questions: could Carr magentise the human brain, could he magnetise a glass of water, and could he magnetise a stick? Carr answered 'I can' to each of these questions. Bayne then proposed 'that the man who declares that he can magentise or mesmerise the human brain, a glass of water, or a bit of stick, is a humbug, a swindler and an imposter.'

Challenges like this must have become very wearing. It's possible that a hostile public was behind Carr's hurried exit from South Australia. On the other hand, there might have been another reason.

Some nine months after Carr left Adelaide, a boy called Arthur Charles Guthrie Carr Kidman was born to Emily Kidman, in the same city. His father's name was recorded as Thomas Guthrie Carr.

No record exists that the mesmerist ever financially supported or communicated with his illegitimate son.

IV

From Adelaide Carr slowly made his way to Sydney. He passed through Moonta in September 1867, Bendigo in October and Castlemaine in November. In Eaglehawk, Victoria, he gave his subjects a 'galvanic shock' without the aid of a battery. Then he popped back down to Melbourne for the Duke of Edinburgh's visit, late in the year. But that trip was a failure; according to a local authority, 'the balls, illuminations, public dinners &c., took away a good many people who usually went to the theatres'. In Heathcote, he had good houses but a very poor reception. According to one local paper, he utterly failed to impress his audience.

'The singing of the boy Johnny was the only redeeming feature in the whole affair,' it said.

Next came Beechworth, where Carr was subjected to a withering review. A local paper complained that he was not genuine, not scientific, and not well read. 'As to his so-called lecture on Sunday night,' it declared, '. . . we must confess that we never listened to such a mixture of ignorance, impudence and folly.' The paper was particularly shocked that Carr, after opening with a prayer, should have concluded by holding out his hands 'in a most theatrical manner' and blessing the audience. This was regarded as going a bit too far.

In the same issue, a Dr Alyara L Slater declared that he had never pronounced one of Carr's subjects to be insensible during a recent performance, as the paper had earlier reported. 'The pupils of the eyes were not insensible to light,' Slater wrote, 'and this I stated to Dr. Carr, when asked a question by that gentleman.' Slater was adamant that Carr's so-called subject had not been in a coma, and that any claims to the contrary were utterly untrue.

After Beechworth came Albury, then Yass. By February 1868, Carr had reached Wagga Wagga, where he gave a couple of lectures at the Mechanics' Institute. Just before boarding a coach to Gundagai, he scribbled out a cheque for the hall rental and gave it to Andrew MacLean, who passed it on to the secretary of the institute.

But the cheque bounced. So Carr was arrested in Boorowa, for uttering a valueless cheque with intent to defraud.

'That one possessed of almost magical powers permitted himself to be arrested at all, and especially in consideration of a ridiculously small sum, must have astonished his admirers,' the *Age* smirked. 'It now turns out, according to the explanation of the *Yass Courier* (equally ingenious and ingenuous) that it was "all a mistake".'

Apparently Carr had forgotten to alter the name of the bank printed on his cheque. As soon as he'd realised his error, he had notified Andrew MacLean, who had then asked the institute's secretary, Joseph Thompson, to withhold presentation for a couple of days. Carr wanted to alert his bank in Sydney, so that funds could be placed to his credit in the bank on which the cheque was drawn. But it was too late. By the time Thompson had received Carr's note, the Joint Stock Bank of Wagga Wagga had already dishonoured his cheque.

Carr appeared before the Boorowa court, and was granted bail. Before he could be dragged off to Wagga Wagga, however, all charges were withdrawn. Someone, somewhere, had decided against prosecuting. 'We are informed,' the *Age* concluded, 'that an action is to be commenced by Dr Carr against the parties who procured the warrant, as its issue has occasioned him serious pecuniary loss, as well as the injury it is likely to cause in other respects.' Carr was always vindictive, even in victory.

But this wasn't his first arrest in New South Wales. In Wagga Wagga he had already been charged with the illegal possession of a swordstick. The swordstick actually belonged to Dr Clark, who had appeared with Carr on stage in Adelaide. And it had been stolen by Carr's former assistant, Edwin Turner Osbaldeston.

By that time, Osbaldeston was already in Yatala stockade, serving seven years for a series of petty thefts that had been described as 'incredible'. His recent history was very odd. After leaving the mesmerist's employ, he had become shampooer to Prince Alfred, the Duke of Edinburgh. Prince Alfred was visiting Adelaide at the time, and Osbaldeston's wide experience in bathhouses had probably played a part in his appointment. His service was so exemplary that he soon attained the position of valet. But on 17 November 1867, a certain Corporal Doyle of North Adelaide police station visited a jeweller's shop in Rundle Street. Here he discovered a music box that had been left for repair just a few days earlier by Mrs Osbaldeston. Doyle recognised it instantly as belonging to Joseph Kirkpatrick, who had been robbed of it in April that year – along with a gold pencil case, a locket, a paint box, several coats, several jackets, a muslin dress, a baby's braided dress, and a handkerchief.

Kirkpatrick identified the music box as his. So Doyle secured a search warrant. Then he went with two other policemen, Constables Besley and McCaffery, to a house in Grenfell Street, near Hindmarsh Square, where Osbaldeston was living with his wife and children. Mrs Osbaldeston answered the front door.

'Does Mr Osbaldeston live here?' Doyle demanded. When she replied that he did, Doyle asked if he was at home.

'No; he's at Government House,' she said.

At Doyle's request, she let him in, confirming that she had left a music box to be repaired at Mr Pfaendler's shop. Doyle wanted to know where the box had come from. 'I really can't say, sir,' the woman answered. 'Mr Osbaldeston could tell you where he got it . . .'

But Doyle had already recognised the jacket she was wearing. He sent for Kirkpatrick, who had been waiting in Hindmarsh Square. Sure enough, the jacket belonged to Kirkpatrick's wife. Again, Mrs Osbaldeston couldn't say where it had come from. Her husband had 'bought it from some person'. At that point Doyle decided to pay a visit to Government House. Apparently he had been suspicious of Osbaldeston's activities for months, though his former request for a search warrant had been denied. Now, at last, his hunch had been vindicated.

He left the other two corporals to search Osbaldeston's lodgings, where they found a huge collection of stolen goods – 'two drayloads', according to the *Sydney Morning Herald*. Most of Kirkpatrick's missing possessions were there. So were a colonial oven taken from Edward Lellman of North Adelaide, three chairs stolen from George Gail of Nailsworth, and a concertina and a pair of 'burlesque shoes' thieved from Arthur James Dymond. These last items had disappeared from the dressing room of the Town Hall during an 'Amateur Christy Minstrel' performance. Other objects in Osbaldeston's stash included masonic insignia, a military uniform, a number of maps and anatomical charts, marked linen, a gold watch and lots of jewellery.

Meanwhile, Doyle was on his way to Government House, where he intercepted Osbaldeston on the lawn near the east entrance. Doyle asked him about the music box. Osbaldeston blanched.

'Oh yes,' he said. 'I got it from a person named Evans, I think; but my wife can tell you.' Doyle wanted to know where Mr Evans lived. Osbaldeston couldn't remember. Doyle instructed him to come back home.

'I can't go for half an hour,' the valet replied.

'You must come sooner, if you please,' Doyle retorted.

Osbaldeston said, 'I'll see' and retreated back into Government House. From his expression Doyle expected the worst and immediately applied to 'several gentlemen in the neighbourhood'. These men promptly searched the great house, but they were too late.

The fugitive had escaped through the western side of the building, climbed down into a quarry at its northern end, passed through a 'police paddock', skirted the barracks and made his way to his own house – where he was immediately captured by Corporals Besley and McCaffery.

Osbaldeston was then stripped of his official uniform. Doyle dragged him all over Adelaide in an attempt to identify the stolen objects found at his house. Back in his own lodgings, Osbaldeston promised to find the name of the person who'd sold him the music box, and searched 'for some time' in a memorandum book. According to Doyle:

> *He said that Evans had got a sister and a brother-in-law who kept a pledge-shop in Melbourne. He pointed out the name of Shuttleworth in the book, and said that's the name of the sister; that he had several times seen Evans, alias Shuttleworth, about the Theatre, and dined at his house several times. He could not tell where they lived, but Abbott was the name of his brother-in-law, who kept the pledge-shop.*

Doyle was having none of it. He cautioned Osbaldeston, then began to search the parlour. Besley was searching the bedroom. McCaffery was in the passage, but soon followed Mrs Osbaldeston into the kitchen at the back of the house, where she had gone to fetch linen for her baby. Suddenly Doyle heard the front door slam and the key turn in the lock.

Osbaldeston had escaped again.

He fled down Grenfell Street, into Bent Street and across Rundle Street, before scaling a high fence and running across an open paddock. Finally, he ended up in the chief secretary's garden on North Terrace. After climbing another fence, he hid in a clergyman's hayloft. But it wasn't long before Doyle tracked him down and took him off to North Adelaide police station.

A few days later, two members of the prince's suite inspected Osbaldeston's hoard and retrieved the items he'd taken from them. Also retrieved were several articles belonging to the Duke of Edinburgh, as well as a red silk cushion embroidered with the Prince of Wales' feathers and his motto, 'Ich Dieu'. 'Three flags which were missing recently from the poles erected in honor of his Royal Highness . . . were found among the plunder,' the *Launceston Examiner* reported, adding that, when Osbaldeston had been living in North Adelaide earlier that year, he had written a letter to the *Advertiser* about the recent spate of robberies, complaining about the 'insufficiency of police protection' in the area.

On 21 November, Osbaldeston tried to hang himself in his police cell. He was immediately put in a straitjacket. At around the same time, his wife disappeared. His future looked gloomy. But as it turned out, Osbaldeston's extraordinary adventures had barely begun.

In 1926, at the age of ninety-three, he was charged in New Jersey with stealing a horse some forty years earlier, while he was travelling through the United States under the alias 'Edwin Turner'. Nonagerian Osbaldeston claimed to be the son of the former Earl of Onslow, raised in London by tutors in the company of Edward, Prince of

Wales. He insisted that the matter of the stolen horse was 'a case of mistaken identity'.

In the sixty-odd years that had elapsed between his first arrest and his last, Osbaldeston had been in court over and over again.

On being released from prison in South Australia, he'd travelled to New Zealand, where he'd lectured on 'hydropathy' as Dr Edwin Turner. Convicted of theft once more, he'd served a brief term of imprisonment before being rearrested on another theft charge. After breaking out of prison he'd been hunted down and arrested again, after which he'd jumped bail and disappeared altogether, 'believed gone to San Francisco'. There is some evidence that he may have returned to Melbourne, then travelled to England as a ship's surgeon before ending up in the United States.

By 1893 he was a massage therapist and chiropodist on West Forty-Sixth Street, New York – where his ten-year-old son reported him to the police for abuse. Apparently, Osbaldeston had repeatedly assaulted all four of his young children, though he was never convicted of it.

Then, in 1903, the following item ran in New York journal the *Malone Farmer*:

> *Mrs Frank Lugas is barricaded in her home at 6,319 Broad Street* [Pittsburgh], *fearing death at the hands of an assassin. Prof. Edwin T. Osbaldeston says he is her husband. He boarded at her house when she was a Miss May. Osbaldeston followed his wife and child to Oberstein, Germany, and found his wife the housekeeper for a manufacturer named Wirth. Osbaldeston killed Wirth and a servant who interfered. The German courts released*

> *him on the plea of insanity. He wrote from Germany that he was coming here to claim Miss May as his wife. Two days ago he wrote from New York saying he was coming to kill her. He sent her a piece of bloody shirt, which he said was taken from his victims in Germany. The police are watching every train to arrest Osbaldeston and are guarding the house of Mrs Lugas.*

In fact, Louisa Lugas, nee Weiss, alias Metzgar, had once been Osbaldeston's massage student in Malone, New York, before she'd borne him a child and was arrested with him for shoplifting in Montreal. He'd skipped bail and she'd escaped from prison to Germany, where Wirth had employed her. From Germany, she'd moved back to America and married Frank Lugas . . .

Osbaldeston's life was almost as strange as the autobiographical fantasies he'd dreamed up. It says something about Thomas Guthrie Carr that he should have hired such a very peculiar man. Their association certainly raised a few eyebrows, one newspaper wondering how deep the connection was between Carr and Osbaldeston. How far, it asked, was the subject under the inspiration of the master? 'Whose will was the ruling passion that impelled the surreptitious taking of the clothing, jewellery, -&c,' it slyly inquired. 'Was the great medicine man acting on the organ of acquisitiveness of the slave . . .?' Had Carr's departure from Adelaide had anything to do with Osbaldeston's arrest? Some people recalled that Dr Carr had been invited to Government House, the scene of Osbaldeston's predations. Did *this* have any significance?

To put an end to all speculation, South Australia's governor sent a private telegram to the *Argus* in December, announcing once and for all that Thomas Guthrie Carr was *not under his patronage.*

But the question of the stolen swordstick was apparently settled to the satisfaction of everyone involved. Carr must have convinced the authorities that he was an innocent party, because he was never convicted. Instead, he left Wagga Wagga for points east, arriving in Sydney sometime in March of 1868.

He was joined there by Andrew MacLean, who soon set up as a 'surgeon and practical dentist' in Lauriston Terrace, Phillip Street. John Huxtable also came to town, on business connected with his latest venture, The Aerated Bread Company. Starting a week after Carr's first Sydney lecture, Huxtable acted as Carr's unpaid agent for about a fortnight, receiving only a 'present' in return. But somewhere along the line Carr had shed both his Maori assistant and the long-suffering Johnny. Instead, he started to look for replacements, engaging people like Miss Brooks and Prince Tommy, the Aboriginal boy who was described in the press as a 'coloured young gentleman from Fraser's Island'. In April a lad called James Dalton was also hired; William Roberts later described him as Carr's 'buttoner' – a slang term usually applied to a sharper's assistant employed to entice dupes.

It was during this search for assistants that Carr eventually stumbled upon Eliza Jane Gray, and became embroiled in the affair that led to his arrest on a capital charge.

PART III

AFTER THE INCIDENT

I

On Monday 21 and Thursday 24 September 1868, Eliza Gray continued her testimony at Thomas Guthrie Carr's committal hearing. She faced a barrage of questions, delivered in a scattershot way that was probably designed to confuse her. But the story that finally emerged was simple enough.

A few days after the alleged assault on 18 March, she had begun to feel ill. This was unusual, because she'd always been very healthy. Her only other bout of illness had involved congested lungs, and though she admitted to being 'liable to faints', the sensation she experienced normally when fainting was very different from the lack of consciousness she'd succumbed to in Carr's rooms. As for the new complaint, it was unprecedented. But although she described its symptoms to the court at some length, they weren't published. Every time anyone referred to her mysterious illness the details were passed over, or branded not fit for publication.

What Gray had contracted – or what she was *believed* to have contracted – was some kind of venereal disease. An exact diagnosis is impossible because we don't know what her symptoms were. She might have had gonorrhoea, or chlamydia, or even syphilis. She might not have had a venereal disease at all; the complaint that was so quick to affect her might have been a simple urinary tract infection. A misdiagnosis is unlikely, however, because nineteenth-century doctors were familiar enough with the signs of sexually transmitted diseases. And although Carr later claimed that she was not suffering from 'the complaint she had mentioned, but from another', the effects of the illness left Gray in no doubt as to where it had come from.

As soon as she began to feel the symptoms she went straight to Carr and accused him of infecting her. She wanted him to 'remedy the injury'. According to Gray, Carr promised he would. He declared that he would come to her house and 'make it all right'. She thought he was offering her a cure.

'I always threatened him with the law,' she deposed, 'from the first instance.' But the law was double-edged. On the one hand, as Carr himself later admitted, exposure could ruin a 'public man'. On the other hand, for a woman, the consequences could be even worse. In his summing-up of the case, William Roberts took care to remind the Bench that Gray had delayed reporting the incident for the best of reasons – because doing so 'might have militated greatly against her future happiness'. Gray herself insisted, over and over again, that if Carr had kept her well supplied with medicines and money, she would not have 'exposed herself' by prosecuting him.

A few days after she first accused Carr, she was undressing in her bedroom at about eleven o'clock at night when she looked out of the window and saw him descending from a cab. So she went down and opened the front door. 'I let him in because I thought if he made a noise it would create scandal,' Gray said, 'and he had done me enough injury without that.'

She was questioned vigorously about this nocturnal visit, made while her husband, William, was away on the steamer *Fire King*. She had met with Carr in the front room, she said. They had gone nowhere else. There was a bed in the room, but it had been occupied by one of Gray's sleeping children. She didn't know how long Carr had stayed, or what time he'd left. He had wanted to stay all night, but she'd refused to let him. Obviously, if he'd given her any advice about her condition, it hadn't helped her very much.

But his cheque for thirty shillings certainly had.

Shortly afterwards, William returned home from his trip to the Manning River. He was forty-two years old and a native of the Orkney Islands. At the age of fourteen he'd been a farm servant; by 1845 he had a seaman's ticket, issued at Newcastle-on-Tyne. Two years later, he jumped ship in New Brunswick, Canada, and vanished for a while. But in 1853 he married Eliza Jane Shields at St Mary's Cathedral, in Sydney, and by 1866 they'd had eight children together.

According to William's testimony, his trip on the *Fire King* had taken place 'subsequent to the 18th of March', which was a Wednesday. Since his steamer 'generally left

Sydney on Monday and got back on the following Friday', he must have left home on Monday 23 March. During the voyage, William too had fallen ill – and he wasn't happy about it. In later testimony, he declared that he 'remembered the night of the 22nd of March; until that time nothing had occurred to mar the peace and happiness of his family'.

This all suggests that, if Eliza *had been* infected by Carr, she had passed the complaint onto her husband within four days of the assault. William, in turn, must have fallen ill within four days of their congress. On returning from the Manning River he had accused his wife of infecting him; Eliza calculated that this confrontation must have happened 'more than a week after the occurrence on the 18th of March'. Though her response was to blame him for his own misfortune, she later admitted that her accusation was false, made because 'he was spiteful and threatened to take my life'. Carr, she insisted, was the real cause of her sickness. 'I told him that I had to blame my husband through him,' she fretted.

Her testimony was a little vague as to whether she'd told William about her own illness when he confronted her. But even if she had, she certainly hadn't told him that Carr was responsible for it. 'I was afraid to tell my husband that it was Dr Carr for fear he would blow his [Carr's] brains out,' Eliza Gray revealed.

William only discovered that Carr was the actual culprit a few days before the committal hearing, when Eliza finally laid charges.

Even so, William had obviously been suspicious for some time. After 22 March, he stopped sleeping with Eliza. Then he moved out. He also went off to a chemist for help, though his wife seemed under the impression that he'd gone to a doctor. She herself soldiered on until the end of April, when she fainted in the Cohen Brothers' workroom and had to be taken home. After that, she said, she was forced to resign her position because of poor health. 'I was very ill, scarcely able to walk, when I went to see Dr Bell . . .' she related. 'I swear that Dr Carr was the sole cause of my illness. I swear that positively.'

To confirm her statement, Dr William Bell was called upon to testify. Described in press reports as 'legally qualified', he advertised himself as both a general practitioner and a government vaccinator, with thirty years of practice under his belt. A member of the Royal College of Surgeons, he was also the author of various published essays: one on 'The Wear and Tear of Human Life', another on 'Small Pox and Vaccination' and yet another on 'infantile education', in which he argued at length that children shouldn't be sent to school before they were seven years old. After many years spent knocking around rural New South Wales, he had come to Sydney in 1863, where he'd taken up residence at 463 Pitt Street. In 1866, he'd advertised an unusual subscription service, offering unlimited treatment for five pounds a year.

Eliza Gray may have taken advantage of this offer.

According to Bell, he had been tending the Gray family for two years when Eliza Gray came to him in April, complaining of a 'certain ailment'. No doubt he had been treating her children, off and on; if she'd previously been as fit as she claimed, this may have been the first time she'd consulted him about her own health. He saw her five or six times after the initial visit, at intervals of three or four days. The fact that she was still sick in September suggests that his treatments hadn't worked. But since medicines containing mercury were commonly prescribed for venereal disease at the time, it's possible that by September Gray was suffering from the side effects of mercury poisoning.

She was now a jobless invalid, with seven children and a husband who wanted nothing to do with her (though he was still supporting his children). Dr Bell may not have been charging her fees, but she would have had to pay for her medicines. So it's not surprising that she applied to Thomas Guthrie Carr for help. She had nowhere else to turn.

Exactly how many times she went to see him became a matter of much debate. James Dalton, Carr's 'agent', claimed to have met her in April. He said that she had visited Carr thirty or forty times. Other ladies had called on Carr at the School of Arts, he deposed, but Gray had been the most frequent visitor. Gray denied strenuously that she had been there so often. She admitted that she had gone several times to ask Carr for money to pay for her medicine 'which sometimes he gave her and sometimes he would not'. She insisted, however, that she'd taken Elizabeth Hook with her on these occasions. 'He was vexed with me for bringing Miss Hook with me because she used to laugh and giggle,' Gray declared. 'This was after the 18th of March. I went to the School of Arts several times after the occurrence.'

But then Carr moved. His run at the School of Arts had finished towards the end of April, around the time that James O'Farrell had been hanged. It had been a highly successful series of engagements; even towards the end of March, his shows were being described as 'unpleasantly crowded'. One columnist even wondered if he would have to secure a larger building, thanks to his popular appeal. So after leaving the School of Arts he didn't leave Sydney. Instead, on 6 May, Carr advertised three 'grand sensational seances' at the Prince of Wales Opera House in Castlereagh Street – an impressive venue with all the latest in theatre equipment, including gas footlights. He moved his lodgings, too – down the harbour to Watsons Bay. And he also leased a set of consulting rooms at 94 Hunter Street, opposite Shadler's Bakery. Here, among all the birdstuffers' shops and photographers' studios, he continued to draw teeth and give phrenological assessments.

It was almost as if he was trying to avoid someone.

Carr's Prince of Wales engagement was lavishly promoted. From 7 to 9 May, a special steamer left Watsons Bay every night at 6.30 pm and returned from Circular Quay at 11.30 pm, for the express purpose of transporting people to Carr's entertainment. 'Passengers taking tickets for the Dress Circle or Stalls will be conveyed free of charge,' Carr promised. He ran a series of testimonials in the Sydney *Empire*, quoting satisfied customer after satisfied customer. 'I beg to state that Dr. Carr extracted a tumour from my face on the public platform at the School of Arts and the operation was accomplished without pain,' wrote Henry Hollebone, of 62 York Street. 'I beg to state that I had a finger amputated while under the mesmeric influence and that I did not feel the slightest pain whatever,' wrote Ellen Sweetman, on 24 April. Mrs Henry Hockney Dawson, the headmistress of a girls' school on Elizabeth Street, wrote, 'Doctor Carr has extracted four (4) teeth from my daughter while under mesmeric influence, and I have much pleasure in stating she showed but very slight signs of feeling the operation.' It's possible that Mrs Dawson was a neighbour of Carr's; one can't help feeling concerned about the welfare of her students, if, in fact, the letter was genuine.

After the Prince of Wales shows, Carr turned his attention to the suburbs. On 23 May he advertised a 'farewell performance' at the Balmain School of Arts. Two nights later he was at Newtown Oddfellows Hall, and on the 29th he was in Woollahra. But he kept his Hunter Street rooms open for private patients. 'Early application is necessary, as Dr Carr's stay in Sydney will be of limited duration,' the advertisements warned.

Meanwhile, Eliza Gray was getting desperate. She needed more money. Exactly how much she eventually received from Carr was a point of contention. She acknowledged that, after the first cheque for thirty shillings, he had given her another £2.2*s.* The defence claimed that he'd also given her five pounds for her rent, but she denied it. On the contrary, 'she never told him that she owed rent; she told him that through him she had to leave her husband'. That, she testified, was when he'd given her the cheque for £2.2*s.* Some of this money she later used to pay her rent. But when the defence declared that, on 5 June, Dalton had given her one pound in an envelope, she refuted that claim, too:

> *I got an envelope from Dalton with 'I am sorry it will not be convenient for me until Saturday' written inside the envelope, but there was no pound in it. On the Saturday following I went and saw Dr Carr, but we had a dreadful row.*

She insisted that he gave her no more money, then amended this statement under cross-examination. She thought he might have given her one pound when he sent her to Dr Charles Eichler, of Bridge Street. This was on 5 June, after their 'dreadful row'. Obviously, Gray's health wasn't improving under Dr Bell's treatment, so Carr wrote a note to Dr Eichler. It read: 'Dear Doctor, will you kindly advise bearer about something which I cannot attend to.' He then promised, in writing, to pay Eliza Gray's fees, and asked Eichler to make sure his chemist billed Carr for any medicine. After his signature, Carr added a suspicious-sounding postscript: 'That lady is much better.'

The next day Eliza Gray went to see Dr Eichler, who later testified that she was suffering from 'a certain disease'. He examined her, but could not identify the precise origin of the complaint. 'Mrs Gray came to me six times,' he said. 'After she had been three or four times at my house, she said it was all Dr. Carr's fault. Up to that time she had never mentioned Dr. Carr's name.' To the best of his recollection, Gray had first referred to Carr on 3 August.

By that time, Carr had already left town. He was touring New South Wales. But he hadn't paid Dr Eichler before leaving, and he hadn't left money for Gray's medicines. It was this last omission that rankled the most. 'If he had left the money . . . with Dr Eichler, to get the medicines, I should not have brought him here now,' Gray declared in court.

Her next move was to approach Andrew MacLean, who was still working as a dentist on Phillip Street. She had seen him with Carr, though she never specified exactly where. When she wrote to MacLean, she inquired as to

Carr's whereabouts, giving her address but not her name. 'If I had done so I thought he would not call,' she said, adding that she had *not* made an appointment for nine o'clock at night, nor asked him to come to her house, as the defence claimed. 'Dr MacLean called the same evening on which I wrote the letter, about eight o'clock,' she related. He then gave her Carr's address, inscribed on a card. It was a Dubbo address.

The card was produced in court, along with Gray's letter to MacLean. 'I also asked him if he was writing to Dr. Carr, to tell him to write to me,' Gray added.

If Carr did write, she never mentioned it. But he probably didn't, because around that time he was having troubles of his own.

II

By the middle of June 1868, Carr was in Bathurst, attracting 'much popular attention'. Here he was reported to have amputated *two* fingers belonging to the same young man, over two evenings. The young man in question told Carr's audience that he had felt no pain until four hours after the first operation; the second also appeared to be painless. A certain Dr Grant of Mudgee helped Carr to dress the young man's wounds, after which Carr excised a cancer off an old man's lip and compelled his other mesmeric subjects to enact a death scene. During the performance, Carr referred to certain 'unworthy imputations' that had been made against him.

By July, he was advertising his show in Grenfell, where he was described as 'a very eloquent man, his manner being dignified and commanding'. The *Mining Record and Grenfell General Advertiser* related in awestruck tones that Carr had not only drawn several teeth in front of a sizeable audience, but had also removed a tumour from the neck of an assistant blacksmith well known around the town. This tumour had then been deposited on the shoulder of the patient, who'd later walked off the stage and announced to his friends that he had not felt the slightest pain. 'As to the subsequent mesmeric experiments,' the paper concluded, 'it is undeniable that some persons were successfully acted upon . . . but it is also clear that some were acting a part.'

Nevertheless, Carr was complimented on his clever, instructive lectures, and on the eloquence and grace with which he condemned 'the shallow and frivolous pursuits of young people of the present age'.

By August, Carr was in Forbes. And it was here that he made a bad mistake. During one of his shows a man named Ingram – who refused to be mesmerised – volunteered to have a tooth pulled. When the tooth broke off in his mouth, Ingram went to the local police court. He charged the mesmerist with assault, because Carr had told the audience that he'd broken the tooth on purpose.

'I was one of a number of volunteers that went forward on the stage to have my tooth extracted,' Ingram testified, 'and Dr. Carr broke it off by the gum, and said to the meeting that he had done this to punish me.'

A startled magistrate demanded, 'Punish you? For what?'

'For my impudence,' Ingram replied. He was asked if he had suffered much pain. He answered that it was not what he had suffered, but what he *might* suffer in the future, when he had the roots removed.

'Did you feel any pain at the time?' the Bench wanted to know.

'I did,' said Ingram.

'Were you mesmerised?' the Bench queried.

'No,' said Ingram.

'When you sat down to have your tooth extracted, did you expect to feel any pain?' was the next question put to the plaintiff.

Ingram admitted that he had. Then Thomas Guthrie Carr rose to cross-examine him, beginning with, 'Were you drunk upon the night that I broke your tooth?'

'No,' Ingram rejoined. 'I cannot say that I was.'

'Were you drunk?' Carr repeated.

Ingram amended his statement slightly. 'I had taken a nobbler or two . . .'

'*Were you drunk*?' said Carr, at which the Bench intervened.

'Yes or no?' was the stern query made of the plaintiff. Ingram finally confessed that he had been drunk.

'Did you swear, and smoke your pipe upon the stage during the interval that I was absent, and annoy my subjects?' Carr then inquired. Ingram allowed that he had been smoking. He also claimed that he could recall what had happened that night. He remembered Carr breaking his tooth. He remembered swearing and smoking before the audience.

'I was not swearing at you; it was at the pianist,' he assured Carr.

'When you sat down to have your tooth drawn,' Carr continued, 'while I was in the act of placing the instrument did you throw your hands up violently and force mine away?'

'Yes I did,' said Ingram, 'it was high time, because you hurt me.'

Carr then asked if he had told Ingram that he was mesmerised, or that he would feel no pain. But before the plaintiff could answer, Carr suddenly turned to the Bench and argued his case:

> *Will your Worship permit me to explain that all the punishment I wished to inflict upon this man was the pain consequent upon tooth extraction. I extracted other teeth that night upon the stage without pain, while the subjects were in a mesmeric state. This man admits that he knew he would feel pain, that he was perfectly conscious, and that I had given him distinctly to understand that he would feel the pain; he did not care, he would insist on having it out. It was not my intention to break the tooth. It was my wish to extract it, but owing to the violent resistance of this drunken man the tooth was broken off by aveolar process.*

The magistrates heard him out. Then they retired for five minutes. When they returned, the police magistrate, William Farrand, stated that most of the Bench regarded this as a clear case of assault. If Ingram *had* been guilty of misconduct, the police should have been called. Carr had no right to take the law into his own hands. 'Dr Carr's statement to the audience that he had done this to punish the plaintiff clearly proved an assault had been committed,' Farrand declared.

Only one magistrate, Charles Cropper, dissented. He didn't believe that an assault had taken place, because the plaintiff had been warned about the pain he would feel and had (in the words of one newspaper), 'brought on himself all that occurred'. But despite Cropper's objections, Carr was found guilty and fined forty shillings.

He announced that he would apply to the supreme court for a writ of prohibition, overturning the judgement.

By this time, however, he had another court case to worry about. In Victoria, a Scottish 'delineator of character' named William Gourlay was seeking damages of £1000 from Carr and a man called Ambrose Kyte. According to Gourlay, Kyte had agreed to let him St George's Hall during the Duke of Edinburgh's visit in late 1867 – but had let the venue to Carr instead.

Kyte contested this claim. He argued that Gourlay had changed his mind, asking for the hall to be re-let because he was 'afraid there would be too many amusements in town at the time of the Duke's visit for Gourlay's entertainment to pay'. Kyte had therefore given the hall to Carr, on identical terms. 'Carr played six nights,' said Kyte, 'and he gave me a cheque, which was dishonoured.' According to Kyte, Carr had been very successful during his first run at the hall, in 1866, but not in November 1867. On the first night of the prince's visit, the mesmerist's earnings had amounted to no more than three pounds. Whether this failure was due to a recent, scathing review in the *Argus*, Kyte couldn't say, since he seldom read theatrical criticism. In fact, the review had described Carr's audience as being comprised of 'shopboys and servant girls'. It had condemned Carr's dreary lecture and clumsy illustrations, poured scorn on his severe references to 'some Adelaide clergyman', and concluded that the whole entertainment 'was in the worst possible taste'.

'When Carr failed, I suggested to him that Gourlay might take the hall off his hands,' said Kyte. Instead, Gourlay had applied for an injunction to stop Carr from performing. And when Gourlay's application was refused, he had sued for damages instead.

The jury returned a verdict for the defendant, and the plaintiff's bill was dismissed with costs. But the whole matter must have weighed heavily on Carr's mind as he traipsed around the colony, from town to town. And on finally returning to Sydney, he had barely installed himself in his new consulting rooms when Eliza Gray turned up, on 10 or 11 September, demanding recompense.

Carr's new rooms were at 11 Bridge Street, the last in a line of four-storeyed terrace houses occupying the space where the Burns Philp building now stands. The houses all had dormer windows and shops on the ground floor. Carr shared his premises with Arthur Cubitt, a house and shipping agent. Charles Eichler's consulting rooms lay further east, on the corner of Young Street.

Eliza Gray confronted Carr at his new address on a Friday or Saturday afternoon. But she had to get past James Dalton first. According to his testimony, she had already visited once that morning and been rebuffed. When she reappeared a few hours later, Dalton escorted her into Carr's office – and remained there for most of the interview, though she objected to his presence more than once. What happened next is hard to disentangle. There were several visits to Bridge Street, and differing accounts of what took place there. Clearly, however, Gray was in a state of tremendous anxiety.

She had already told Dalton that she was ill. When asked by the mesmerist what claim she had on him, she replied,

'You know what claim; I am very ill.' Conscious, perhaps, that Dalton was listening, Carr declared, 'You never said this to me before.' Then Gray remarked obliquely, 'You know something that took place in March.' Carr, in response, looked very surprised. 'I cannot understand why you have come here today,' he said.

Dalton, at the time, knew nothing of the 'affair in March'. But he heard Gray tell Carr that she was very ill, and that she'd been obliged to leave her situation as a consequence. Carr's response was to assure her that she wasn't suffering from 'the complaint she had mentioned'.

'Whatever it is, Doctor, I am very ill,' she said. Then, according to Dalton, she announced that if Carr gave her twenty pounds, she would let the matter drop.

'I won't give you a halfpenny, Mrs Gray,' Carr retorted.

Gray vigorously denied Dalton's version of events. She insisted that she had asked for no specific sum but had told Carr that unless he gave her something, she would take him to court. Then the exchange had got ugly. He'd said that she was a common woman, adding that 'if all the respectable married women in Sydney are like you there is not one respectable'. She'd called him a rotten man, 'worse than Bertrand', because Louis Bertrand had shot only one man dead to take his wife, whereas Carr was trying to murder two. 'I may have said a great deal more,' Gray confessed. But she had never promised to revenge herself on Carr, had never used abusive language and had never said she was cleverer than other women. 'I may have told him that he was not dealing with a fool,' she conceded.

Whatever she did say, it had rattled Carr. He'd threatened to summon a constable. She'd threatened to send him a lawyer's letter. 'He then threw 10s. into my hand, and said "There's money to pay for it",' she testified. 'I would not have taken it only my children had not tasted bread for two days. Dr. Carr asked me how much I would take as a recompense, but I did not name any amount. I would have taken anything rather than bring disgrace upon myself and my children, and keep them from starving.'

Up in the witness box, she burst into tears.

Dalton remembered the scene differently. From what he could recall, when warned that Gray would send him a lawyer's letter, Carr had answered, 'As many as you like, so long as you leave me alone; don't bother me; what will it cost?' Then he'd given her ten shillings. Dalton claimed that Gray had seemed 'quite pleased' with this payment, thanking the mesmerist and reminding him to 'send Dalton on Friday', as he'd promised. At that point, said Dalton, Carr had asked Gray, 'If you will write me a letter apologising for your violent conduct, as you are poor, I will send you £5.' Whereupon Gray had repeated her request for twenty.

In Gray's version of this exchange, Carr wanted her to apologise for calling him a 'Bertrand'. Though he had offered five pounds for a written apology, she'd turned down his request because her conscience 'would not allow' her to comply. Dalton didn't remember Gray calling Carr a 'Bertrand' to his face. Referring to her afternoon visit, Dalton mused, 'I swear she made no reference to Bertrand. She said to me in the morning that Dr. Carr was worse than Bertrand.' Obviously the 'Bertrand' moniker was a mortal insult, hard to forgive. Comparing anyone to Henry Louis Bertrand was to accuse him of being a liar, a satyr and a homicidal maniac.

By 1868, the 'Mad Dentist of Wynyard' had become a household word. Three years earlier, on Monday 2 October, Dr Charles Eichler had been called from his office on Bridge Street to a house in the suburb of St Leonards. Here a thirty-five-year-old man called Henry Kinder, who worked at the City Bank, was lying with a bullet in his head. He was partly conscious, but after examining his wound, Eichler held out no hope of a recovery. The doctor believed that Kinder had shot himself. From the reports of the attending witnesses, Eichler judged that the deceased was an 'imbecile'.

The attending witnesses were Kinder's wife, Maria, a family friend named Henry Louis Bertrand, and Bertrand's wife Jane. According to Maria, her husband had been a heavy drinker, and irrational. He'd threatened to take his life a week before he actually did it. They'd had a violent argument shortly before the occurrence, when he'd threatened to leave her. A little while later she was entertaining her friends and doing some needlework when her husband had walked into the room and blown a hole in his head. No one, she admitted, had tried to stop him.

Bertrand also testified. He said he'd met with the victim once or twice a day for the past ten months and thought him 'the strangest man in the world'. He also said that, although he'd gone for a doctor after Henry Kinder had shot himself, he'd found no medical practitioners at home and had finally left word with Dr Eichler. For that reason, although the incident had occurred between five and six o'clock in the evening, Eichler hadn't dressed Henry's wound until eleven o'clock that night.

Nevertheless, Kinder survived, fully conscious, for five more days.

The Coroner's Court declared the shooting a suicide, committed during a fit of temporary insanity. But within two months, Louis Bertrand, his wife, Jane, and Maria Kinder had all been charged with murder.

Henry Bertrand was then twenty-five years old. He lived and worked as a dentist at number seven, Wynyard Square – where he'd first met Maria Kinder. She had come to him as a patient and they soon became romantically involved, exchanging passionate love letters that formed the basis of the case for the prosecution. Bertrand's growing jealousy drove him to several murder attempts; according to his assistant, Alfred Burne, Bertrand had at one point bought a 'red crimean shirt' (that wouldn't show blood), blacked his face, armed himself with a hatchet and rowed across Sydney Harbour with the aim of breaking into Henry Kinder's house and crushing his skull. But that hadn't worked. Neither had Bertrand's numerous attempts to poison Kinder. Burne recalled Bertrand saying 'that he had often before given him poison, and that it had never taken effect.' Even the shooting hadn't gone as planned, though Bertrand had prepared meticulously for the task. He'd disguised himself as a woman to buy the gun. He'd practised his marksmanship by filling a sheep's head full of bullets that he'd made in a plaster mould. But despite being shot, Kinder wouldn't die. He lingered on for days, telling a constable that he hadn't shot himself, but refusing to name the person who had.

At last, the adulterous lovers took matters into their own hands and poisoned the invalid with belladonna. Bertrand admitted as much to his sister, Harriet Kerr. He told her that his wife had actually mixed the poison, that it would never be discovered and that 'he had enough poison in the house to kill half the people in Sydney'. Jane Bertrand's involvement was very puzzling to strangers, but not to Harriet. 'His treatment of his wife was everything that was bad, wicked and cruel,' she said, describing how, on one occasion, Bertrand had urged Jane to write a suicide note, and had threatened to brain her with a stick. 'She used to sleep a great deal,' Harriet revealed. 'I thought it was not natural sometimes; it was more like a stupor.'

Other people speculated that Bertrand had mesmerised his wife. One of Bertrand's friends, Alexander Bellhouse, certainly thought so, stating that Bertrand 'said he was a powerful mesmerist, and had great power over people that way; that he had great influence over his wife, and could do what he liked with her.' Most dentists of the time had more than a passing acquaintance with mesmerism, since it was regarded as a form of anaesthetic. But it's unlikely that Bertrand actually needed to mesmerise Jane – not if she was the victim of prolonged domestic violence. According to Harriet Kerr, he used to 'beat his wife most brutally'.

In the end, the charge against Jane Bertrand was dropped. Maria Kinder also escaped prosecution, owing to a lack of evidence. Only Bertrand eventually faced court, where witness after witness testified to his bizarre behaviour. One of them was a woman called Mrs Mary Agnes Robertson, who had become the focus of Bertrand's attentions while Maria Kinder was away in Bathurst. Like Harriet Kerr, Robertson had heard Bertrand confess to shooting Kinder. Unlike Kerr, however, she had reported his confession to the police. By that time she was terrified of Bertrand, who had already threatened her with a knife and a 'steel'. He had once coerced her into kissing him by promising to flog his wife if she didn't.

'I never told Bertrand that I was very fond of him,' she insisted, before going on to claim that the dentist had tried to mesmerise her in her own room, completely against her will. 'I fancy I felt the effects – a kind of galvanic shock; Mrs Kinder was present, but no one else; when I felt a dizziness in my eyes, I ran out of the room; I know he has tried to mesmerise me by following me about the place and looking at me.'

Maria Kinder also alleged that Bertrand was able to make her do things against her will, owing to a 'sort of clairvoyance over her'. In fact, the idea of mesmeric influence dominated Bertrand's whole trial, much as it did Carr's. 'In the course of the investigation,' the *Sydney Morning Herald* declared in an opinion piece on the Bertrand affair, 'statements have been made of mesmeric influence, by which it is alleged that the minds of certain persons are captured to the will of others. We doubt if this subject can long escape the jurisdiction of Courts. It is a dreadful power if it exists at all.'

Mesmerism became a popular scapegoat for the crime, as did the fact that Bertrand was French – and Jewish. A defence of mental derangement found some sympathy in the newspapers too. But like today's pundits, those of the 1860s were quick to condemn popular entertainment as the real culprit:

> *Bertrand himself is an insignificant common-place fellow in appearance; and seems to be rather proud than otherwise of the sensation he has created. He is an admirer, apparently, with the worst characteristics, of the French school of romance, and thoroughly imbued with the depraved spirit which pervades the work of Eugene Sue and similar*

authors. The most charitable explanation of his conduct is that, being a weak-minded person, he has set himself up to imitate some hero of the worst class of literature that ever disgraced a civilised community.

Coincidentally, both William Roberts and Julian Salomons were involved in the Bertrand case. Roberts represented the Bertrands at their committal hearing; Salomons defended Louis Bertrand during the appeals process, so ably that Bertrand's death sentence was later commuted to life in prison.

But by September 1868, the two counsels were on opposing sides, battling over the innocence of Thomas Guthrie Carr.

III

Carr's gift of ten shillings didn't satisfy Eliza Gray for very long. She was back at his Bridge Street office the next morning. Dalton blocked her at the foot of the stairs and told her that Carr wanted her to stay away. When that didn't work, he explained that Carr wasn't in.

She didn't believe it.

'When Dr. Carr came in, he asked her to walk upstairs,' Dalton deposed, 'but she remained outside talking loudly and abusively, saying the matter should be made public.' It was, he admitted, the first time she had ever been abusive. Her noise attracted quite a lot of attention.

Carr must have been scared off because he retreated upstairs. Gray soon followed him, after telling Dalton to leave the house. On arriving in Carr's rooms, she discovered that a gentleman was already there. The mesmerist asked her what she wanted. She refused to speak in front of a witness.

Then Dalton joined them, doubling the number of witnesses. He heard Carr tell Gray to leave. When she wouldn't, Carr bade Dalton fetch a constable. 'He gave her two minutes to go,' Dalton recalled, 'but then told me to go for one.'

Dalton obeyed. On failing to find a constable, he returned to find Gray 'walking round the room'. He managed to get her away somehow, he recalled, but she came back at five o'clock to confront the mesmerist.

This meeting was to be their last.

'He said to me "You are poor, are you not?"' Gray testified. 'I replied, "You have made me poorer than ever I was." He said, "You know how to get money like all other poor women." He also said he would bring a man to swear before my husband that I had behaved improperly. I said he should prove it. I told the prisoner that I had always worked hard and honestly for my living, until he made me unable to do so.'

Dalton's account of this exchange differed slightly from Gray's. According to Dalton, Carr offered to help Gray because she was poor, but warned her that this was not the way to get money. Carr also said, 'You know I am a public man, and think an exposure would ruin me, and that by threatening me you will frighten me.' At this point Gray must have become rowdy again, because Carr once more sent for a constable. 'A constable came,' Gray related, 'and I went out with the constable, who told me if I had any claim against Dr. Carr I could summons him.'

So that was what Gray did. She finally went to 'lay the information'. William Roberts wasn't the first lawyer she approached but he was obviously the first one who agreed to take her case. Shortly afterwards, she told her husband that Carr had raped her. 'My husband was in Sydney the day I laid the information,' she revealed, 'but I did not know he was home the day I saw Mr Roberts.' In other words, William Gray didn't go with her to press charges.

Here Eliza Gray's story ended. Salomons, however, wanted more than that. Scattered throughout her testimony were answers to a host of thinly veiled accusations that were obviously designed to impugn her character and testimony. Having declared that she had only once before been ill, she was questioned closely about any other doctors she might have consulted besides Carr, Bell and Eichler. She was asked about a black velvet jacket she had bought, costing £2.2*s*. She denied vehemently that Carr had ever given her two pounds to make three shirts. 'He offered me an order for some shirts, but I refused to take it,' she said.

Then Salomons mentioned a Mrs Greenfield. Yes, Gray replied, she knew a Mrs Greenfield, who had married a baker's boy called George James Lees. Gray had no idea how long they'd been married, though it was certainly more than a year. Lees was about nineteen or twenty. He had often been to Gray's house. 'He knows nothing of me, if that's what you want . . .' she spat. 'Nothing improper ever took place between us.'

In answer to another question from Salomons, Gray insisted that she had not spoken to Lees since her last spell in the witness box. She had, however, gone to confront a couple of cabmen – one of them named Thackall – who were witnesses for the defence. Whatever their story was, it clearly involved a hansom or 'patent safety cab'. 'I intend to "pull" both of them, as I was never in a patent safety in my life,' Gray declared. 'I told his [Thackall's] wife that if he gave false evidence I would pull him afterwards for perjury.' She'd also remonstrated with Lees' brother-in-law.

Salomon immediately requested that the court instruct Gray not to go near any more witnesses.

During the proceedings, he reeled off various other names, most of them male. Sullenly Gray acknowledged that she did know Constable Patrick Kelly, of Redfern police station. He had often come to her house, where he would sit and have a glass of ale with her, late at night. 'He was there one night the worse for drink,' she recalled, 'and I had a job to get him out. I can't say how long he stayed there. I swear he has never been in my bedroom.' She then began to cry again, accusing Carr ('that wretch, there') of making her life a misery. This was on the Monday. On the Thursday, she had to face the same smear campaign.

Yes, she had seen Constable Kelly since the start of the hearing. She didn't know anyone named Donald McLeery. She'd been acquainted with Edward Walsh since she was a child; they'd gone to school together. 'He has been in my house,' she conceded, though not as late as midnight. She knew a person called Lucas. She didn't know whether he had been to her house alone – but she wasn't about to give the court a history of her life just to please 'that villain'. She was alluding to Thomas Guthrie Carr, who must have reacted, because she suddenly lost her temper. She accused him 'of being drunk the other day and grinning and waving his hand'. The Bench had to rein her in.

Salomons' questions continued. She knew a Sullivan, but he'd never been to her house. A man named Crummey certainly had, but only with Gray's husband. No, she wasn't familiar with anyone named Wearne. She knew a James Kennedy, because his sister had worked for her. Kennedy had never been to her house alone. Shipman? She didn't know him.

'If you had told me the other day that you wanted the whole history,' she sniped, 'I would have written it, and brought it with me.' Yes, she'd occupied the house of a Mrs Priest, in Newcastle. Did Mr Salomons want to hear the lady's character? 'I did not bring sailors home there,' Gray argued. 'My husband was at home with me every night, except one week when I came to Sydney.' She had *not* been turned out of the house for bringing sailors home; it was because she had stopped buying bread from the landlady, who didn't want another baker driving up to her door. 'I don't know what all this has to do with the case,' she complained, obviously seething.

At last she was told to step down. Then Elizabeth Hook was briefly recalled. Salomons questioned her about 18 March and about her more recent contact with Eliza Gray. Hook confessed that she had gone with Gray the previous week to see William Roberts. They had spoken again that morning on York Street. Gray had chided Hook about a mistake in her evidence and had told her that William Roberts would examine her that day. 'I also said that it was a great pity . . . that my name was mixed up in it,' Hook remarked. 'We had no unpleasant words.'

Her memory of Gray crying 'Oh, good God, Lizzie, I've been mesmerised!' was something she'd only mentioned to her friend's legal team that very morning.

Once Hook had finished the case was adjourned until Monday 28 September. By this time, of course, news of the case had spread all around the colony. It had even reached New Zealand. But where past accounts of Carr's tribulations had often been characterised by a slightly arch tone, these latest reports contained no trace of frivolity.

Matters had become too serious for that.

PART IV

ANIMAL MAGNETISM

I

The case against Thomas Guthrie Carr revolved around the power of mesmerism. Without this power, according to Eliza Gray, he couldn't have assaulted her. But was Carr really capable of mesmerising Gray against her will? Was *anyone*?

From the very first, mesmerism had been the subject of endless debate. Almost a hundred years after Frederick Mesmer concocted his theory of animal magnetism, people were still challenging it. 'Mesmerism has scarcely advanced an inch since the days of its discoverer. It has always rested under a stigma of quackery,' wrote the anonymous author of an article about mesmerism who may well have been Carr, since the piece first appeared in the Sydney press while he was living there. The piece began with an awestruck summary of the 'wonderful power' being exhibited nightly at the School of Arts, then proceeded to attack those who were sceptical about it. How *could* there be collusion? Who on earth would submit to having his finger amputated, or his teeth extracted, for nothing more than a modest fee? The writer argued that doctors were largely to blame for mesmerism's notoriety:

> *Why should they sneer at and ridicule a power the existence of which is no longer doubtful . . .? While so many forms of chronic disease exist to baffle their skill and laugh at their pharmacopoeia, how do they justify their conduct in neglecting a power which might be the means of filling up the immense gap in their professional system?*

But animal magnetism *was* still in doubt. Despite years of investigation no one had yet proved conclusively that mesmerism really worked. A French Royal Commission of 1784, chaired by Benjamin Franklin, had found no scientific basis to the theory. Some fifty years later, in 1831, the French Royal Academy determined that 'the existence of a uniform character, to enable us to recognise, in every case, the reality of the state of somnambulism has not been established'. In other words, the academy ruled that it was impossible to tell whether someone was faking a mesmeric trance or not. Even so, it admitted that some effects observed during its inquiry 'appeared to depend upon magnetism alone'. It also deduced that magnetism didn't seem to affect healthy people, and often didn't act on sick people, either. It calculated that the time needed to mesmerise someone varied from one minute to half an hour. And it stated that 'we only saw one person who fell into somnambulism upon being magnetised for the first time.'

In the 1830s, when interest in the phenomenon was at its peak, Professor John Elliotson of London's University College Hospital became an exponent of mesmerism, lending it an aura of respectability. It was Elliotson who described the first British surgical procedure performed using mesmerism as an anaesthetic. The patient, a labourer from Nottingham, apparently lay like a statue while his leg was amputated. 'The placid look of his countenance never changed for an instant; his whole frame rested, uncontrolled in perfect stillness and repose,' Elliotson marvelled. But he had trouble convincing his fellow doctors that mesmerism was legitimate – especially after he began to treat the Okey sisters. These epileptic young women soon became notorious, claiming all kinds of bizarre (even mystical) powers. Elizabeth Okey, who was supposed to be clairvoyant when mesmerised, was alleged to have predicted the fates of other patients confined to the hospital where she herself was living; her predictions were written down and given to the hospital apothecary, on Elliotson's orders. Eventually Elliotson's use of her so-called diagnostic powers, and his association with mesmerism in general, led to his expulsion from the hospital wards. But he still had a lot of supporters. In 1843 he began to publish *The Zoist: A Journal of Cerebral Physiology and Mesmerism*, which survived for another ten years thanks to the public's enduring fascination with Mesmer's teachings.

At around the same time, Dr James Esdaile was busy converting hearts and minds in India. He started removing scrotal tumours while his patients were mesmerised, and continued to do so for twenty years. A committee appointed by the deputy governor of Bengal could find no evidence that seven of the patients it investigated had suffered any pain during their procedures. Esdaile's success was a triumph for the supporters of mesmerism. He was often cited in its defence.

But the concept of animal magnetism was already under attack from another quarter. Scottish surgeon James Braid didn't believe that mesmeric trances were induced by external 'operators', or by the manipulation of magnetic energy. He argued that such states were caused by mental suggestion and that they could be self-induced. His name for the process was 'hypnotism' and it caught on fast. The battle was now being fought on two fronts: as well as having to prove that mesmeric trances were genuine, mesmerists had to demonstrate that they themselves elicited these states with their own powers. The fight between James Maughan and Thomas Guthrie Carr wasn't just a fight between two opinionated blowhards. It was a fight between the proponents of hypnotism and the supporters of mesmerism.

Though hypnotism finally won, the struggle dragged on for decades. In 1860, two French doctors named Jean Nicolas Demarquay and Félix Giraud-Teulon conducted their own experiments. They discovered that out of eighteen patients, only one – an hysteric – became insensible under the attentions of a mesmerist. From this study they concluded that magnetic sleep, magnetic somnambulism and hypnotism were all identical, and that they worked only on people suffering from hysteria. Even passionate advocates of mesmerism were willing to concede that there might be an overlap. 'Electro-biology, Electro-psychology, and Hypnotism are essentially the same with Animal Magnetism, although there is probably some difference with precise characters of the state produced,' wrote Dr William Gregory in 1851. Gregory didn't share the sceptical attitude of Demarquay and Giraud-Toulon. On the contrary, he was an enthusiast and saw mesmerism as a gateway to clairvoyance. He accused James Braid of not believing in clairvoyance because he hadn't been able to produce it by using the hypnotic method. 'Mr Braid's process . . . may not produce certain powers, which could perhaps appear in the same cases under influence of a different operation,' he argued.

This creeping tendency to associate mesmerism with clairvoyance and spiritualism (and with people like Thomas Guthrie Carr) was a big factor in the triumph of hypnosis. James Braid had always made a huge effort to disassociate his theory from Mesmer's, if only to avoid the 'whiff of fraudulence' that still clung to animal magnetism. But old associations were hard to shake off. The medical establishment wasn't won over. And even where the genuineness of trance-like states was accepted, their morality was questioned. From the outset, people had been afraid of what might happen if a male mesmerist treated female patients. If animal magnetism really worked, surely it was too dangerous to use?

'I have my doubts whether Mesmerism does afford the easy opening for misconduct with which it has been taxed,' George Sandby, a Suffolk vicar, declared in 1844. He insisted that profound torpors were unusual, and that 'more generally, *if not always*, the Mesmeric state produces, on the part of the patients, such a high tone of spirituality and sense of right, as to make them less than ever disposed to an acquiescence in what is wrong.' Even so, he grudgingly allowed that mesmerists should be people of character and principle, and that the process should always be conducted in the presence of a third party.

Sandby's contemporary, Joseph P F Deleuze, went even further. He suggested that only women should mesmerise women. And if no female 'magnetisers' were available, strict rules should be followed:

> *When a physician intends to magnetize a woman who keeps her bed, the clothes ought to be kept over her. If she can rise, she ought to be clad in the most decent manner. The physician will not touch her except to take her thumbs, or to make frictions along the feet outside her garments. All the passes will be made at a distance . . . It would be proper to have a nurse near the bed during the sitting.*

Other practitioners agreed wholeheartedly. Australia's first professional mesmerist, Caroline Harper Dexter, established a Melbourne practice in 1858 under the pseudonym Madame Carole. But she eventually found herself treating only female patients, thanks to a persistent, widespread concern about the propriety of men and women placing each other in a trance. Though this concern meant that both mesmerists *and* hypnotists were regarded with suspicion, mesmerists were definitely worse off. It was the mesmerist, after all, who was thought to be wielding a mysterious and slightly sinister power.

Even where a mesmerist had a stainless character and the best of intentions, some critics argued that damage could still be done. It was widely accepted that a kind of transference happened between mesmerist and subject, so that the subject's 'very lively affection' for the mesmerist would continue to trouble her when she was awake. George Sandby acknowledged this fear while disputing it. He claimed that the affection induced was more like a sister's love than anything else. Furthermore, he said, the 'great increase in the moral perceptions' brought about by mesmerism would ensure that the subject wouldn't be led astray.

Assurances like this fell flat – and for good reason. Mesmeric experiments often involved asking subjects to do things they wouldn't normally do. And as more and more cases involving trance-like states trickled into the courts, the morality of mesmerism (and hypnotism) became an increasingly hot topic.

In 1860, the *Gazette Médicale de Paris* reported that an eighteen-year-old girl had found herself pregnant four months after visiting a mesmerist. This man was convicted when it was somehow proven that a woman could be impregnated during a 'magnetic sleep' without her knowledge. In 1868, Maria Kinder claimed that Louis Bertrand's mesmeric hold over her had been the cause of her involvement in the murder of her own husband. And in 1888, a woman named Madeleine Grille was found lying beside twenty-three-year-old Henri Chambige in Algeria. Grille had been shot twice in the head. Chambige claimed that they had undertaken a murder-suicide pact, but her family insisted that he had mesmerised and murdered her.

'So far, hypnotism has only made a casual appearance in a court of justice,' psychologist Alfred Binet and physician Charles Féré observed in their 1888 work, *Animal Magnetism*. 'But this state of things might change at any time, and suggestion may become an instant of criminal practices.' Back in 1865, a concerned columnist had expressed much the same sentiments in the *Sydney Morning Herald*. During the interim, however, no concerted effort had been made to prove the genuineness of trance-like states in any court of law. As Binet and Féré themselves pointed out, the question of 'proof' had not been considered by those writing on the subject:

> *They have not asked under what conditions judges would admit the reality of the facts of hypnotism brought before them. They have not understood that in a medico-legal study, the demonstration of the hypnotic state is the first question, and the most important of all; the others are comparatively unimportant, since if the hypnotism is not proved, all the consequences which may be drawn from it become illusory.*

According to Binet and Féré, the complaint of a victim could only be regarded as legitimate once it was proved 'experimentally' that he or she was susceptible to hypnotism. They themselves weren't sceptics; on the contrary, they believed that a hypnotised subject could undergo all sorts of violence without remembering it. 'We even think it possible that a subject might be violated in the hypnotic state, in which she would be unable to offer any resistance,' they declared. Their concern was simply that false accusations could be made – and upheld – if the proper rules of evidence weren't followed.

During Thomas Guthrie Carr's committal hearing, no one tried to establish whether Eliza Gray was susceptible to mesmerism by sitting her down and actually mesmerising her. A few of the witnesses, however, were asked for their opinions on the subject. Dr Charles Eichler gave his views at some length – perhaps because he was regarded as being properly qualified to do so. He revealed that he had attended Carr's show on several occasions and had seen Carr extract teeth and jab people with pins. Whether these people were in collusion with Carr, Eichler couldn't say; he had merely seen them being selected from the audience. To all appearances, they had become insensible to pain once Carr's 'mesmeric influence' had placed them under his control. Naturally, a woman under such control would be very vulnerable.

'If a female submits herself to a mesmerist,' he mused, 'she is in a state of unconsciousness, and is entirely at the disposal of the mesmerist, and he can do whatever he likes with her.' He himself had experimented with mesmerism, but had only succeeded in his efforts on a single occasion. And he didn't believe that anyone could be mesmerised unwillingly:

> *I doubt very much whether it would be possible for Dr. Carr, or any other mesmerist, to mesmerise Mrs Gray, or any other woman, without her consent. This is my opinion from my knowledge of mesmerism. It would take a person thirty minutes or a great deal more to mesmerise another person of a moderately strong constitution. I have heard Mrs Gray's evidence. I do not think it possible for Dr. Carr or anybody else to mesmerise her by waving his handkerchief before her face in the manner she has described.*

Eichler's views on mesmerism echoed those of George Sandby, who refused to accept that anyone could be forcibly magnetised, except in 'most rare cases of extreme sensibility'. Sandby reminded his readers that certain conditions were necessary for mesmeric sleep: silence, stillness, and a fair amount of time. 'With many patients the Mesmeric action must be renewed for several days in succession before any effect be procured,' he stated.

Binet and Féré, however, were less optimistic. They agreed that someone who had never been hypnotised, and wasn't susceptible, would only succumb if consent was given. But those who *were* susceptible ran a great risk. 'They may be taken by surprise when naturally asleep and hypnotized by pressure on the eyes,' the two physicians warned, 'and in a waking state they may be intimidated . . . and may even receive dangerous suggestions without being put to sleep.'

Carr had described Gray as a good subject. This might have meant that she was susceptible. But did it mean that she could be mesmerised against her will?

Gray herself might have thought so. After reading about Louis Bertrand, and watching Carr up on stage, she may well have believed that a mesmerist had extraordinary powers at his command. Dr Eichler himself seemed willing to concede that mesmerism worked – and that it could be used against helpless females. By 1868, even in a far-flung colony like New South Wales, mesmerism was burdened with a sleazy aura of sexual licence.

Perhaps that's why Eliza Gray felt confident enough to accuse Carr of raping her. Whether or not she was telling the truth, she may have assumed that she had a good chance of winning her case, simply because Carr's occupation put him at a disadvantage. To convict him, however, she would have to prove, not only that mesmerism really worked, but that she could have been mesmerised against her will. And even if that *were* established, the question still remained: could *Carr* have mesmerised her against her will? All the dazzled reviews and wholehearted endorsements he'd garnered over the years suggested that he could.

It wasn't easy to see, at first glance, that Carr might have been a total fraud.

II

On 7 January 1869, Thomas Guthrie Carr appeared before the Resident Magistrate's Court in the New Zealand town of Hokitika. Twenty-one-year-old John Campbell Kerr had brought an action against him, to recover £19.19*s* in back-pay. Kerr wanted four weeks' wages, plus an extra week in lieu of notice.

Described by the *Age* as someone who combined 'the qualities of a smart check-taker and an impressionable "medium"', Kerr was a young, unemployed journalist when his friend William D'Arcy Leigh approached him on 28 November 1868. Leigh had arrived in Hokitika eighteen months earlier. Before being hired as Carr's agent, he'd been waiting tables at the Royal Mail Hotel. During his testimony at Carr's Hokitika trial, he twice swore under oath that he had never been convicted of a criminal offence in Australia.

'I had a conversation with [the] plaintiff about his nervous condition of the eyes,' Leigh declared, 'and I told him I thought mesmerism would do him good. I therefore introduced him to Dr Carr.'

Carr recalled this meeting very well. According to the mesmerist, Kerr had come to him as Leigh's friend, complaining about his eyes. Carr's advice had been simple: stop smoking, stop drinking and start attending Carr's séances in the assembly room of the Post Office Hotel, since this might eventually lead to a cure. Carr promised not to charge the plaintiff any fees 'on condition that he should submit to mesmeric treatment, so as to become a mesmeric subject.' Carr added that he had made 'no engagement whatever with Mr Kerr'.

Kerr begged to differ. He insisted that Leigh had asked him to visit the mesmerist at the Empire Hotel because Carr wanted to see him. Though Carr had offered to treat his eyes, the younger man wasn't interested, having suffered from his affliction since childhood. 'He certainly said my eyes looked weak,' Kerr said, 'but he did not ask me to come down on account of my eyes. I did not become a subject on condition that he should treat me for my eyes. He gave me some stuff that was to cure me in a week, but I did not use it.' Later, a chemist determined that this so-called medicine contained only gentian and rhubarb.

Kerr's first meeting with the mesmerist took place on a Saturday. That was when Carr 'punctured' Kerr on the forehead (to treat his ocular condition), gave him the remedy that was supposed to be otherwise unobtainable in the southern hemisphere (but was practically worthless) and asked him to attend a séance. Kerr did so the following Monday, after meeting with Carr once again. But nothing much happened to him during the show. 'I was not then initiated,' Kerr observed.

The next day, Leigh told Kerr that the mesmerist wanted to engage him as a subject. When Kerr asked how much they intended to pay him for his services, Leigh referred him to Carr, who then referred him back to Leigh. 'They kept referring me from one to another,' Kerr said. Though he saw Carr almost every day after that, to plan each evening's performance, Kerr could not get a straight answer about his salary. He couldn't even get

Carr into the same room as Leigh, except on one occasion when Carr suddenly disappeared before they could discuss terms. At last Kerr lost his temper:

> *I spoke strongly to Leigh . . . and he came to my bedroom on a Sunday morning and put ten shillings on my pillow, and said he would give me the rest in the evening. The next day he gave me a cheque for 30s. The cheque was signed by Dr. Carr.*

Shortly afterwards, the mesmerist told Kerr to get himself appointed as a correspondent to the *Hokitika Daily News*. Kerr dutifully obeyed. He promised the newspaper's editor that he would send stories back from the nearby town of Ross. On reaching Ross, however, Kerr spent most of his time working for the mesmerist by regularly appearing on stage.

'I was mesmerised at Ross with a coin,' he revealed. 'I went up to the front seats and held a coin in my hand.' This was a technique that Carr often used and it indicated that he was more of a convert to hypnotism than he would have liked his public to believe. He had an excuse, though, for having his subjects sit and stare at a coin or button for fifteen minutes before he brought them up on stage. 'This was explained to be merely a means of preventing their eyes and attention wandering,' one reviewer noted.

But it didn't mean that his subjects were mesmerised. Kerr denied that *he* ever was. When he took part in a piece of street-theatre arranged by Carr, who wanted to throw Hokitika into 'a state of excitement', he was simply following instructions. According to Kerr, the mesmerist told him to come to the Post Office Hotel and 'do the arm-stiffening business', before walking across the street with a troop of Maoris, then running away as if he were scared.

Finally, on returning to Hokitika from Ross, Kerr stopped being a mesmeric subject. Instead he became Carr's agent, replacing Leigh, who had gone to Christchurch.

'I saw the Doctor generally before the performances,' Kerr explained, 'and he instructed me what I was to do. I was certainly never under the influence of Dr Carr. The performances were all arranged beforehand.'

George William Harvey was Carr's lawyer. He stood up to cross-examine the plaintiff, who insisted he had never once told Carr's audience that he'd been mesmerised.

'But you made a fool of yourself generally?' Harvey inquired.

Kerr agreed that he had.

'And you have not left that off yet?' Harvey snidely asked him.

'Yes,' said Kerr. There was laughter in the court.

'Do you mean to say,' Harvey continued, 'that Dr Carr engaged you to simulate that you were under the influence of mesmerism?'

'Yes, by his agent, Mr Leigh,' Kerr replied. 'He said if I was any sort of subject, I should travel with Dr Carr. Dr Carr was perfectly aware that I was only shamming . . .'

He added that, being unemployed, he had not been in a position to refuse Carr's offer.

'So if the public chose to be gulled,' said Harvey, 'you were willing to assist him in gulling them.'

Kerr agreed that he had been. 'But I consider I have more pluck than many to come here and expose it,' he retorted, explaining that he hadn't known he was doing anything illegal. 'I thought it a lark,' he said. Then he went on to describe how one night in Ross, a subject had publicly claimed that he'd only pretended to be mesmerised during several earlier performances.

'So there was another rascal?' Harvey asked him.

'So it appears,' Kerr replied.

There was more laughter.

Under questioning from Harvey, Kerr refused to concede that he had ever been turned out of the Empire Hotel, either by the mesmerist or by his secretary. Nor, Kerr said, had he ever denied on stage that he'd received money from the mesmerist. 'I never spoke except when I made stump speeches, which I composed myself,' he testified, claiming that the mesmerist had discharged him, not for being drunk, but for neglect of duty. And no one had *ever* promised him six pounds a week, he said. He had simply been told by Leigh that he would be well paid.

'I had another motive in coming here besides that of recovering what I consider I am entitled to,' Kerr informed the Bench. 'That motive is to prevent Dr Carr from continuing his entertainments.'

Kerr concluded his testimony by insisting that he had not asked Carr in person for £21.15*s* before taking out his summons, because he'd had no opportunity to do so. Instead he had sent the mesmerist a bill and a letter. During a recent conversation he'd had with Leigh, he'd warned his old friend that he was going to court.

Leigh had told him to look out that he 'did not get into trouble'.

Here the prosecution rested. Harvey immediately proposed that Carr had no case to answer. Where an action was founded on an alleged fraud, he said, the plaintiff could not recover payments. Besides which, Kerr was a liar. 'Could it be believed that he would go down to the Post Office Hotel to act lies without having first made an arrangement as to salary[?]' Harvey demanded. If Kerr had gulled the public, Harvey went on, he had gulled Carr as well. And the contract between them was totally void, because it was founded on fraud.

Walter Reid, who later became New Zealand's first solicitor-general, was acting for the plaintiff. He disagreed with Harvey's interpretation of the law. Mesmerism, he said, was 'but a dreamy kind of thing; a sort of half and half science'. It was, in fact, an entertainment – and Kerr had exhibited himself for the entertainment of the public, who knew well enough what they were going to see when they went to a show. While Reid admitted that a contract should be void if it was opposed to the public good, there was a difference in this case.

The Bench listened, then ruled that the defence should proceed. So Harvey called Thomas Guthrie Carr to the stand.

Carr told the court that on first trying to mesmerise Kerr he had been unsuccessful. But Kerr had later come to him and said, 'Oh! Dr Carr you almost had me. Why did you not go on?' After that, the young man had fallen into a trance every time he'd mounted the stage. Carr had stuck pins into him, had made him dance the 'nervous cure' and had compelled him to deliver speeches. 'I believed myself that he was mesmerised,' Carr deposed, 'and if he was not, no one would be more deceived than I was . . .'

According to Carr, everything he'd ever said to the plaintiff had been said on stage. There had been no private conversations. Kerr had not gone to Ross *with* the mesmerist; he had gone there as a correspondent for the *Hokitika Daily News*, to report on a volunteer ball. Carr had never paid the plaintiff any money. On one occasion, however, Kerr had come to him and said, 'The newspaper has not yet made any arrangements with me, and I am unable to get to Ross for want of means.' Out of the goodness of his heart, Carr had then authorised his secretary to lend the plaintiff some cash to pay his horse hire and hotel bill.

'He attended some of the séances at Ross,' Carr declared. 'He was, however, so dissipated that I was obliged to tell him that I would not permit his coming to my séances any more. I do not think there were any other persons at Ross who attended my séances there, who had been under mesmeric influence.'

Walter Reid must have raised his eyebrows. 'Did not Mr Cooper go?' he asked.

Carr immediately corrected himself. Yes, of course – Thomas Cooper, a Hokitika stationer, *had* attended a few séances in Ross. He'd been there for the volunteer ball. But Carr had never given Cooper or the plaintiff any wages. On the contrary, Kerr was always loafing around Carr's hotel, asking for hand-outs.

'He came to me and said that Mr Hiscocks, with whom he was lodging, had turned him out,' Carr said. 'So, as an act of kindness, out of humanity, I instructed Mr Leigh to give him a cheque for £1.10*s* . . .'

'Then you were under his influence!' Harvey interjected, triggering a burst of laughter.

'He was poor,' Carr went on, ignoring the interruption, 'and so, as an act of kindness, and out of pure humanity, I gave him the money.'

'Do you call paying his expenses at Ross humanity?' Reid inquired, with delicate sarcasm.

Carr didn't know anything about that. He'd never paid Kerr's expenses. He admitted, however, that he *had* asked Kerr to carry some 'instruments' to Ross. 'He came to me as a beggar, and I gave him assistance,' Carr reiterated. 'There are plenty of others that I have defended in the same way. I do not deny that certain sums of money have been lent to Mr Kerr. He was in poverty, and was continually representing his want of money.'

'Do you deny,' Reid pressed, 'that the sum two pounds, set down in this account as having been paid to the plaintiff on 16 December, was paid to him?'

'I swear it was not given to him as wages . . .' Carr insisted. He then described how the plaintiff had come to him that very morning, demanding fifty pounds to settle the whole matter before it went to court. But Carr had simply opened the door and told him to get out.

'Did he call upon you for any other purpose?' asked Reid.

'No,' said Carr.

'Did he not serve you with a subpoena?' Reid demanded.

Again Carr had to amend his statement. Yes, Kerr had thrown a paper at his feet. Yes, Carr *had* authorised a certain gentleman to give the plaintiff some money, simply to get rid of him. 'He was disturbing me and preventing my attending to my patients,' he said.

When questioned further, he confessed that he himself had written out a cheque for thirty shillings, to give to Kerr.

Dr James Grant had been present during this exchange, which he described to the court after replacing Carr in the witness stand. He'd seen Kerr hand over the subpoena. He'd heard Carr order the plaintiff downstairs. But Grant wasn't an innocent bystander. He was one of the mesmerist's associates – and a disreputable one, at that. Five months later he was in court again over a debt he owed to a tailor. Apparently, Grant had asked the tailor to send some new clothes to his hotel, promising that he would pay for them directly. He had even come to the tailor's shop a little later, dressed in his new clothes, and requested a hat. (He was very particular about the hat, explaining that his head was a strange shape owing to its huge bump of 'conscientiousness'.) Before leaving the shop again Grant had promised to settle his account within the hour. But ten minutes later the tailor had seen him pass by on a coach out of town.

Grant insisted that it had all been a mistake. He'd understood that Carr would pay for the clothes. Grant himself had been penniless at the time, having gambled away his own money in expectation of a sum that Carr owed him. The magistrate, on hearing this, gave Grant two weeks to settle his debt. Grant must have done so because he didn't appear in court again.

Carr had a lot of associates like Grant, whether he acknowledged them publicly or not. One of the witnesses who testified at Carr's Hokitika trial was Thomas Cooper, the stationer who claimed to have been in Ross to attend the volunteer ball. He'd gone to Carr's shows as well, he said, but not because he'd been paid to.

'I never made any arrangements with Dr Carr that I should . . . sham to be under the influence,' he deposed. Yes, his expenses in Ross had been partly covered by Carr. Yes, Carr had sent him a ticket to the ball. But he'd never told anyone that he was going to Ross to attend the séances. People had simply *assumed* that.

'I have received £2 besides,' he revealed. 'I received a coat also, to replace one that I destroyed at one of the séances. I decline to answer whether I was ever under the mesmeric influence of Dr Carr. I have made a "stump speech". It was my own composition, with the exception of two words which were supplied by the plaintiff.'

Despite Cooper's assurances that he wasn't in Carr's employment, he was subjected to so many curious inquiries that he wrote to the local paper about it. 'I may state that I am as ignorant of the affair as the parties who have so much bothered me,' he bleated. A few months later, however, someone called Cooper, who was 'suffering from a disease of the hip', threw away his stick after being mesmerised during one of Carr's shows and proceeded to jump about 'in a very amusing manner'. Though Cooper is a common name, it's hard not to be suspicious . . .

Another associate who testified was William Maddison, who claimed that he had been with Carr for three years. In 1868 he had admitted to sailing from England with Carr, and it was true that he had been working for the mesmerist in Bendigo. But since he didn't make an appearance at Carr's Sydney trial, or in Carr's Sydney advertisements, there may have been a gap on his résumé.

Whatever their history might have been, Maddison loyally backed Carr's version of events. He described how he had encountered the plaintiff 'loafing about in the passage' of Hokitika's Princess Theatre, two nights after Carr's return from Ross. 'I told him he had better go in and sit down, or go away,' Maddison declared. 'Dr Carr told me to pay [the] plaintiff's hotel expenses. I expect it was a loan. It could be no other.'

Maddison admitted that he had once lent Kerr seven shillings of his own money. 'He said, "Pay seven shillings for me," and I said, "all right, old boy," and paid it,' Maddison recalled.

Like Maddison, William D'Arcy Leigh – the man who'd introduced the plaintiff to the defendant – remembered once or twice giving Kerr the odd sum 'out of charity'. He denied having paid Kerr any wages. But he *had* asked Kerr to attend Carr's shows. 'It is usual, if you find a plastic subject, to request him to attend,' Leigh explained. 'I have been in the habit of attending the séances myself. I did not know that he was shamming. I did not engage him to sham . . .'

Harvey then questioned several other witnesses. Andrew Gibson, a miner, had been present during the séance at which a 'German boy' had said he was only pretending to be mesmerised. In response, Carr had asked his other subjects if they had been paid, or were shamming. They had all denied it – including John Campbell Kerr. Charles Strasser, a local café owner, swore that he had once asked Kerr how he felt after his performances. Kerr had replied that he felt 'queer'. Strasser himself had witnessed Kerr sitting cross-legged, like a tailor, while under the mesmeric influence – but when urged to do it again, Kerr had been unable to adopt the same pose.

'I have frequently met him when he has been going down to the séances,' Strasser added, 'and he has said that he tried to keep away, but he could not resist the influence: he was obliged to go.'

Having finished with Strasser, Harvey pointed out that there were at least two other people in the room who could be called upon to give similar evidence. But why waste the court's time? Instead Harvey requested that the plaintiff's case be dismissed. 'He comes to the Court and says, "I am an imposter; I have assisted Dr Carr to deceive the public, and I have deceived them myself,"' Harvey exclaimed, referring to Kerr. How, he asked, could such a man be believed?

Reid's response was blunt. It was ridiculous, he countered, to argue that 'Dr Carr, Dr Grant, and the others who came here merely for a time and went away – who were a mystery to all and to themselves as well – whose trade it was by these séances to make money – should give money to [the] plaintiff merely out of charity.' If, on the other hand, the defendant wanted to argue that a contract based upon fraud was void . . . well, then Carr would have to face the consequences of such notoriety. Reid wondered if he would ever 'recover' from it.

In the end, the court found for the defendant. Kerr was ordered to pay Carr's costs. But as Melbourne's *Age* pointed out, the mesmerist didn't exactly win – not after Kerr's 'pretty revelations' were broadcast around the colonies:

> *Is this Kerr the same youth who, in company with the exemplary Maori (made a leetle too much of, by-the-bye), so astonished a crowded audience in St George's Hall? The Maori, a most inoffensive-looking creature, would in his mesmeric throes utter the wild war-whoop of his tribe and brandish a formidable putty-knife over the doctor's head, but was sure to quail under the glance of that terrible eye. The ecstasies of the civilised youth developed themselves in stump speeches, ingenious imitations of animals and (what was always sure to take immensely) the man going to be hanged – forming altogether an agreeable relaxation after*

> *the displays of the Maori, whose forte lay in the heavy business. We cannot find that this last-named gentleman, who made the biggest hit of all here, was ever introduced in New Zealand.*

In fact, the gentleman in question had remained in Victoria – and was still there in 1870, when he finally opened up about his time with Thomas Guthrie Carr.

III

The *Geelong Advertiser* broke the story. It reported that a 'splendidly tattooed' Maori had been seen about town, and had been approached by someone who recognised him from Carr's shows. When asked about his performance, the Maori had replied that mesmerism was 'all humbug'. Carr had paid him three pounds a week to be pricked with pins, he said, and he'd liked the money.

This bit of news travelled all the way to New Zealand, where it was duly reported. By that time, however, Carr's honesty was already under attack. Not long after his highly publicised disagreement with Kerr, in 1869, a newspaper in Nelson reviewed one of Carr's shows with a slightly jaundiced eye. It described how a very large audience had gathered to watch Carr mesmerise a group of Maori subjects, who 'obstinately refused to part with their self-control'. One of them appeared to be partly mesmerised until a pin was driven into his arm – whereupon he flinched. Another man, when told to sleep, immediately closed his eyes, then opened one of them again as soon as Carr's back was turned and winked. As the show unfolded this man could barely suppress a smile. His sides were seen to shake with laughter.

It wasn't the first time that Carr had failed to impose his will on stage, and it wouldn't be the last. Years earlier, in Bendigo, he had made a very embarrassing error. After compelling all his young, male subjects to engage in a boxing match, he had stopped them with a word before turning to his audience. 'Tonight,' he had announced, 'I am going to show you my great power over the best boxer in the class. He is now under my influence and I will tell him he is the champion boxer of Bendigo, and that he is to fight me, and I will make him imagine I am the champion of the world.'

Carr had gone on to say that, no matter how much the young man swung at him, these blows would never land – because he, Carr, had willed it so. Then the sparring had commenced. As promised, neither Carr nor his subject had actually landed any punches, though they'd gone through the motions nimbly enough. Finally, a high-spirited Carr had told his opponent, 'I will give you leave to hit me if you can.' Whereupon the younger man had replied, 'Doctor Carr, I am not under your influence, and can hit you, so look out.'

Carr had thought this great fun. He'd said as much to his audience, in a loud voice. Suddenly a fist had shot out and struck him a 'terrific blow' that had sent him head over heels into the orchestra pit. As he'd smashed a hole in the big drum, the miners in the audience had all leapt to their feet and cheered.

Furious, Carr had immediately jumped up and chased his young subject across the stage, into the wings, out of the theatre and along an alley. His subsequent performances at

Bendigo had been ill attended and he had left the town soon afterwards.

'The general public are apt to suspect collusion between lecturers and some of their "subjects",' the *Wellington Independent* warned in June 1869, after noting all the sceptics populating Carr's audience at a recent performance. 'One or two, on Thursday night, were very generally criticised; and in the interests of science, it will be well for Dr Carr, this evening, to prove even more fully the absence of anything like collusion.'

By September 1870, when another of Carr's agents – one Edward Wrixton – publicly announced that mesmerism was 'false', the accusation barely caused a ripple. This may have been because Wrixton was in court, charged with embezzling £2.5*s*. But it may also have been because Carr's deceptions, by then, were old news. They were certainly old news in Victoria. As far back as February 1868, a Beechworth entertainment had featured someone impersonating 'Dr Dionysius Carr', whose valet John had 'proved himself quite as much an adept at "coma", and nearly as good a singer, as the original John.' The word 'humbug' was used, and various tricks alluded to. Then, in 1871, a man named John Bignell claimed that he knew what had happened to Carr's mesmeric power.

The Nunawading Messiah had stolen it, he said.

James Cowley Morgan Fisher, the Nunawading Messiah, was an escaped convict living under an assumed name. A farmer and charcoal burner in Nunawading, near Melbourne, he had taken over his mother-in-law's religious sect, changing its name from 'the New Church of the Firstborn' to 'the Church of the Firstborn'. Fisher followed the teachings of Englishman John Wroe, who had a worldwide following as the leader of another sect called the Christian Israelites. While Wroe was dying in Melbourne, in 1863, Fisher tried to claim his title. But Wroe refused to acknowledge the upstart charcoal burner, and Fisher's attempt failed.

Fisher, however, wasn't the only one who wanted to step into Wroe's shoes. So did another follower called John Bignell. When Bignell also failed in his bid to take over the Christian Israelites, he transferred his allegiance to Fisher, joining the hundred or so disciples under Fisher's command. This modest flock included a man named Andrew Wilson, who later calculated that he'd given Fisher about eighty-five pounds during his spell in the church. But in 1871, Wilson had a change of heart. He went to the police and charged Fisher with obtaining money under false pretences by claiming to be the Son of God.

According to Wilson, Fisher had been going around saying that he would never die, and that those who believed in him would never die, either. When Fisher's mother-in-law *did* die he had an explanation for those who questioned him; he had felled her with a paralytic stroke, he said, because she had lied about having money in the house. Wilson believed this, at first. Gradually, however, he lost his faith in Fisher.

This may have been because Fisher failed to cure his child of a fatal illness, as was generally reported. Or it may have been (as Wilson later maintained) because Fisher was eventually fooled by someone. A man told Fisher that a Danish lodge of Freemasons was eager to offer its allegiance to the Church of the Firstborn, and Fisher believed it. When the trick was finally revealed, the trickster laughed in Fisher's face. 'That shows what an imposter you are,' he said. 'If you were Jesus Christ, you would know that I had been gammoning you.'

Later, a theory arose that John Bignell himself had encouraged Wilson to lay the charge, because Bignell was trying to oust Fisher by claiming he was the lineal descendant of Moses. Whatever the reason, Wilson took Fisher to court. The case created quite a scandal. Wilson accused Fisher of believing in polygamy. He said that Fisher had once shown his followers a hole in his hand, made when he was hanging on the cross. Fisher denied that he had ever claimed to be the Messiah. He also denied that he had been bedding his wife's sisters. And in the middle of all this, James Bignell gave a public lecture at Nunawading, endorsing Wilson's accusations.

Bignell told the assembled crowd that, although Fisher's mother-in-law had preached and railed against him, he'd had an 'extraordinary power' over her. The secret to that power, Bignell insisted, was mesmerism:

> *Many people believed that Fisher deprived Guthrie Carr of his mesmeric power; I do. When Carr was in Melbourne, Fisher went to one of his performances, with the express purpose of taking the power away from him. He afterwards said that he had got Guthrie Carr's power, and it seemed that Carr lost it afterwards, resorting to such contrivances as hiring people to pretend to be under the influence.*

Bignell went on to say that Fisher had once mesmerised a young woman into believing that she was Mary Magdelene, with seven devils in her. According to the *Melbourne Weekly Times*, Fisher himself, though 'commonplace' to look at, had an indefinable quality about him.

'His eyes are shifty, and at times dull,' the paper reported, 'but suddenly, as they become fixed upon some person or object, the pupils dilate; a sombre fire flushes in the orbits; there is a sort of convulsive twitching of the body, and the whole appearance of the man gives one the idea that he is not without a certain amount of mesmeric power . . .'

In the end, Wilson's charges were thrown out of court. While conceding that some good might come of exposing Fisher, the magistrate declared that it wasn't the law's job to protect gullible fools like Wilson by proving or disproving that a person was the Messiah. 'Such matters are incapable of legal proof,' was the opinion handed down.

The same thing could easily have been said about mesmeric trances.

Clearly, Carr's reputation had suffered. If a religious fundamentalist out in Nunawading had heard that Carr was a fraud, then the mesmerist must have been facing some pretty hostile audiences. In his defence, however, it should be said that he wasn't the first stage mesmerist to resort to trickery, and he wouldn't be the last. In 1872, in the New Zealand town of Kyneton, a certain 'Professor Nash' was imitating Carr's methods. Nash put a youth called Richardson under the influence, then made him dance a jig and sing a verse of 'Tell me, Mary, how to woo thee'. But suddenly Richardson, without any kind of encouragement, launched into a speech. And when Nash placed a hand across his mouth, commanding him to be silent, Richardson's response was to announce that he'd had enough of this 'farce'. He informed the audience that Nash was an imposter who knew nothing of electro-biology, and that no one on stage was really mesmerised.

At this point, half of Nash's other subjects wandered away.

Taken aback, Nash called Richardson a humbug himself, insisting that he'd never claimed he could influence *everyone*, and that if people pretended, he 'could not be held answerable for the pretence'. Then one of Nash's subjects suddenly snapped out of his trance, came forward and kicked Richardson off the stage. Richardson tried to protest, but was told by an angry spectator to sit down and hold his tongue. Richardson was hurt. He 'appeared to think he was a benefactor to all mankind', one reporter noted, and kept arguing with Nash until the mesmerist threatened to charge him with defamation of character. That was when another mesmerised subject sprang to life and told the audience that Richardson had once confessed to 'playing possum' for the mesmerist Madame Sibly for two pounds a night.

Richardson denied this vehemently. He insisted that he had genuinely been under Madame Sibly's mesmeric influence. 'Ah, but then she was a woman,' cried a voice at the door, evoking a burst of laughter. Nash immediately tried to demonstrate his power by sticking a pin into someone. But at the other end of the hall, Richardson did the same. He drove a pin into a man he claimed was 'under his influence', right up to its head. 'This rivalry appeared to annoy the "professor" very much,' the *Kyneton Observer* remarked, 'and he protested against Richardson opening shop in his shop.'

The title of this story was 'Another Dr Carr'.

It wasn't the first time Nash and Carr had been compared. In January 1868, while Carr was heading for Sydney, Nash was in Victoria. 'Professor Nash, who is about as much a professor as Dr. Carr is a doctor, gave three mesmeric séances at the Star, Beechworth . . .' the *Ovens Constitution* commented. It described how a local sweep named Jones, who was supposed to be under the influence, had his 'organ of tune' touched by the lecturer, and must have thought that Nash intended to wake him from his magnetic sleep. Jones was about to become 'very lively' when Nash again darted forward and whispered a few magic words in his ear – at which point the subject launched into 'The Bonnie Hills of Scotland'. 'Little casualties of this sort will, however, occur in the best regulated mesmeric lectures,' the paper concluded. 'In every mesmeric lecture which we have yet heard, whether from Vernon, Russell or Stone in the old country, or from Bushell, Carr or Nash in Australia, there has been a certain amount of quackery, which by no means alters the fact that there is a good deal of reality in mesmerism itself.'

In other words, when it came to mesmerism, the jury was still out. That may have been why the whole issue of animal magnetism wasn't rigorously examined at Carr's committal hearing. Salomons and Robert may both have concluded that doing so would lead them nowhere useful, since nothing could be proven one way or another.

Instead, they concentrated on attacking – and defending – Eliza Gray's credibility.

PART V

MARRIAGE PROBLEMS

I

The proceedings against Thomas Guthrie Carr continued on Tuesday 28 September 1868.

The first witness called to the stand that morning was William Gray, Eliza's husband. He testified that for the past three months he'd been travelling to Queensland and back on the steamship *Lady Young*, as a fireman. Before then he'd worked on the *Fire King*, for £8.10*s* a week. Now his wages were only £7.10*s*. He had always given most of this money to his wife, for the support of his family. He'd kept very little for himself.

'I recollect the last night that I slept with my wife I was in good health,' he said, referring to the previous March, when he'd still been working on the *Fire King*. 'Then I was living happily with my wife and family, with nothing to disturb the comfort of my home. I have had reasons for not living with my wife since.' After 18 March, during his trip to the Manning River, he'd fallen ill. And on returning to Sydney he'd gone to see Mr Watson, his chemist.

William Gray explained that his wife had only told him about Carr's assault the day before he'd left for Queensland on the *Lady Young*. They had been at home, he said, but after telling him the truth she had 'flown'.

'Before this affair I never threatened to murder my wife, or do her any injury,' he declared, his resentment seeping into the flat delivery of the newspaper account. 'I have struck her, but I can't remember the number of times.' The reason he'd hit her was his own business. He had never, he insisted, accused her of going with other men.

He'd arrived back in Sydney the previous Saturday, at about ten in the evening. Heading straight for Botany Road, he had stayed the night there – though not in his wife's bedroom. 'I am now staying with my children, but not with my wife,' he said, 'but she stays in the same house.' Though he *had* been back in Sydney when Eliza Gray approached William Roberts, he hadn't gone with her. Nor had he discussed the matter with his wife. 'I have not spoken to anybody about getting damages from Dr Carr,' he informed the court. 'I have been damaged enough through him.' He hadn't even read about the case in the newspapers.

Asked about his knowledge of Carr, William Gray admitted that he had gone to see the mesmerist's show in March – though he didn't specify the exact date. It may even have been after the alleged assault on his wife. He had paid for a ticket and had visited Carr in his rooms beforehand. During the performance, Carr had made a blindfolded woman follow him about on stage. 'He also drew two teeth from two little girls, who took the teeth round to the audience and showed them,' the witness recalled. 'I saw the teeth. They appeared to have been really extracted.'

Cross-examined by Julian Salomons, William Gray confessed that he had been served a summons to appear in court while he was on board the *Lady Young*; he wouldn't have come, otherwise. When questioned about this, he bristled. 'I didn't like to come for reasons of my own,' he growled. 'I decline to give the reason.' It was his own business, he said. But Salomons kept pressing until finally the witness blurted out, 'If I left my work, without showing a cause for so doing, I would lose my situation and be deprived of the means of supporting my children, who would have to go begging.' He acknowledged that he had not been asked to give evidence before the subpoena was served.

Salomons then raised the subject of domestic violence. William Gray insisted that he had struck his wife only two or three times. He had never knocked her down. But when pressed, he retracted this claim. 'I won't swear I have not threatened her or knocked her down since March,' he admitted. On Salomons asking him if he knew that Carr had come to his house, the witness denied it. He claimed that he didn't know a man called Lucas. He might know him by sight, perhaps, but not by name. He had never seen Lucas at his house.

In answer to a final query from the Bench, William Gray couldn't recall that his wife had ever told him she was going to have her bumps read. Then he stepped down.

The next witness called was Dr Charles Eichler, who gave an account of his dealings with Eliza Gray before offering up his opinion of Carr's mesmeric skills. He was also asked whether Carr could have anaesthetised Gray by dousing a handkerchief in chloroform.

'Chloroform in a handkerchief would lose its effect at a distance,' he replied, 'but the greater the quantity of chloroform, the longer and heavier the sleep.' He pointed out that a person under the influence of chloroform was relaxed, whereas mesmerism induced rigidity. 'If there were chloroform on a handkerchief,' he continued, 'and it was passed from one hand to the other in the manner described by Mrs Gray, it would have as much influence over the person holding the handkerchief as the person before whom the handkerchief was held.' He had never, he added, seen chloroform administered in such a way.

As a sidebar, William Roberts raised the subject of Carr's letter to Eichler. What was the meaning of its postscript, in which Carr mentioned that a 'lady' was much better? Eichler assured Roberts that the 'lady' referred to was not Eliza Gray, and that she was not suffering from the same disease as the plaintiff.

After Eichler had been dismissed, the case for the prosecution closed. The police magistrate put the usual questions, after which Salomons submitted that there was no case to answer, unless the magistrates were of a different opinion. They were. So the hearing was adjourned until eight o'clock.

When its cast reassembled at the Central Police Court that evening, the first witness for the defence was the 'baker's boy' referred to by Eliza Gray. His name was George James Lees and he caused quite a stir, even among the jaded court reporters. 'This witness, quite a youth, without a shadow of down on his face,' the *Empire* marvelled, 'gave his evidence, disgusting as it was, without even a blush, and smiled or grinned all the while.' To say that he made a bad impression was an understatement.

George James Lees was born in Newcastle in 1848, to George Lees and Susannah Priest. At the age of eight, by his own admission, he was arrested for forgery – but on appearing before the Quarter Sessions, he was discharged. In June of 1867, he was arrested again. This time he was accused of embezzling from his employer, a baker named Alexander McLean, of Redfern, Sydney. According to McLean, Lees had delivered bread to McLean's customers and had also collected money owed by them. But Lees had kept some of this money for himself. He had retained £1.16*s*.4*d* from a man named Joseph Haigh, two pounds from a woman named Mary Lapton, and six shillings from another woman named Jane Nutter. For this crime he was sentenced in October 1867 to nine months' hard labour in Darlinghurst Gaol. '*You* ought to know,' Lees said to William Roberts, 'you pleaded for me.' Then, with cheeky irreverence, he added, 'I have read reports of this case in the newspapers. I knew you were pleading. Dick Furlong told me so. He said you would give me a good overhauling!'

Lees was released from prison in April 1868. By that time he was already married to Charlotte Catherine Greenfield. Charlotte had been born in 1847, and had married Lees shortly before his arrest. By September 1868 she'd had one child by him, and would go on to have eight more – though not all of them would survive to adulthood. According to Lees, Charlotte had worked at Eliza Gray's house; he thought that they might have been 'in partnership'. This suggests that Charlotte, too, was a seamstress, though it begs the question: why had Eliza Gray called her 'Mrs Greenfield' when cross-examined by Julian Salomons? Mrs Greenfield was surely Charlotte's mother, Elizabeth.

In 1897, Elizabeth Greenfield's funeral notice mentioned that she'd lived in Botany Road, so she and Eliza Gray had probably been neighbours. In the mid-nineteenth century, Chippendale was not a very desirable neighbourhood. It contained a slaughterhouse, a large distillery and many 'third class' houses, some of them log huts 'indescribably disorderly and ugly in their appearance'. A fetid stream of sewage ran through a wasteland in the middle of the suburb. Yet scattered among the destitute inhabitants were large numbers of respectable tradesfolk – shoemakers, carpenters, butchers, laundresses and, of course, seamstresses. The Botany Road neighbourhood was obviously an important part of Gray's life; hints of it keep popping up in the testimony. She sewed for her neighbour, the local saddler, Robert Lucas. She worked with her neighbour's daughter, Charlotte Greenfield. In 1870, long after the Carr case had ended, Gray found herself in court again after trying to help another neighbour's girl. Margaret Thomas, who lived near Gray, was married to the second officer of the steamer *City of Brisbane* – and her daughter by a previous marriage, Mary Ann Silvey, was giving her trouble. Mary had already been sent to Newcastle Industrial School for Girls because of her ungovernable behaviour. When she returned home at the age of seventeen she soon came knocking on Gray's door. Apparently Gray had known her since she was a child, and after hearing that Mary had been ill used by her mother, Gray agreed to take the girl in until she found a 'situation'. But a day or so later, Mary went off to inquire about an advertised job – and never came back. Gray then discovered that her husband's watch and chain were missing from the bedroom. They were worth five pounds.

Mary received twelve months' hard labour in Darlinghurst Gaol for this theft. She also received a further three months for stealing forty shillings' worth of clothing from a lady she lodged with in Castlereagh Street, under the alias 'Isabella Webster'. Described in the *Police Gazette* as a prostitute, Mary Ann Silvey was a bad lot, whose prospects never improved. But thanks to her trial report, we know that two years after the Carr affair William and Eliza Gray were still, to all appearances, married. Eliza was described as 'the wife of William Gray'. She was keeping his watch and chain in her bedroom. Despite everything that had happened they were muddling along as best they could.

No more children were born to them after 1866.

'I was two months courting,' said Lees, when questioned about his own marriage. 'My marriage was a sudden arrangement.' He then went on to relate that even while courting his wife, he had been carrying on a 'criminal intimacy' with Eliza Gray. 'I know Mrs Gray,' he declared. 'I have known her for seven years. I live on Botany Road. I have been to her house several times. I have been criminally intimate with her on several occasions.'

At this point Eliza Gray could keep silent no longer. 'Oh, you wretch, you insignificant little vagabond,' she shrieked, 'you know you are telling a lie, you know you never were. Oh my God!' She dropped to her knees, then rose again, clapping her hands and raving. 'By God, you never had improper intimacy with me, if I might be struck dead in this spot! Oh, oh, I cannot stop and listen to that!'

Much of Lees' testimony wasn't reported; it was considered unfit for publication. Possibly there was details in it that Eliza Gray found excruciating. But despite her outburst, Lees continued with his story. He said that he had known Eliza Gray since he was a boy, and had frequently visited her on his way back from 'singing rooms'. (A singing room was a kind of early music hall, usually attached to a pub.) She had introduced him to his wife, and he claimed to have bought them both lemonade whenever he dropped in. He calculated that he had first been improperly intimate with Gray in November or December of 1866, while he was working for Alexander McLean.

'Before the occurrence between Mrs Gray and myself, on the first occasion, we were larking while we were drinking, but I can't give you the remotest idea of what the larking was,' he declared. 'I can't recollect the first act of familiarity between us.' He couldn't really remember their second coupling, either, though he thought that there might have been one or two months between the first and second acts. 'I am so conscientious that I can't fix the date of the second occasion,' he cheerfully admitted. 'It might have been in January or February. I was married in April.'

He told the court that he would generally visit Eliza Gray at about nine o'clock and stay until midnight, but that he didn't go there by appointment; she had never actually invited him to her house. Nevertheless, when he 'attempted liberties', she didn't repel them. He mentioned that she would call him 'Jim', and sometimes 'George'. He hadn't given her any money, he said, but he had seen other men in her house at night. He had no idea if anything improper had occurred between these men and Eliza Gray.

His wife, he insisted, knew exactly what he'd done.

William Roberts then questioned Lees about Thomas Guthrie Carr. Lees admitted that he had been to several of Carr's séances. He said that he believed in mesmerism. But he insisted that he had never had any dealings with Carr. Nor had he ever claimed that Carr would pay him fifteen shillings for coming to testify. 'I have said that I would ask Dr. Carr for it because that is my day's wages,' he explained, adding with breezy impudence, 'I might be a member of parliament yet!'

Next, William Roberts asked him if he had a cousin living with Carr. No, Lees replied, he did not. His cousin was merely living in the same house, as a servant. In other words, his cousin worked for the landlady, not for the mesmerist. Though Lees had gone to visit his cousin at Carr's house on Sunday week, he hadn't met with Carr there.

Lees denied that he had discussed with anyone the evidence that he was going to present in court. Moments later, he corrected himself. A man named Stephens, who claimed to be a private detective, had spoken to Lees on the street, telling him that he knew more about the matter than Lees realised. Stephens had then taken Lees to a public house. 'I let some out,' Lees confessed. 'I do not know what I let out, but when I found I had let it out, I made "tracks" home.'

Suddenly he laughed.

'Why are you laughing, sir?' William Roberts demanded.

'I am laughing at Mrs Gray,' said Lees. 'She's shaking her fist at me.'

Roberts then asked if Lees had ever been to any 'dancing saloons' since his marriage. Lees confirmed that he had – and that he had taken girls with him, too. A dancing saloon was regarded as a haunt of prostitution. Two years later, in Adelaide, an article was published on the subject: it described several of the local dancing saloons in great detail. The Shamrock, for example, was entered through a narrow door to a filthy backyard. Visitors had to pick their way through pools of stagnant water and patches of fetid mud until they reached a parlour about thirty feet long, with a small gallery at one end for an orchestra made up of a drum, a cornet and a fiddle. The parlour was attached to a bar where liquor could be purchased. The women occupying the settles along the wall were of the lowest possible class:

> *Some have been notorious street-walkers for the past ten years . . . They have acquired the muscle of prize-fighters, possibly not without some practice of the art. They have passed the voluptuous stage years ago; they are no longer even sensual; the heavy, callous stupidity of their faces is almost brutal. Moral consciousness does not betray itself in a single look or gesture. The idea of shame has ceased even to suggest itself to them. They are little better than animals, who live for a purpose, which they don't care who knows. They drink without getting drunk – or very rarely. They dance mechanically without evincing any more pleasure than if they were on a treadmill. They speak without allowing a gleam of intelligence to break through their torpid vacancy. They herd together in the adjoining hovels, rows of which are leased to them by the landlords of the Shamrock and the Albion. They are, in short, the lowest type of prostitute . . .*

To suggest that Lees went to dancing saloons was to besmirch his character in a big way. To say that Eliza Gray went to them was to label her a whore. But that's what Lees did. 'I have seen Mrs Gray at these dancing saloons,' he said. 'Mrs Gray did not dance. She came with another married woman.'

Lees suggested that Gray 'may' have stayed at the saloon until midnight.

By this time it was quite late, so the case was adjourned until the following Thursday. But Lees wouldn't be called back. He disappeared from the narrative entirely – and from the pages of the *Police Gazette*, as well. His misspent youth apparently didn't result in a life of crime or an early death. When he died in Redfern in 1907 he was lavishly mourned by his entire family, who published five 'in memoriams' a year later. Charlotte lamented the passing of her 'dearly beloved husband' with the words:

So full of life, in perfect health.
Not thinking death was near.
Not having time to say goodbye
To those he loved so dear.

His children were equally keen to commemorate their 'dear father' – so he obviously did something right, even if he spent too much time in dancing saloons with other women.

William Gray also disappeared from the witness stand. He probably went back to the *Lady Young*; according to its crew manifest, he was still working on board as a fireman in December 1869. As for Eliza Gray, she would have needed a stiff drink after hearing Lees' testimony. She must have been wondering what she'd got herself into, and dreading what new horrors Thursday would bring.

Thomas Guthrie Carr would also have been worried about the hearing on Thursday. But it's likely that by 28 September he was wrestling with an even thornier problem: the problem of his approaching marriage.

A girl he knew was pregnant – and this time he couldn't run away.

II

Jane Ann Ireland was born in 1844. Her father, John Ireland, was a convict when he arrived in Australia, having been sentenced to seven years' transportation. By 1828 he had been assigned to Dr David Ramsay, a Scottish physician turned general merchant and wool broker. Ramsay and his partner, Thomas Paine, had been successfully working out of an office on the corner of Bligh and Hunter streets, in Sydney, since 1823. But in 1828 Ramsay dissolved the partnership. He turned his attention to his land holdings, which included the sprawling Dobroyde Estate, in Petersham. This land had originally been granted to wealthy emancipist Simeon Lord. When Lord's daughter married Ramsay she had brought the estate with her as a dowry and in 1826 she and Ramsay moved into 'Dobroyde House', a timber cottage that was replaced by a large stone mansion thirty years later.

This mansion is now Yasmar Juvenile Remand and Detention Centre, on Parramatta Road in Haberfield.

Ramsay described his new home as 'one of the finest places in New South Wales, the oranges in the orchard alone are worth £100 per year'. In 1816, the house had been advertised in the *Sydney Gazette* as 'an excellent villa fit for the reception of a small, genteel family with suitable detached kitchen, dairy, stable, coach house, piggery, cow house and stock yard, together with a most productive garden containing some of the finest fruit trees in the colony.' Ramsay greatly improved this garden and in the 1830s established Dobroyde Gardens Nursery alongside a nearby creek. With so much work to do on the estate, it's not surprising that Ramsay had convicts like John Ireland assigned to him.

But Ramsay didn't confine himself to horticultural pursuits. Towards the end of the 1820s, he had an inn constructed on Parramatta Road, near its intersection with Liverpool Road, Ashfield. Officially known as the Speed the Plough Inn, it was commonly referred to as 'the Plough'. Ramsay himself was too busy to get involved in its day-to-day management, so he leased it to various innkeepers. Charles Jordan ran it between 1830 and 1835. In 1836 it was leased to John Ireland – who remained its landlord until his death in 1847.

Clearly, John had proven himself a valuable and trustworthy employee. By the time he took over management of the Plough he'd been married for ten years, to Sarah Ann Blades, and they'd had five children together: Mary Ann, Sarah, John Henry (who died when he was an infant), John Thomas and James Bede. Since all of these children except Mary were born at the Plough, it seems that John Ireland must have been working there long before he became its landlord.

Five more children were born to him during the eleven years he presided over the Plough: George, William

Henry, Thomas, Jane Ann and Isabella. By the time Jane arrived, the inn was a two-storeyed brick building with a shingle roof, a wide veranda, and a single-storeyed wing at each end. Two horse troughs carved out of logs stood near the pole out front that bore its sign. In 1849, after John Ireland's death, the new landlord described his property as having a large and spacious yard, extensive stabling, wool sheds, stores and coach houses, and several enclosed paddocks (with plenty of water) for cattle, sheep, horses and 'teams'.

This handsome spread was Jane's playground when she was a toddler. In the early 1850s, just a few years after her father's death, an English visitor described the Plough in admiring terms:

> *After travelling fourteen miles along this uninteresting road, you are agreeably surprised by suddenly emerging into the Parramatta Road, about six miles from Sydney, and opposite one of the most characteristic roadside inns that we have seen in the country. Here, as we mingled amongst the pedestrians, horsemen, carts and carriages . . . we no longer supposed ourselves travelling in the land of gold and gum-trees, tea and damper. There was so much of what is called civilisation in the aspect of the people and the roadside scenery, so much that looked thoroughly English, that it required no great stretch of imagination for us to suppose ourselves conveyed to a turnpike road in the mother country . . .*

In the *New South Wales Directory* of 1837, John Ireland was complimented on his 'jolly appearance', which was likened to that of 'a roadside host in England'. The word 'jolly' might have been code for 'corpulent'; apparently he carried a lot of weight, though he wasn't a tall man. He was, however, hugely energetic. Despite the fact that it was strategically placed on a main road, the Plough was a little too close to the city to attract any overnight custom – except that of bullock drivers, who found it hard to travel more than ten miles a day. As for the inn's local clientele, it was limited by the fact that Ashfield was still a small, rural community. As a consequence John Ireland had to work hard to drum up business. He started his own coaching line, running a light, four-wheeled carriage twice a day between Ashfield and Sydney. He also became involved in the establishment of a nearby racecourse. For twenty years, punters from the city would come to Ashfield, blow their money at the races, then repair to the Plough for a drink. Apparently, turf-related arguments would often be settled there by dumping people in the horse-troughs.

Other sources of business for the Irelands included local boxing matches, local livestock auctions and a mail contract, which John shared with a man called John Titterton. One route ran between Sydney and Goulburn, along Liverpool Road. At first, Ireland's coaches used to stage at the Bark Huts, a small settlement halfway between Sydney and Liverpool. Then he and Titterton bought a hotel called the Angel, in Enfield, and turned *that* into a staging post. Ireland's other route, to Bathurst, was probably the first mail coach ever to run over the Blue Mountains. His coaching business became extensive; in 1836, he and the 'clerk' of his Sydney booking office, Michael Doyle, were charged with assault for hauling George Shepherd, a wine and spirit merchant, out of Ireland's 'Campbell Town Coach'. Apparently, there had been a ticketing mix-up.

The arrival of these coaches at the Plough was another source of income. Ashfield residents would always flock to the inn whenever a coach turned up with its cargo of passengers and news. Sometimes, when two coaches arrived at once, there would even be a race into the city – or so the story goes.

As a child, Jane probably had a lot to do with horses and with the day-to-day running of the inn. Even after her father died, her mother, Sarah, continued to manage the Plough until 1849, when it was leased to a man called Fraser. But the Ireland family remained in Ashfield. When Jane was seven years old her mother married Samuel Lucas – who in 1852 opened another inn directly opposite the Plough. It was called the Bird in Hand. The Lucases followed John Ireland's example, trying to build their business by becoming involved in the local races. One popular race that was held for several years in the 1850s, called the 'Woodman's Purse', began at Battle Bridge and ended at the Bird in Hand.

But for all the Lucases' efforts, their venture failed. While the Plough remained a local landmark until the early twentieth century, by 1865 the Bird in Hand was gone. So was Sarah, who died in 1856. What happened to Jane after that is hard to say. She might have stayed with Samuel Lucas. She might have gone to live with her sister Mary Ann, who was already married with children. John Ireland had left a great deal of property when he died – including forty-eight square miles of land near Molong, New South Wales – and apparently Lucas tried to secure it for himself after Sarah's death. He failed, but his efforts must have caused some ill feeling, which in turn might have dictated Jane's movements. In 1861, when she was sixteen, her brother William Henry Ireland married Julia Seale, whose family owned the New Inn on Liverpool Road, Burwood. William took over this establishment in 1865, so it's possible that Jane might have spent some time there.

On her marriage certificate, however, she gave her usual place of residence as 'Sydney'. This suggests that she was living in town; had she been living in Ashfield or Burwood she would have said so, because they weren't a part of Sydney at the time. The one thing we *do* know about Jane is that, by 2 October 1868, she had definitely met Thomas Guthrie Carr – because that was the day they got married.

Exactly how and when they met remains a mystery. We can't even be sure that he was the father of her child, though his personal history suggests that he probably was. Two and a half months after their marriage, on 14 December, Carr was performing in Hokitika, New Zealand, when the man chairing his show announced that Mrs Carr had given birth to a daughter that day. So it's likely that Jane was at least six months' pregnant at the time of her wedding, which occurred while her new husband was on remand for rape. If that was the case, then the child would have been conceived around the time Carr first arrived in Sydney. He might well have met Jane in Ashfield, while he was passing through on his way from western New South Wales. Or Jane might simply have gone to one of his early shows, like Eliza Gray.

Poor Jane must have been at the end of her tether. The fact that she was heavily pregnant when she married Carr suggests that he was a reluctant participant. It might even have been a shotgun wedding. William Ireland showed an abiding interest in his little sister. Some twenty years after her marriage, he was involved in organising her funeral, and was a witness at her daughter Monica's wedding a year later, so he may have taken it upon himself to make sure that Jane wasn't cast off. But if that was the case, why on earth did he wait until she was six months' gone? Was it because Carr had spent so much time away from Sydney? Was it because Jane had kept her pregnancy a secret until it began to show? Or was it because she didn't actually want to marry Carr, but finally bowed to family pressure?

If Carr raped Eliza Gray, he might also have raped Jane Ireland. And though forcing a woman to marry her rapist might seem a little extreme, Jane's position, as a nineteenth-century single mother, was desperate. On the other hand, Jane might simply have been besotted. We just don't know. All we know is that, once married, she and Carr stayed that way until he died.

They were wed at Scots Church, on York Street. A Presbyterian minister presided, though both the bride and groom were eventually buried according to Anglican rites. (Carr had been raised a Presbyterian.) The wedding must have been a very quiet affair. One of the witnesses was related to the minister – and the other one wasn't a member of Jane's family. On her marriage certificate Jane gave her age as twenty-two, despite the fact that she was older. This wasn't the last time that she would smudge the facts on an official document. In 1886, Carr's death certificate gave his daughter's age as sixteen, implying that she was born in 1870. Monica herself might have gone through life believing that she was a year or so younger than she really was. On her mother's death certificate, dated 1891, Monica's age was given as twenty-one.

Even after so many years, the shame of that early pregnancy still cast a long shadow.

It's possible that Jane brought some property into her marriage, eventually if not immediately. Her father's landholdings were divided between his children after Sarah Ireland's death, though none of them became wealthy as a consequence. James was a butcher. George, like William, was a publican. William took out a coaching licence in 1870 and transferred his New Inn licence to the freshly built Ireland's Hotel, just up the road, ten years later. Mary Ann's brother-in-law, Andrew Hardie McCulloch, was a lawyer, and his son became a politician. They were a solid, respectable, quietly prosperous family, despite their convict origins. Jane's predicament must have appalled them.

Once married, however, she kept a low profile. Though her husband was always in the newspapers, Jane barely made an appearance. In November 1868 her name was published when she and Carr arrived in New Zealand on the steamship *Egmont*. In 1871 she was presented with a 'small parcel of nuggets' at a public meeting convened by the inhabitants of a remote country district in New Zealand, where Carr was also presented with a testimonial for all the lecturing he'd done there. A few years later it was reported that Mrs Carr had suffered a severe injury to her left arm after she was thrown from a horse. But for the most part she remained hidden by the dominating figure of her loud, overbearing husband. This was hardly surprising, since Carr had his own views about a woman's place in the world. He once gave a lecture called 'Woman and Woman's Work' in which he argued that a woman's proper sphere was the household, and that her greatest pleasure should be watching over and training her children.

Only in the later years of their marriage did Jane finally begin to surface. That was after she had settled in Morpeth, New South Wales, where she seems to have made a reasonably pleasant life for herself. In 1882 a local paper related how Mrs Carr, of Northumberland Villa, had placed a newly hatched chick beside her tortoiseshell cat and its kittens, because the chick was cold and weak. The cat immediately adopted this chick, clasping it snugly between its front paws. 'When the cat left her young for water or food and the chicken strayed,' the paper revealed, 'pussy at once picked it up between its jaws and gently replaced it.'

A few days later, when the next brood emerged, Mrs Carr put them in a box by the fire – where her cat soon found them. It wasn't long before all five chicks were tucked cosily into the cat's basket. 'When that cat dies,' the paper concluded, 'Dr Carr will be induced to explore the region of its philoprogenitiveness to see if there be anything abnormal in its development, for pussy displayed equal solicitude for the chickens as for her own offspring.'

This gentle little story hints at Jane's domestic life, with her cat and her chicks and her (by then) teenage daughter. But it was only after Carr's death that she at last received her due. Within six months of his passing she decided to return to Sydney, where her family still resided. Morpeth, however, was sad to see her go. A meeting was organised at the Morpeth School of Arts to present her with a testimonial.

One hundred and fifty people turned up, many of them women. The mayor of Morpeth, Joseph George White, opened the proceedings by paying tribute both to Jane and to her husband. He recalled how Jane had once cared for the child of a dying woman 'as if it were her own, without the slightest expectation of any reward'. He could not praise the good doctor's widow enough, he said. And although they were about to lose her, he was comforted by the fact that she would simply be carrying to another place 'the kindness and labours she had extended to the sick and poor in Morpeth for the last six years'.

There followed a burst of enthusiastic applause, after which White read to Jane a prepared address. In it, the citizens of Morpeth expressed their high appreciation of her sympathy, tenderness and Christian charity towards the suffering and the sick, particularly among the poor:

> *By the bed of sickness, without fee or hope of earthly reward, you were always nursing and tending, and aiding and cheering those who were in pain or affliction. We desire to express our deep sympathy with you in the recent sad bereavement of your excellent husband, the late Dr. Thomas Guthrie Carr, whose kindness of heart and tenderness to the sick, and other amiable qualities, we all remember and bear cheerful testimony to.*

Jane was presented with a gold watch, the inner case of which bore a grateful inscription. Several aldermen then came forward and spoke at length about her many virtues. One of them declared that the only person with whom she could be compared was Florence Nightingale. 'Whenever a case of sickness or distress was made known,' he added, 'the only question with Mrs Carr was "Can I help?"' Jane had always given free medicine to the poor, and tonight's testimonial 'was poor indeed in comparison to her gifts'. At one point, he said, he'd been afraid that the death of her husband might have felled her, and impaired her usefulness to others – but he was glad to see that in the midst of her own sufferings, she seemed to find relief in attending to the sufferings of her fellow man.

In conclusion, the mayor described how the testimonial had come about. His daughter had suggested it, he explained, and he had gone with her to 'solicit subscriptions'. In four hours they had collected nearly all the money required. One person, on being asked if he could afford the sum he'd donated, had simply replied, 'whether I can or not . . . she deserves it'.

Soon after this event, Jane, her daughter and her 'adopted daughter' – whose existence was once or twice alluded to in the press, but whose name was nowhere recorded on any official documents – were escorted to the Sydney train by a great crowd of their friends, many of whom were 'visibly affected' by the parting. There can be no doubt that Jane had made a huge impact on the community, and that her loss would be keenly felt. To all appearances, she was a very nice person.

So how did she end up with Thomas Guthrie Carr?

The mayor of Morpeth, in his testimonial speech, described Carr's great kindness and generosity, 'especially to children'. A fellow alderman declared that Carr had always been one of the most benevolent men in town. Since they were talking to his bereaved widow, they could hardly have said otherwise – but it's not as if Carr didn't have *any* redeeming features. We know for a fact that he once gave money to a ten-year-old beggar, and his gifts to local charities were repeatedly mentioned throughout his career. In fact, collecting for charity seemed almost a default mechanism for Carr. In New Zealand once he was at a race meeting when a young boy was thrown from a horse. The 'plucky little fellow' immediately picked himself up and claimed not to be hurt at all. But Carr started collecting money for him anyway, as a reward for his manliness . . .

It's possible that Carr got a kick out of making donations. For one thing, it put him squarely in the limelight. A common feature of his good deeds is that they never went unnoticed. In 1876, he remitted a telegraph money order to Whanganui to pay the funeral expenses of a former secretary, Charles B Levett. Some two weeks later, he published a letter in which he thanked the people who had represented him at the funeral, mentioned that he himself had paid for it and observed that he had donated Levett's linen, socks and new suit to the local hospital – along with a generous sum from his own pocket. Then he went on to praise Levett's kindness and generosity.

This letter stuck in the craw of at least one local observer, who accused Carr of making a parade of his own sorrow, gratitude and liberality. While choosing to publicise his gift of money, clothes, linen and even socks – 'the Doctor is proverbially accurate as to details' – Carr had at the same time neglected to supply Levett with cash while he was alive. Instead, the deceased had been forced to seek subscriptions so that he could pay his hospital deposit. 'But who can blame him [Carr] for making professional capital out of another's misfortune?' the angry columnist concluded. 'Has it not been the same throughout the chapter, and will be so probably to the end?'

Levett's death certainly proved useful to Carr. A few days after it occurred he sent a telegram to the *Wairarapa Standard*, explaining why so many people hadn't received the phrenological charts for which they had paid him:

> *I left my secretary, Mr Levitt* [sic], *in Wanganui, with all my notes. Mr Levitt, who was unwell, I have expected weekly. Each mail he promised to come to me, and assured me he would forward me the few charts I have been unable to complete. Mr Charles Levitt died in Wanganui last Monday morning, 17th. My papers are not yet sent me.*

So Carr's generosity was not, perhaps, entirely without an ulterior motive. But his physical courage can't be doubted. In Wellington, New Zealand, he once came to the aid of a policeman who was being assaulted by two other men. During a show in Dunedin, he personally ejected a drunken audience member who had tripped up a mesmerised subject and injured him. In Hawke's Bay, New Zealand, Carr entered a burning building to help save its contents – and he did exactly the same thing ten years later in Port Macquarie, New South Wales. This shows how brave and impulsive he was. It also shows a slightly suspicious pattern of behaviour, though there's really no proof that Carr was an arsonist. Fires were a frequent occurrence in the days of kerosene lamps, and Carr was just the sort of person who would be drawn by a large, public conflagration. Fires and fights – Carr wasn't fazed by either.

Even being shipwrecked didn't disturb him unduly.

On Sunday 28 December 1879, the paddle steamer *Agnes Irving* ran aground on the south spit of Macleay Heads, New South Wales, near Trial Bay. She had left Sydney the day before, carrying fifteen passengers. Carr was one of them. He wrote an account of his experience that was later published in Sydney's *Evening News;* this article was calm, clear and highly complimentary of the vessel's master, Captain John Magee. According to

Carr, the *Agnes Irving* had been racing against another steamer, the *Elamang*, all the way from Sydney, and was just drawing ahead when a great wave drove her stern against the sandbar where she fetched up. At that point enormous breakers punched a hole in her starboard side and drenched the people on the quarterdeck. In the saloon, chairs and benches were overturned. Crockery crashed to the floor. The ship canted over and began to make a bed for herself in the sand. 'A few ladies were in abject alarm,' Carr reported, 'and a few gentlemen, who ought to have known better, heightened their apprehension by vague surmises and prophecies.'

Soon the fore-hold and cabins were filling with water, which rushed in despite the blankets that were hurriedly wedged into cracks and holes. The *Elamang* passed by on her way to Brisbane without even pausing to help; another ship called the *Mary Cochrane* did much the same thing. For about three hours, Captain Magee stood on the bridge with his feet planted firmly apart and his hands on the rail, issuing orders. Finally, at six o'clock, he signalled to the pilot, spread his arms and announced that he could do no more. The engine frame had been dislodged and the ship was sinking.

He ordered that the first lifeboat be lowered into the sea.

'The ladies were with no little danger placed safely on board,' Carr wrote, adding that they were landed without incident, thanks to the efforts of four seamen and the chief mate, who was acting as coxswain. 'The pilotboat next conveyed a number eager to get ashore, with equal success,' he continued.

> *I secured a seat in the third boat; the pilot, as he passed us, shouting to one of his men on shore to take us to the station. At this time it was half-past 7 o'clock, and clear to everyone that the Agnes would never leave the sandspit on which she was fixed. At about 10 o'clock she was abandoned to Providence and the elements, as fine a steamer of the size as ever I sailed in, and I have travelled in hundreds, of all sizes and sorts, from a frigate to a steam launch.*

Carr went on to relate that Magee had almost been dragged from the ship by the pilot, who was praised by Carr for accommodating some of the stranded passengers in his own house that night. Others, like Carr, had to sleep in the pilot station. Carr's short digression on the subject of the fleas in this building shows not only a well-developed sense of humour, but a sort of unquenchable vivacity that may account for his social success over the years:

> *New Zealand fleas are fatter, heavier and more formidable-looking; but, like other phlegmatic persons, they are slow, and of easy temper. The fleas on the pilot station are small; they have indomitable pluck and audacity, and their activity, energy and voraciousness are equalled only by their vigilance and cunning . . . You may cover a brigade of them by an instantaneous motion of your hand, your eyes will sparkle with contemplated revenge; you will work that hand as careful as you will, and be ready for a grab with the other, you must give it up. I tried it lots of times. The fleas are away by magic.*

The quirky charm of this extract might explain why Jane Ireland attached herself to Carr. He may not have assaulted her at all; he may simply have seduced her. He was a practised manipulator with a 'gift of the gab', a lot of energy and a commanding onstage presence. Even if this glamorous façade was misleading, it could easily have beguiled a country girl from honest, hardworking stock.

On the other hand, there's no question that Carr could be dangerous. His size, his strength and his impulsive nature meant that, physically, he was rather brave. But these same characteristics, when combined with his short fuse, also made him a violent man. Violent, touchy, even a little sadistic . . . Carr wasn't exactly an ideal husband.

Wherever he went, people seemed to suffer – and Eliza Gray wasn't by any means the first of them. There was a pattern to his dealings with others. Over and over again, he left a trail of victims behind him. And many of these victims, like Gray, had been subjected to the full force of his highly destructive character.

PART VI

THE ORGAN OF DESTRUCTIVENESS

I

Mesmerism wasn't Carr's only source of income. He was also, of course, a very successful phrenologist. 'Dr Carr has, I understand, been so busy here with private professional practice – principally phrenological – as to induce him to remain a day longer than he intended,' one New Zealand journalist observed in 1877. Carr's lectures on phrenology were, in many respects, just advertisements for his personal consultations.

Like mesmerism, phrenology was a slightly disreputable, eighteenth-century pseudo-science that enjoyed great popularity during the Victorian era. Its inventor, Franz Joseph Gall, had identified twenty-seven 'organs' within the brain that governed different human faculties. Each organ was represented by an area on the surface of the skull. To read a person's character, one simply had to measure the irregularities of his or her head. If a bump was small, it indicated that a certain faculty was weak. If large, then the faculty was strong.

When lecturing on the subject of phrenology, Carr always stressed its usefulness. It was the perfect tool for planning a child's future, he said. A skilled phrenologist could advise parents if their son had the makings of a mechanic, a lawyer or an artist. On one of his printed phrenological charts Carr claimed that phrenology was 'the good parent's good friend', because it uncovered the 'temper, disposition, capacity and talent of their offspring'. The same document explained how phrenology helped women acquire domestic virtues, and helped men improve their capacity for thought. Phrenology, he declared, assuaged the passions of the turbulent and modified the violence of rage. It did this, presumably, by identifying behaviours that needed curbing.

Archibald Sillars Hamilton, another colonial phrenologist who happened to be Carr's contemporary, went even further. He argued that prison inmates with dubious bumps ought never to be released. 'Every degree and character of crime,' wrote Hamilton, '. . . are the result of fixed laws.' Phrenology, he said, would 'enable mankind to understand these laws and thereby assist in preventing the manufacture of criminals, and in rightly governing those who are already criminals.'

As it happened, Hamilton was a bit of an expert when it came to crime. In 1860, he was charged with trying to rob a grave in Maitland, New South Wales. His purpose had been to obtain the skull of a recently executed Aboriginal man named Jim Crow, to add to his collection. Over the years, Hamilton managed to acquire about fifty skulls, many of them Aboriginal; he maintained that, being a man of science, he needed skulls the way a geologist needs rocks. The jury at his trial found this argument convincing enough to acquit him. But shortly afterwards he must have crept back into the East Maitland churchyard where Jim Crow was buried and dug up the controversial skull. Because by 1862, Crow's skull had become a prop in Hamilton's lectures.

Surprisingly, there's no evidence that Thomas Guthrie Carr ever did any grave-robbing, despite the fact that he ended up with a collection similar to Hamilton's. In the early days of Carr's phrenological career, he'd been forced to borrow his skulls from the Sohiers. Even in 1870, he was using skulls that belonged to other people. By 1877, however, he had started to promote his own exhibition of 'skulls and casts of well-known murderers and criminals', as well as a gallery of one hundred and fifty cartoons. Unfortunately, not long afterwards, he lost his box of skulls on a coach and had to advertise for it. 'Any person giving information concerning the same . . . will be rewarded,' he promised plaintively.

Unlike Carr, Hamilton was never a stage mesmerist, though phrenology and mesmerism were always closely associated. In his enthusiastic treatise on mesmerism, George Sandby described how, when an operator touched particular spots on the heads of his mesmerised subjects, they would exhibit 'marked and sometimes violent manifestation of certain mental faculties'. In other words, by exciting the organ of 'tune', you could make someone sing. This, Sandby concluded, was seen by some as proof that phrenology really worked.

Whether it was proof or not, it was certainly entertaining. Carr frequently employed such 'phreno-mesmerism' in his shows. Hamilton didn't – and this was only one point of difference between them. 'Is the science of Phrenology correct?' someone named George J Neal wrote to the *New Zealand Herald* in 1869. 'If so, how is it that the delineations given by Dr. Carr are in direct opposition to those of Mr Hamilton? Are the manipulators at fault, or is the science all humbug?'

The same correspondent had asked the same question during Carr's most recent performance and Carr had reacted with unusual restraint. He'd pointed out that the three-year gap between his reading and Hamilton's would naturally have seen the subject's skull change as his faculties developed. But in print, Carr was far sharper. After dismissing the letter as 'commonplace' and 'beyond the range of criticism,' he went on to speculate that Neal might have been told something unflattering by Carr – something that might have been 'carefully withheld' by Archibald Hamilton. Carr was, in effect, accusing Hamilton of dishonesty. Hamilton happened to be in Australia at the time; that may be why he didn't weigh into the argument. Like Carr, he had a habit of lashing out whenever he was impugned or contradicted. In 1862, a letter sent by Hamilton to Brisbane's *Courier* was so vituperative that it prompted comment from the Editor:

> *We would remind Mr Hamilton that scurrility is not argument. He seems to regard every disputant who questions his conclusions, and seeks to argue with him upon phrenology, as a personal enemy . . . We make these remarks merely because we consider that Mr Hamilton is damaging his reputation by the manner in which he replies to those who wish to argue the point with him.*

Carr was equally thin-skinned, as can be seen from his correspondence with Thomas Buddle. Buddle was an Auckland solicitor. Having requested a private phrenological analysis from Carr, he received in response a letter and a printed chart. Most practical phrenologists had their own charts printed (Hamilton certainly did), and Carr seemed particularly proud of his. At one point he was advertising freshly printed 'Superior Illustrated' charts for five shillings apiece. A chart *and* an 'estimate', however, cost ten shillings. And for a chart, an estimate, analysis and advice, Buddle was asked to pay double that.

But he didn't seem to think he'd got his money's worth.

On one side of Buddle's chart were three drawings of phrenological heads, showing the locality of the 'organs'. On the other side a list of the different faculties was provided, organised into neat little groups: animal, domestic, intellectual, semi-intellectual, reflective. 'Selfish propensities' and 'selfish sentiments' were stashed in the animal group. They included destructiveness, combativeness, secretiveness and 'bibativeness' (i.e. intemperance). Carr had given each of Buddle's faculties a mark out of seven. The solicitor's mark for 'inhabitiveness' (love of country and home) was a high five. His mark for 'approbativeness' (love of praise) was only three and a half.

Next came the letter. In it, Carr informed Buddle that his brain was a little larger than normal, with a phrenological development that indicated 'a respectably furnished cranium'. He then went on to describe Buddle as bilious, nervous and sanguine, hasty and of petulant temper, outspoken, tactless and possessed of little caution. According to Carr, Buddle had great moral energy, aided by combativeness, but wanted 'the strength of mental grasp, of solid understanding'. Like his father, Buddle was brave and daring, but he lacked his father's calculation and penetration. 'You are honest in your feelings, your affections, your likes and your dislikes,' Carr wrote, '. . . but why not methodise, why not act with greater measure of speculative energy, in which mind more than passion or feeling operates . . .?' Carr advised that Buddle should venture into some sort of speculative business, since he was governed by impulse and recklessness. Why not, perhaps, open a general store? Or become a land agent? 'You are constituted for action, not for dreaming,' Carr went on. 'Nature has not made you an artist nor a hero . . .'

Thomas Buddle's response was politely couched, but utterly bemused:

> *My object in undergoing the examination was perhaps more to satisfy curiosity than with a view of marking out a course for the future – my pursuit in life being pretty well fixed – and your report is so utterly at variance with my own estimate of my faculties and inclinations, as well as that of every friend I have shown it to, that I am free to confess that what little confidence I previously had in the science of Phrenology is not a little shaken.*

Painstakingly Buddle pointed out every error in the reading. He had always been considered overly cautious. He was 'the greatest duffer imaginable' when it came to accounting or business. Since childhood, it had been a struggle for him even to cut off a fowl's head, yet Carr had given him a five for destructiveness! On the whole, he regarded Carr's delineation as being completely off target.

Carr replied promptly, using the back of Buddle's own letter. In a wild, almost indecipherable scrawl, he accused Buddle of telling Charles Levett, Carr's secretary, that Carr had deferred writing his chart until he had gleaned more information about Buddle. This charge, Carr said, was unworthy of a gentleman. 'I had not the least knowledge you were a solicitor till Levett informed me,' Carr wrote, adding snippily, 'I understood you were a draper's assistant.' He insisted that, no matter what Buddle might say about his reluctance to chop off a fowl's head, 'yours is the destructiveness that wounds deeper and is more deadly'. Carr stood by everything he had said. Buddle *was* impulsive. He *was* petulant. And Carr denied absolutely that Buddle really knew himself.

Again and again, over the years, Carr exhibited this same explosive touchiness. He simply could not ignore a challenge. Whether it came from the Reverend James Maughan or from some anonymous newspaper hack, he seemed to have trouble restraining himself when confronted. Early in 1876, a journalist at the *Wairarapa Standard* paid for one of Carr's phrenological examinations. Carr had promised to send a chart by first post, the journalist reported, but it had never arrived. After running this complaint, the paper received a telegram from Carr. 'If I am indebted to you, please telegraph and say for what,' he demanded. In response, the paper pointed out that diligent inquiries had uncovered several customers in the Greytown and Carterton areas who had paid for charts they'd not received.

This, apparently, wasn't a new tactic for Carr. Way back in 1869, fellow phrenologist Professor James H Hume had publicly accused Carr, in Melbourne, of scooting off to Sydney without sending people the phrenological charts for which he'd been paid. In 1871, down on New Zealand's South Island, Carr had been blamed for defrauding customers in the same manner. Some twenty inhabitants of Alexandra had paid him fifteen shillings apiece for phrenological charts that had failed to materialise. The local paper had roundly condemned Carr's conduct, calling it 'dastardly', but the *Wairarapa Standard* was more playful in its approach. 'Can we do more than make this admission?' it chaffed. 'Or shall we characterise your conduct in the matter as truly honourable – perhaps a little eccentric, but merely the eccentricity of genius, the sportive effervescence of a noble soul?'

Carr erupted like a volcano. To the editor of the *Standard* he gave his 'well-known' whereabouts, and remarked that if he should die without fully discharging his debts, then it would be time enough for the paper's representatives to 'degrade their honourable editorial office in practising vulgarity and insult'. The journalist who'd had his bumps read soon received a refund (in frankly insulting halfpenny stamps) and a letter that was published all over the colonies:

> *Sir . . . During the twenty-five years which I have been in active practice, I have examined all kinds of heads, from the head of a sucking pig to that of a barber's pole, but your head is, without doubt, the most extraordinary phenomenon of the kind I have ever witnessed. But for the fact that you presented the thing to me poised upon a pair of human shoulders, I should have imagined you had made a mistake, and brought the forequarters of a jackass to be operated upon. I have often heard your readers complain of the unmitigated twaddle with which your columns are filled,*

but if they had read your head as I do, they would not be in the least astonished.

Carr never minced his words. When challenged to discuss the merits of phrenology by Dr James Sibley, Carr pronounced this well-respected (and highly qualified) medical practitioner to be 'a rash and presuming young man'. In a letter to the press, he declared that the impudence of Sibley's challenge amounted to 'madness'. But at least Sibley wasn't physically attacked, like the Bendigo boxer, or the drunk with the broken tooth. Anyone who defied Carr face to face risked a beating.

That became obvious to William McLean, a clothier in Wellington, New Zealand, when Carr burst into his shop complaining about a pair of gloves one day in 1871.

II

Carr had bought the gloves from McLean a few days earlier. Though they were the size he'd ordered, they didn't fit him; he wanted McLean to pay for the larger pair of gloves that he'd had to buy, or that he *would* have to buy – McLean wasn't quite sure if the gloves had been bought or not, because Carr was in a very excited state. 'He was inclined to create a disturbance,' McLean later testified, adding that Carr had apparently visited the shop on a previous occasion, while McLean was out, and had used a lot of disgraceful language.

'I must have the exact words,' Carr demanded in court. But McLean didn't know the exact words. He went on to say that, when Carr had threatened to go to the law,

McLean had told him that this was probably the best thing to do.

'What's that you say?' Carr had cried, before grabbing McLean's nose and shoving him backwards against the shop fixtures. McLean had ended up with a badly swollen lip. When cross-examined by Carr, he insisted 'I gave you no provocation.'

Several witnesses were in the shop at the time and they confirmed McLean's story. A local inspector of post offices thought that McLean had endured Carr's abuse with great patience. Another witness, Richard White, described Carr as 'bouncing, swearing and damning' as if he wanted to frighten McLean. Under cross-examination, White took issue with the word 'tweaked'. Marks had been left on McLean's nose, he said. That was no tweak.

'Were you present during the whole of the affair?' Carr asked him. 'It is very remarkable that you remember so much in detail against my case, and so much in favour of Mr McLean. Can you remember what I said?'

'Yes,' White replied, 'you came into the shop in a very bouncing way – your usual way, I believe.'

'Do you remember whether I made use of any foul language?' Carr demanded.

The witness couldn't recall.

'Swearing implies vulgarity,' Carr continued. 'I should like you to state to the Court what I did say.'

White answered that he already had. Then Carr wanted to know if McLean's nose had been tweaked very hard.

'I don't know,' said White, 'but I should not like you to have hold of my nose as you had hold of his.'

In his own defence, Carr made a long statement about buying a pair of gloves that weren't labelled correctly, then being irritated by McLean's 'excessive civility' and attempts to convince him that he was wrong. He denied using any foul language, though he might have said 'damn it, it's a shame after paying 5s not to be able to get a pair that fit'. He was sorry for the assault and had told McLean so, but it had been a tweak – a mere tweak. If he'd wanted to hurt McLean, he would have boxed his ears and left a mark that wouldn't have faded so quickly.

The final witness was police Inspector Atcheson, who testified that McLean was a quiet and inoffensive man. When Carr interrupted the inspector, complaining loudly about his conduct, Atcheson stood firm. He informed the Bench that McLean had come to him after the assault, whereupon Atcheson had approached Carr – whose response had been to threaten Atcheson with the same punishment he'd dished out to McLean.

'I only wish you had,' the policeman added, turning to Carr. 'I'd have given you more than you bargained for, big as you are. I wish I had seen the assault. I'd have arrested you myself.'

The court found for McLean, fining Carr five pounds and costs. Then, after a brief interval – during which the Bench tried a case of furious riding – Carr was brought in again, to answer a charge of threatening language. McLean testified that Carr had called him a low, mean, damned, contemptible hound.

This time the Bench bound Carr over to keep the peace for six months, with two sureties of twenty pounds each. As he left the court, Carr was heard to mutter something about the judgement being 'infamous'.

'Recent news from New Zealand contained the announcement that at Wellington, a Dr Carr had been fined £5 for breaking a draper's nose for selling him a wrong-sized pair of gloves,' the *Australian Medical Journal* noted. 'Is this the same Dr. Carr who some time since escaped from the Yarra Bend lunatic asylum?' It wasn't, of course. The asylum inmate was one Dr Alfred Yates Carr. Thomas Guthrie Carr wasn't a lunatic, even though he sometimes behaved like one.

Thomas Guthrie Carr was a bully.

A year earlier, he had become embroiled in another assault case. The plaintiff, a man called King, had tried to sue Carr for fifty pounds in damages. They had met at a hotel where several other men were locked in a dispute. A fight had broken out and King had taken part as a 'second'. Carr's objection to the affair had gone unheeded; during the scuffle that ensued, a window was broken. Later, Carr had accosted King, demanding that he help pay for the damage. King, who hadn't touched the window, had nevertheless promised that he would stump up twenty-one shillings if Carr would do the same. On this understanding, they had returned to the hotel together. But King had then withdrawn his offer and 'high words' had been exchanged. Carr had given King either a blow or a push – opinions differed – and, according to King, had kicked him in the face when he'd fallen down. But no one present had seen the kick and no trace of it was left on King's face. Though the magistrates had found for the defendant, they had awarded only 'nominal damages'.

Carr had been fined just one farthing, and both parties had been ordered to pay their own costs.

Carr, however, failed to learn his lesson. Years later, in 1877, he was hauled into court once again for unlawful assault. A man named Francis Porter, from Ipswich,

Queensland, testified that he had gone to one of Carr's shows. When Carr had invited members of the audience to come and have their bumps read, Porter had followed his friend Keogh up onto the stage. Something about the plaintiff's manner must have irritated Carr, because he'd told Porter, 'We don't want you here; pick up your hat and go away.' Porter had immediately turned to the audience and declared, with drunken wit, 'Ladies and gentlemen, this is the man that told the man that I was the man that gave the man the bad sixpence!'

Then he'd returned to his seat.

Unfortunately, he'd seemed unable to keep his mouth shut. 'Why was the reason you wouldn't have the Grampian Hills phrenology?' was the question he'd loudly (and incoherently) asked not once, but three times. Losing patience, Carr had finally stormed over to him and said, 'I want to speak to you.'

'Very well,' Porter had replied, at which point Carr had grabbed him, tearing his collar and the buttons off his wrist. Porter had offered no resistance, even when Carr had shoved him into the arms of two local constables. On his way out, Porter had heard the doorkeeper say, 'I was instructed to return your money.'

When Carr cross-examined him, Porter insisted that he hadn't been drunk, though he *had* been drinking. Nor had he rushed onto the stage in a violent manner. 'I did not hear you ask me to leave the hall quietly,' he told Carr. 'I did not drag the forms out with me when you attempted to put me out.' He had injured his finger during the fracas.

Porter's friend Keogh testified that the plaintiff had seemed excited on reaching the stage; a person who didn't know him, Keogh conceded, would have looked at him swaggering about and thought him drunk. According to Keogh, Porter had started talking loudly when he returned to his seat – so loudly that other members of the audience had cried, 'Put him out!' After Carr had done so, the audience had cheered.

The Bench dismissed the case, but with a word of warning to Carr; the mesmerist was reminded – not for the first time – that he shouldn't be taking the law into his own hands. If Carr heeded the advice, it wasn't evident. Half the time he seemed to think he *was* the law. The rest of the time, he just seemed to enjoy throwing his weight around.

This might have been why he became a phrenologist in the first place. As his letter to Thomas Buddle amply illustrates, phrenological analysis was the perfect excuse to insult people. 'This man,' Carr was reported to have said after publicly examining somebody's bumps, 'would cheat all the week and preach on Sundays, and would make an excellent parson.' Another man, on another occasion, was described as 'obtuse, very obtuse, even to the verge of stupidity'. Someone had an 'indolent brain'. Someone else was 'not to be trusted with either man or woman.' A certain hapless architect was judged to be an epicure, a glutton, too fond of sleep, and wanting in 'constructiveness'. Then there was the poor fellow whose small head was condemned as 'a mere pimple', and who was accused of being unable to draw two straight lines – even though he happened to be a draughtsman. 'Dr Carr, in trying to prove that man descended from the same race as donkeys, examined the head of a well-known burly Wellington editor, and said there was no doubt of the soundness of the theory,' the *Evening Star* reported in 1877.

Exactly how much offence this kind of banter caused is hard to say. Some people didn't like it. One audience member complained that Carr's readings 'revelled too much in the development of animal propensities'. Another accused him of failing to find a single good point in any of the heads he examined:

> *When a phrenologist gives a lecture he should remember that the success of the lecture greatly depends upon having some volunteer heads to examine and in so doing he should not be so harsh as to pick out all the faults and bring them conspicuously before the public and hardly mention the good qualities. It must be very distressing to the person concerned, though it may afford some amusement to the audience, which was evidently the lecturer's purpose.*

Other critics went even further. They published their own analyses of Carr's bumps. Somebody writing under the pseudonym 'Stella' proposed that his facial development indicated love of sensual pleasures, and 'modesty in the proportion of three percent'. Stella also suggested that Carr was passionately fond of amusement, but chiefly at the expense of others. His temper, though soft and agreeable when cool, was harsh, stern and unbending when inflamed. With ladies he was dangerous, 'artful rather than open'. The bump of affectation was well developed.

'Vera' was even less complimentary, condemning Carr's head as a very bad type, with animal propensities that were far too large. His organs were cramped, especially towards the region of benevolence. His coronal region was small, indicating a lack of moral sentiment. He was over-developed in love of approbation, self-esteem, combativeness and destructiveness. 'Love of approbation and self-esteem is [*sic*] the ruling element in the Doctor's character, with love of sensual gratification,' Vera diagnosed. 'His enormous self-esteem, combativeness and firmness . . . make him vindictive, harsh, cruel, cynical, obstinate, self-opinionated and unsparing to either friend or foe.'

Carr would probably have argued that he was simply trying to educate his subjects by pointing out the defects they were trying to hide. But the fact is, there was a market for this kind of roughhousing. Some of Carr's more boisterous audiences frankly enjoyed it when people were insulted on stage. At one show a reviewer was disappointed when it didn't happen to a colleague, and wondered how another subject could bear the weight of all the talents and virtues ascribed to him. Luckily, Carr went on to describe a third man as being devoid of any powers except a taste for women, and a fourth as having a very good opinion of himself. 'The doctor said that Mr Stevens was fond of his glass . . . but Mr Stevens himself says that he has never tasted a glass of liquor of any kind since he was eight years of age,' the reviewer went on. 'We trust the doctor's hint will not prove to be a temptation, as if so, Mr Stevens will go "the whole hog" for drinking, as Dr Carr said he went also for eating.'

Another reviewer found it very amusing to watch the change of expression on Carr's subjects as their characters were delineated. Any desire on the part of these subjects to thump the mesmerist was quickly dispelled by a glance at the 'Herculean frame' towering over them. Meanwhile, the audience fairly screamed with delight as foible after foible was uncovered. 'However excruciating the public reading of a bad head may be to its owner, certainly the onlookers enjoy it immensely,' the reviewer acknowledged.

Carr sometimes analysed politicians' skulls, and this tended to go down very well too. The same day he assaulted William McLean he publicly made 'an amusing comparison' between parliamentarians Charles Haughton and Thomas Shepherd, disparaging the latter at the expense of the former. Then he sat down and let a local phrenologist named Watson read his bumps. According to Watson, Carr's head showed a high degree of mental power, but with a 'more than corresponding degree of undesirable faculties'. Since Carr didn't try to argue the point, it's likely that the entire stunt was arranged beforehand, to get a laugh.

Exactly where theatre ended and real violence began is sometimes hard to judge, with Carr. The more serenely he responded to a challenge, the more likely it was to have been engineered for publicity purposes. In 1868, for example, Carr wrote to *Bell's Life in Sydney*, explaining how a defiant man named Thompson, who'd chaired his last séance, had publicly offered fifty pounds to any charity if Carr could mesmerise him at his next performance. Carr had promptly staked £150 against Thompson's fifty that he would be able to mesmerise Thompson in the space of an hour. Unfortunately, Thompson didn't turn up to meet the challenge, and Carr wanted to know what to do. 'Not having heard that Mr Thompson has advanced the sum of £50 to the charities in question,' Carr concluded, 'I wish to know by what process the payment of such a debt can be enforced.'

Was this a stunt? It's hard to tell. Thompson might *not* have been in Carr's employ; it's possible that the mesmerist simply took advantage of a lucky break. More suspicious was the incident in 1877, in Charters Towers, Queensland, when Carr was challenged to read people's bumps blindfolded. He was then presented with a disguised pumpkin by a bunch of 'wags'. 'The good gentleman had no sooner placed his outspread fingers on the vegetable than he shouted out in the most genuine German, "Mein Gott in Himmel, it is an Alderman!"' a witness related. No doubt this routine brought the house down.

It's likely that the wags in question were some of Carr's young associates.

Then there was the time in Wellington, New Zealand, when a local worthy went to Carr's hotel, called him a fraud and dared the mesmerist to put him under the influence. Apparently a large audience turned up that night to watch Carr mesmerise his challenger, who 'got the needle properly', much to everyone's satisfaction. The climax came when the subject was told to stamp on his own watch. According to the (possibly faulty) memory of a spectator writing twenty-five years later, the owner of this watch went to court afterwards, seeking restitution and damages, but was unsuccessful. 'I wonder now whether this was a "put-up job" or not,' the writer mused.

It could have been – though someone who had broken a man's tooth on stage would hardly baulk at smashing a watch. On the other hand, the challenge had been made in a way that ensured it would attract a large, expectant audience. And there was also the question of whether Carr really *could* mesmerise his subjects . . .

One thing is certain: Carr's aggressive nature had found a perfect outlet. As a phrenologist, he was able to insult people with impunity. As a mesmerist, he was able to indulge, not only his love of mayhem, but also his taste for blood.

Because by this time, mesmerism was a battlefield in every sense of the word.

III

In her book *Mesmerized: Powers of Mind in Victorian Britain*, Alison Winter describes English mesmeric demonstrations as 'tumultuous, embattled scenes'. Sceptics often attacked mesmerists physically, or were kicked out of venues themselves by angry audience members. Some 'anti-mesmerists' would assault not just the mesmerists themselves but their subjects. As if the demonstrations themselves weren't violent enough, opponents would set upon mesmerised subjects to prove that they weren't really under the influence. At one English performance, a hostile doctor suddenly took out a lancet and thrust it under a boy's fingernail. Though the boy displayed no discomfort at the time, he apparently 'suffered a good deal after he was awakened'.

Mesmerists were considered fair game in the colonies, too. An American electro-biologist called Professor Bushell, who beat Carr to Australia by several years, took Beechworth saddler Alfred Bonnett to court in 1864, charging him with assault. After pretending to be under the influence at one of Bushell's séances, Bonnett had suddenly thrown a glass of water at the mesmerist, calling him an imposter. Six years later, the electro-biologist Madame Sibly (whose real name was Marie Element) faced down a hostile sceptic in Bendigo. She was about to stick a pin into one of her subjects when, without warning, an audience member came up and bit the subject's hand. Whether the victim reacted or not wasn't reported; what interested the press was Madame Sibly's response. She 'hit out direct from the shoulder, both right and left', giving the offender a couple of black eyes. Then she waved a hand at her gang of mesmerised youths, who immediately rushed at their target 'like a pack of hounds'. They overturned seats as women screamed and children cried. Luckily, while the fugitive made his escape, his friends were able to block the path of Madame Sibly's bodyguards.

After peace had been restored, the mesmerist promised her audience that she would horsewhip the man who had caused such a disturbance at the very earliest opportunity.

Many of the people who attended Carr's shows were probably expecting rambunctious behaviour like this. If so, they generally weren't disappointed. Carr's exhibitions became famous for their Keystone-cop pursuits. Sometimes his subjects would chase him around the stage, in the (apparent) belief that he was their mortal foe. Sometimes he would cast one of them as a fugitive and two others as police constables, triggering a stampede through the stalls and into the orchestra pit. Sometimes a subject who had previously declared that he would never again be mesmerised would be cornered after running around the hall. In one instance, a reluctant subject of this kind actually jumped from the dress circle onto the stage.

And then there were the fights that Carr encouraged:

> *For instance, we may mention the case of a young gentleman who went in with the firm conviction that he could not be placed under the influence, and in a short time was most thoroughly under the doctor's control. He was told*

> *that a person standing at the front door had his nose, and he immediately leapt from the stage, rushed down the hall, and with glaring eyes, quivering lips, and pale face, laid no gentle hands on the imaginary robber of his nasal organ . . .*

Carr was reported to have told his audience that his subjects were inclined to be 'fightable'. This was certainly true of a muscle-bound youth who was allegedly drawn towards the stage by Carr's mesmeric power in Hokitika. Crashing over chairs and throwing people aside, this youth finally reached the foot of the stage where he glared up at Carr and pawed at the ground. There followed a grand confrontation. The tall mesmerist stood calmly, his stern gaze fixed on his subject, who trembled with emotion as he tried to resist the unseen power that Carr was exerting. Finally, after a huge struggle, the youth cast himself at the mesmerist's feet.

During another performance, half-a-dozen subjects were apparently made to believe that they were on fire, and at the North Pole, and in the tropics – where a cry of 'Snake!' sent them fleeing, terrified, in all directions. Some of Carr's subjects rode chairs like horses. Some of them *behaved* like horses, frantically bucking and throwing off their jockeys. Frequently Carr would make his subjects swim for their lives on the floor. In New Zealand he once compelled them to climb the scenery, damaging the hall's glass kerosene lamps.

This was all good fun, but it usually ended in tears. During a particularly frantic 'police' chase, somebody put his hand through a glass door and cut his thumb. Another man in Brisbane tried to obey Carr's summons by scrambling over the backs of seats and the heads and shoulders of his fellow theatre-goers, 'knocking his legs about and bruising them considerably'. At a show in New Zealand, Carr sent his mesmerised subjects outside, where they were confronted by a small crowd of children who had been listening at the door. These children began to experiment on Carr's subjects by sticking pins into their arms and legs; one even used an awl on the calves of a person who, 'although he said he did not feel any pain at the time, did not like the appearance of his legs the next morning'.

Children weren't the only ones influenced by the wild atmosphere of Carr's shows. Again and again, people were put out for misbehaving and using bad language. Audiences would often roar with laughter at subjects who appeared to 'suffer acutely' when told that their bones were broken, or that a friend had died. Especially popular were Carr's fake funerals, with their weeping mourners. 'The heartless mockery of the most awful event in our world, disgusts people of taste and feeling, and lowers the mesmerist still further in their opinion,' one Sydney commentator remarked in 1879.

For every bloodthirsty 'lover of the sensational' in Carr's audience there was always someone who cringed. At Beechworth, the press was outraged when a local judge withdrew the pin that Carr had plunged through someone's hand. 'We did not think that his Honour Judge Cope would have been an abettor in such a cruel action,' one onlooker lamented. Though pin-sticking was a common technique among mesmerists everywhere, Carr's demonstrations seemed to strike witnesses as unusually vicious. After his death, he was compared unfavourably to mesmerist and magician Madame Cora Lamond (also known as Adrienne Herrmann and Ursula Bush). 'Dr. Carr . . .

was never, even in his best days, more successful than is Madame Cora,' the *Timaru Herald* declared, 'and while the Doctor was unfeeling in his methods, Madame, like Isaac Walton, impaled her subjects kindly.'

But was Carr *really* impaling his subjects? How much of what he did was truly sadistic and how much of it was sleight of hand? When journalists deplored his on-stage antics, pointing out that 'the Bob Sawyers and Ben Allens of society do not form a sufficient majority to justify the infliction of a spectacle . . . that cannot fail to make the blood run cold', were they shuddering over genuine procedures or clever imitations? Was Carr truly rendering his subjects insensible (as Eliza Gray claimed to have been) or was it all just clever showmanship? Was he a freak or a fraud?

There's no doubt that Carr had a taste for surgery. In 1872, after settling in Waikato, New Zealand, for a few months, he announced his intention of setting up as a 'medical man'. This was just a few days after he was reported to have amputated the diseased finger of one of the earliest settlers in Waikato. Carr always seemed to be amputating fingers, both onstage and off. 'We have been requested to state that Dr. Carr cut off the finger from a Maori girl, on Friday afternoon, in the presence of several gentlemen, and that she felt no pain,' the *New Zealand Herald* reported in 1869. This may or may not have been the same young woman whose fractured finger Carr had refused to amputate in public a couple of weeks earlier, because his audience was too small and his assistant was away. Years later, he was still at it; in Gundagai he claimed to have performed a very difficult operation on a youth named Sheather, part of whose forefinger had been blown off. The resulting stump had given this youth a lot of trouble and he was gradually losing the use of his hand. His parents were too poor to pay other doctors for a consultation, so noble Carr had stepped in and cut out the remaining joint for free.

What can we deduce from this? That Carr was courting more publicity? That he was trying to look like a 'real' doctor? That he enjoyed hacking into human flesh so much that he would do it for nothing? There's no question that he liked to parade his medical knowhow. The *Waikato Times* once mentioned that Carr had set a boy's broken limb. Another story, a few months earlier, had described Carr stumbling upon the scene of a road accident and tending to several of the victims.

Needless to say, it was Carr himself who had informed the press of this incident.

But were all his amputations genuine? And if so, were they performed using mesmerism as an anaesthetic? It's difficult to believe that Carr faked every one of his surgeries; the assault case in Forbes suggests that he was actually pulling teeth. In 1868, before reaching Sydney, he was supposed to have removed a tumour from the forehead of a young man in Queanbeyan, using mesmerism. One local journalist examined the resulting scar and announced that the tumour was still there, though it might have shrunk a little. 'There is the mark of the lancet plainly visible,' he related, 'and the wound which was then inflicted may have caused a bleeding that reduced the size of the protuberance.'

On another occasion, in Whanganui, a pin was put through someone's ear and hand, but there was no blood. This begs the question: was there, in fact, no pin?

Occasionally there must have been; Carr's Maori assistant once claimed that three pounds a week adequately compensated him for the discomfort he'd suffered from being repeatedly jabbed. But it's difficult to say how much physical harm the mesmerist actually inflicted on his subjects by way of pins, lancets and other instruments of torture.

George Francis Sherwood of Wanganui, New Zealand, had no doubt whatsoever that Carr wasn't using mesmerism to anaesthetise his patients. 'Dr Carr may perform valuable surgical operations,' Sherwood wrote, 'but I do not believe that he can do it under the influence of mesmerism, whatever he may do by the aid of "chloroform".' Sherwood was a local watchmaker who later became the first mayor of Patea. In 1869, he attended one of Carr's performances and volunteered to be a subject, fully intending to be mesmerised. He recounted how Carr told him to stare at a coin in his hand for some ten or fifteen minutes. Sherwood did exactly that, eventually fancying that he might be under the influence. But then Carr approached him, made a few passes over his eyes, closed them, and declared that Sherwood wouldn't be able to open them again.

'Of course I did open my eyes, put the coin in my pocket, and walked away, not supposing that the eminent mesmerist would require my services as I was not under the "influence",' Sherwood explained. 'I told him so, but he said that I would be "right enough" when I would "come on".' To Sherwood's surprise, Carr then asked him if he wanted to mount the stage. Sherwood again pointed out that he wasn't mesmerised. Carr replied, 'Oh, yes, you will be right enough when you come on.' He then gave

Sherwood instructions as to what he should do when he appeared on stage, and told him to go and have a glass of liquor, as he was going to have one himself.

During the interval, Sherwood consulted a friend called Day, who revealed that the same thing had happened to him. The two men agreed that they would both go on stage and give Carr every chance to mesmerise them. If he couldn't, they would *pretend* to be mesmerised, 'so as to be afterwards able to convince the public that the part could be acted without being placed under mesmeric influence.'

Sherwood and Day carried out their plan. They went up and found that Carr couldn't mesmerise them. Nobody else on stage was under the influence, either. But the next day Sherwood decided to give Carr one more chance and went to the mesmerist's hotel. Here Carr told him exactly what he was supposed to do that night. First, he was to be drawn from the audience by Carr's animal magnetism. Then he was to act as an auctioneer. Next he was to sing. Lastly, he was to imitate a member of parliament and make a speech to the audience.

Sherwood decided that he would expose Carr while delivering that same speech. But somehow Carr got wind of his intention – possibly because Sherwood had shared it with his friends. The mesmerist ordered Sherwood off the stage and failed to answer his questions in a manner that Sherwood found satisfactory. 'I will conclude by saying that myself, Mr Day, and others, have only one object in view,' he declared, 'and that is to prevent the public being imposed upon.'

This account, if true, shows how Carr manipulated his subjects even when they weren't being paid. It also demonstrates how much sheer trickery was involved in his performances. How he might have faked an excised tumour is unclear, but fraudulent medical treatments were part and parcel of nineteenth-century theatre. Twenty years after Carr's death, in London, a man called Charles Henry Irving brought an action against the mesmerist, hypnotist, medical electrician and 'bloodless surgeon' Dr Walford Bodie (aka Samuel Murphy Bodie) for fraudulent misrepresentation. Apparently, at the age of seventeen, the plaintiff had paid Bodie a £1000 premium to be trained up as a 'qualified doctor'. But Bodie had failed to teach Irving hypnosis, bloodless surgery, or medical electricity. Instead, Irving had learned nothing but tricks and shams.

Irving described these tricks in great detail. He explained that before afflicted patients were brought up to the stage they were carefully screened; unless they could walk off the stage, or lift a paralysed arm a little, they were turned away with a sample of Bodie's liniment. All the men who were hypnotised during the show were employed by Bodie and followed him from town to town. One of Bodie's unpaid subjects, James Bowden, had suffered from a withered leg since infancy. When he'd arrived on stage with his two sticks, ready to be cured, Bodie had broken the sticks across his knee, announcing that Bowden wouldn't be needing them anymore. Then Bodie had passed the toe of his boot up and down Bowden's legs, causing sparks to fly and inflicting a lot of pain. If the orchestra hadn't been playing a 'lively tune', the audience would have heard Bowden yelling.

He wasn't cured, but Bodie gave him a shilling for a cab, to get home.

Bodie's surgery was 'bloodless', so he didn't pull any teeth or slice off any tumours. Nevertheless, his show was infused with the same sense of stealth and chicanery that characterised Carr's séances. The whole issue of collusion was a particularly thorny one. By using familiar faces night after night, Carr raised a lot of red flags. He had to defend himself by explaining that he needed people who were susceptible to mesmerism, just in case no one else in the audience was. But it's clear that Carr's associates were perfectly capable of bearing false witness, or pretending to be patients. The crippled 'Cooper', who was made to throw away his crutches and jump about in 'a very amusing manner' at one of Carr's Wanganui shows, might very well have been the same Thomas Cooper who'd testified in the Kerr case a few months earlier. As for the much-abused 'Johnny', it's worth asking why he stayed with Carr for so long if the mesmerist had really ripped his fingernail off.

Carr's offsiders had a habit of forming tight and rather lawless little gangs. When a mesmerist called Bruce visited Napier in 1875, he found it almost impossible to put his volunteers under the influence – even though some of them had been successfully mesmerised on a previous occasion, by Thomas Guthrie Carr. Things were looking pretty grim for Bruce when someone in the audience suddenly stood up and declared that Dr Carr's subjects had agreed to go on stage 'with the determination not to be mesmerised'. Though this remark was greeted with cries of, 'You are a damned liar!' and 'I never took a penny from Dr. Carr!', the accusation wasn't far-fetched. Carr had a habit of picking shady associates with slightly dubious morals. He was always surrounding himself with people like Edwin Turner Osbaldeston and Dr James Grant. When a false rumour went around that the steamship *Queen of Nations* had struck a reef and almost all of the four hundred people on board had drowned, the source of this 'wicked hoax' turned out to be a man named Woodsin, formerly employed by Thomas Guthrie Carr. 'The public are cautioned against further transactions with JOHN DRYDEN,' Carr advertised in 1870, 'he being dismissed from my service.' This was a few months after somebody of the same name, in the same region, had been charged with obtaining money and a gun under false pretences.

Carr's associates seemed to like guns. In Queanbeyan, New South Wales, one of them was charged with wantonly discharging a firearm in the street. This man's name was Charles Kessler, and he claimed that there had been no bullet in the weapon. Carr backed him up, but other witnesses didn't. A local constable had seen Kessler standing with Carr and a man named William Gregg O'Neill. Kessler was holding a gun. A few minutes later there was the sound of gunfire, and the constable heard a bullet whizz by. He turned and saw Kessler rising from one knee, his gun pointed at the police barracks. 'What's that fellow about, is he going to shoot us?' another constable cried. When confronted, Kessler insisted that his gun had contained only powder.

But witness after witness testified to hearing the bullet pass them. Someone mentioned that there had been children on a nearby recreation reserve. O'Neill admitted that he had lent the single-barrel gun to Kessler, who had loaded it with powder, though O'Neill hadn't seen him put in a bullet. Carr insisted that *he* certainly hadn't. But the defendant was fined £2.4*s* plus costs.

Once again, Carr had ended up in court – this time in a supporting role. Upheaval seemed to stalk him: assaults, fires, thefts, fights, accidents, bad cheques, flying bullets, breach of contract . . . Whether or not he incited violence, it was somehow always hovering over him like a storm cloud. Amputations or no amputations, his brutal streak was a mile wide.

But was it wide enough to encompass rape?

PART VII

THE VERDICT

I

Robert Lucas was the first witness to testify on 1 October 1868 – the second last day of Carr's committal hearing.

Lucas said that he was a saddler and harness maker who lived on Botany Road. Eliza Gray had made saddlecloths for him. He had known her for two years, and had been to her house three or four times on business. Yes, he had been there late – as late as twelve – but never all night. No, he had never been 'improperly intimate' with her. Nor had he heard of anyone else who had.

He'd met with her several times since the start of the hearing, though not at his house.

Dismissed, he yielded the witness box to Constable Patrick Kelly, of Redfern police. Kelly explained that he knew Gray because she had lived in Redfern two years earlier. He swore that she hadn't expelled him from her house for being drunk, though he'd had the odd drink there. 'I was never drunk in her house in my life,' he protested, adding, 'I never in my life was improperly intimate with the prosecutrix.'

When asked if he knew a Mrs Greenfield, he agreed that he did. But he had never told Mrs Greenfield that he considered Eliza Gray a very bad woman. 'I knew Mrs Gray as a hard-working, respectable woman,' he said. At no time had he seen any impropriety in her conduct.

At this point, Julian Salomons requested that he be allowed to cross-examine Kelly as an adverse witness. William Roberts immediately jumped in. 'A witness called for the defence is not to be treated as adverse because his evidence disappoints the person who calls him,' Roberts objected. The Bench ruled that there was no reason to treat Kelly as an adverse witness, so Salomons moved on. He summoned Henry Cohen to the stand.

Cohen was founder and co-owner of the Monster Clothing Hall. He confirmed that Eliza Gray had at one point been a forewoman at his business. Then she'd left, but not because she was sick. Gray had quit after a dispute in the workshop between herself and some of the young women working under her. She had threatened to leave unless Cohen discharged these girls, but he had refused to do so. 'I wanted to know what they had been doing,' he said.

Under cross-examination, Cohen admitted that he didn't approve of Gray. She wanted everything her own way; he thought her obstreperous. 'On the day Mrs Gray left,' he recalled, 'she said she could not stand the young ladies any longer. I told her she could leave or stop, as she thought proper. She may have told me she was sick, but my impression is that she did not. If she had said so, I must have heard her.' On being pressed, he insisted that he was a gentleman, so he wouldn't swear that she *hadn't* told him she was sick. She might have said, 'I am too sick just now to do you justice in consequence of the contention of the girls.' But he couldn't be sure.

According to Cohen there had been a lot of bad blood between Gray and the other staff. Complaints had been made against her, and vice versa. She'd complained that the young ladies weren't doing their work properly. They'd insisted that she was wrong. William Roberts asked Cohen if Gray had targeted anyone in particular. Cohen denied it. Roberts mentioned a certain young lady whom Cohen used to 'see over Pyrmont Bridge'. Cohen confessed that he may have asked one young lady about Mrs Gray. 'I often walk out with young ladies,' he acknowledged, before admitting that Mrs Gray had, indeed, made a complaint against one woman in particular, saying she didn't do her work. 'I did not take the latter's part,' Cohen insisted. 'It would have been against my own interest to do so.'

Cohen could only assume that Gray had received her wages on the day she left, though they were usually paid out on Saturdays at one o'clock. He didn't recall saying to her, 'You left the work in a pretty mess', but if she'd quit on a Thursday, then the work would have been left in a mess. Nor did he remember saying, 'You could not help it, if you were sick', because he hadn't thought her sick. Yes, he had given her a certificate of character when she requested it, having always found that she was attentive to her business and conducted herself well. 'I instructed my clerk to write the character produced, which states that she left of her own free will,' he said.

Gray had asked for the certificate about six weeks after she'd resigned.

'She gave as her reason for requiring it that some of the young ladies had been speaking ill of herself and Dr. Carr, from which circumstance she could not get a situation,' Cohen explained. In other words, Gray's former colleagues were saying that she had been sacked for misconduct.

Cohen denied knowing Carr at all well. They had met once when the mesmerist was ordering a suit. Cohen had also gone to one of Carr's séances, which had been very entertaining. 'He never tried to mesmerise me,' the witness testified, adding that, while attending the show, he had seen boys dancing on stage, and pins driven through subjects' arms, and ladies made to stand motionless for perhaps a quarter of an hour at a time, as if under Carr's control. Carr had claimed that his subjects were insensible to pain, but Cohen didn't know if this was true or not. He didn't know whether the 'representations' were genuine or a hoax.

'I have objected to him coming to our place,' Cohen added, referring to Carr, 'and when he came, it was without my consent.' He'd never heard the mesmerist calling himself the Reverend Dr Carr, BA.

During his deposition, Cohen said that his brother, Benjamin Cohen, might have engaged Eliza Gray and given her sole management of the workroom girls. He couldn't swear to it one way or another. This was the only reference made to Benjamin, who had become Henry's business partner in 1862. Years later, in 1880, the company almost collapsed beneath an annual trading loss of twenty-one thousand pounds, and was subjected to a 'committee of inspection'. After another twelve months or so, Henry dissolved his partnership with Benjamin, withdrawing from the business and leaving Benjamin in charge. But Benjamin wasn't up to the challenge. By 1889 he was a financial agent, living in Newtown with his wife and twelve children.

That was the year his daughter Elizabeth gave birth to an illegitimate girl.

Benjamin obviously didn't want this child in the house, because when she was just nine hours old he had her whisked away and deposited in the care of a 'baby farmer' named Ellen Batts. Baby farmers were women who looked after unwanted infants, either for a weekly sum or a down-payment. Benjamin chose the latter option. His housekeeper recalled that he'd said, 'Get her to do it as reasonable as possible – say about £7.' In the end, Ellen Batts had taken the child for £9.10*s*.

Two months later the baby was dead of starvation, and Ellen Batts was being tried for murder. Twelve children had died in her house over a period of eleven months; she was charged (and acquitted) of killing three of them. Just a few days before the baby's inquest – and about a week after her mother was finally married off to a Redfern boot-maker's son named Richard Crewes – Benjamin died of a narcotic overdose.

The jury found that he had taken too much laudanum 'for the purpose of procuring sleep'. The timing of his death, however, was suspicious. Benjamin was buried in Rookwood Cemetery, near his brother Henry, who'd died two years earlier. It was a sad end to a Sydney landmark.

After Henry Cohen had been dismissed, Carr's old friend John Huxtable was called to the witness stand. He explained that he was an accountant, engaged in promoting his Aerated Bread Company, and that he lived some way down the harbour, in Watsons Bay. On 12 March – the day the Duke of Edinburgh was shot – Thomas Guthrie Carr had lunched at his house. They had caught the 10.15 steamer together from Circular Quay, stopping at Watsons Bay on their way to Clontarf. In the evening they had had caught a return boat from Watsons Bay with several other gentlemen.

Huxtable insisted that he had been with Carr the whole day. 'I left Dr Carr at about half past 9 or 10 at night,' he said. 'I was away from him about an hour . . . I left him somewhere near the Herald office at half past 6 and met him again at the School of Arts at half past 7.' It was possible, he admitted, that Carr had gone to his lodgings during the hour they'd spent apart, and had met Eliza Gray there. But he really didn't know.

He went on to explain how he'd served as Carr's agent, very briefly, but had never taken part in any 'mesmeric operations'. He believed, however, that mesmerism was genuine, and that most of the people he'd seen on stage had been under Carr's influence. 'I can't say whether he has paid imposters,' Huxtable said cautiously. 'There have been several boys night after night going through the same performances. There was a black boy there every night. He was very obedient to the signals.' Some of these boys, he added, had told him that they couldn't stay away.

After describing how he'd first met Carr in Melbourne, Huxtable conceded that he had seen several doctors at the mesmerist's séances. He had also seen members of the Bar there, he added. And with that, he stepped down.

Next up was Henry James Billing, proprietor of the Greenwich Pier Hotel at Watsons Bay. Billing was a well-known and successful businessman. On his father's death, in 1862, he had inherited the family's hotel, menagerie and wharf – which was the only wharf in Watsons Bay. For years, Henry and his father had been luring customers to their 'commodious and excellent' hotel with exotic animals and weekend attractions. They even ran their own steam ferry service. A typical weekend offering at their hotel included swings, quoits, cricket and the Sacramento Minstrels, as well as lions and tigers. At one point, the elder Henry Billing bought two zebras, harnessed them to a 'park phaeton' and drove them around the streets of Sydney. A year later, his keeper was killed when a tiger ripped off the unfortunate man's arm, but that didn't close the menagerie; Henry Billing Senior was soon writing to the *Sydney Morning Herald* to announce that his lioness had just given birth to three cubs, only one of which had survived. The two dead cubs were donated to the natural history museum (though they later ended up in Madame Sohier's waxwork collection). The surviving cub was displayed for a while in a room on Pitt Street, by none other than Henry Billing Junior – who was being trained to run the family business.

When the younger Henry finally did take charge he was as successful as his father had been. In 1864, it was announced in the local press that one of his monkeys had been delivered of a daughter. In 1865, his St Andrews's Day festivities included sack-racing, a greasy pole, the Buckley Minstrels, lions, tigers, leopards, porcupines and Nip Tha Dhu, a 'very handsomely deformed dog' described as a cross between a pig and a pug. By 1866, there was a ballroom attached to his hotel and Billing was charging sixpence to view the menagerie, which was pulling more customers than his hotel could accommodate.

Two years later, Billing was drawn into Thomas Guthrie Carr's orbit. It's likely that the ferry Carr engaged in May, to transport people from Watsons Bay to his shows at the Prince of Wales theatre, actually belonged to Henry Billing. Carr was living in Watsons Bay when he sent Eliza Gray off to see Dr Charles Eichler; she must have cornered him at his workplace because his lodgings were no longer easily accessible. But long before Carr moved into Alfred House, Watsons Bay, he had been spending a lot of time there – as Henry Billing himself testified.

According to Billing, Carr had visited his hotel on the day the Duke was shot. In the evening they had caught a ferry into the city, where Billing had left Carr between 6.30 and 6.45. Then Andrew MacLean made a fleeting appearance in the witness box. He confirmed that he had gone with Carr to Watsons Bay in May, the day after his own arrival in Sydney. But when he mentioned that he had seen Eliza Gray that same day, William Roberts objected, and the witness was dismissed.

All this emphasis on 12 March was rather odd. Carr can't have been trying to establish an alibi, because Gray claimed that he had raped her on the 18th. Possibly the defence wanted to suggest that the plaintiff and the defendant had been having an affair, which was consummated on the 12th. If so, Salomons abandoned this attempt when he called James Dalton to the stand – because Dalton, as he himself pointed out, had first met Carr in April and 'was not there' during the March incident. 'It might have saved a great deal of trouble if I had been,' Dalton remarked during his testimony, which for the most part concerned his encounters with Eliza Gray at Carr's various offices. The only other time she'd spoken to him, he revealed, was when he'd recently spotted her getting out of a hansom cab. 'Ah! Mr Dalton!' she had exclaimed. 'I can see you!'

Dalton also had one or two things to say about his job as Carr's agent.

'I travel with him,' Dalton explained, 'and have just come from Newcastle.' After describing how he had seen Carr publicly extract teeth without inflicting pain, Dalton added, 'He has told me he has fastened me to the floor by a pin through my hand; I don't know how it was done. Generally I was partially aware of what was taking place, but I had no control or power over myself when I was mesmerised.' When asked how this state was accomplished, he referred vaguely to 'passes'. When asked how long it took to mesmerise someone, he replied, 'It all depends on the subject. It took about a quarter of an hour to mesmerise me for the first time.' He then stated for the record that he had never known Carr to mesmerise anyone against his or her will.

William Roberts wanted to know if Dalton was the same young man who, on being drawn from Carr's audience at the School of Arts, had claimed that he'd never seen the mesmerist before. Dalton admitted that he was. But he denied that Carr had asked to see the statement he'd written for the defence. No one had suggested that he write such a statement. On the contrary, he'd provided it of his own free will, because he had some knowledge of the matter.

'I may have said in Newcastle that it was a trumped-up charge, without any foundation,' he conceded. 'I daresay I said I knew all about it.'

In response to William Roberts' query, he agreed that he had a sister, but refused to discuss her. 'I decline to answer irrelevant questions,' he retorted.

At last he stepped down. And since the defence had no more witnesses to call, William Roberts rose to give his closing argument.

II

This case, said Roberts, was a very peculiar one. Nothing like it had been heard of in the colony before. No doubt the defence would lavish a great deal of abuse on Eliza Gray, for not immediately laying a charge against her alleged attacker. But she had been concerned about her family's welfare, and had known that such an action would make things very hard for them.

'She did, however, tell Miss Hook that Dr Carr had mesmerised her,' Roberts continued, 'and did ever a young lady give her evidence in a more straightforward way?' He reminded the Bench that Gray had said to Elizabeth Hook, on the very day the offence was committed, 'Oh, my God Lizzie, I have been mesmerised!' [*sic*]

Why would she have said such a thing unless it were true?

Roberts acknowledged that people were wondering why Gray hadn't told her husband about the assault. But she had described him as an angry man. She had explained how telling him would probably break up the family home. As for William Gray's behaviour in the witness box, it had done nothing to undermine his wife's claim. 'Did he not appear a man of very violent temper?' Roberts demanded, before pointing out that when the plaintiff finally did tell her husband she had been forced to flee.

Eliza Gray, Roberts went on, had exposed herself to the world. She had done a public service in bringing Dr Guthrie Carr – 'this imposter' – to justice, thereby preventing him from carrying out any more of his 'diabolical practices'. Why doubt Eliza Gray? 'Was she not corroborated by nearly every witness,' Roberts asked, 'with the exception of the witness Lees, a scoundrel, who had the impudence to stand up in a witness box, and in the most barefaced way, narrate that he had, from the age of fourteen years, been following a course of life which was not fit to be related in a civilised community?' This boy had visited dancing saloons. He had told his wife that, even while he was courting her, he had been sleeping with a married woman. Why would anyone believe such a villain?

Then there was Dr Eichler's evidence, which corroborated everything Eliza Gray had said. If Carr was innocent, why would he have sent her to Eichler for medical treatment? More importantly, why would he have offered to pay the fees? And what about that postscript on the note he'd sent with her? Who was the mysterious 'other lady'?

Roberts then attacked James Dalton, Carr's 'buttoner' – 'the man who has had pins stuck through him and is fastened to the wall, and doesn't know anything about it. How could his evidence be credited?' He concluded his argument by noting that the magistrates were not supposed to be deciding on the prisoner's guilt, but determining whether he had a prima facie case to answer. If so, Roberts concluded, they were 'bound to commit'.

Then he yielded the floor to Julian Salomons.

Salomons stood up and announced that his defence was going to take some time, because he wanted to make it quite clear that this was a false charge. He begged the honourable magistrates to disregard all reports of the case that had appeared in the local press –

'I have not read them,' the police magistrate interrupted.

Well, they were most unfair to his client, Salomons went on, and might lead to a charge of another nature. If Carr were committed, he said, then half the country could end up accused by a 'woman of the town'. Of course, if the accusation proved to be true, then his client deserved the worst kind of punishment – he deserved death – but it wasn't true. Carr wasn't guilty. And if the Bench convicted him on the evidence of a liar like Eliza Gray, then any one of them might end up in court.

'The evidence would appear wholly on one side to any man who knew how to look at it impartially,' Salomons declared. 'There was not the slightest evidence except the prosecutrix's own testimony, which her own conduct rebutted.' He referred to Lord Hayle, one of England's highest legal authorities, who'd said that a rape charge was the one most easily made, and the one most difficult to refute by the accused party, no matter how innocent he might be. There were never any witnesses in a rape case, and the woman 'had all the game to herself'. He urged the Bench to consider these circumstances before committing a man to trial on such a serious charge.

Next he drew the court's attention to the way Eliza Gray's testimony had varied on different days of the hearing. She'd told one story on the first day. Then, after deciding that it was hard to believe, she had added the account of the handkerchief, insinuating that Carr had used chloroform. But if chloroform *had* been used in such a manner, it would have affected Carr more strongly than his victim. And though Carr was no saint, neither was the plaintiff. It was clear from the evidence that she had been intimate with other men.

Salomons then took issue with William Roberts, who seemed to think that the crime had been proven beyond all doubt. But had it *really* been committed? Almost six months had passed since it was supposed to have occurred. What could be deduced from that?

Salomons reviewed the prosecution's evidence, pointing out various discrepancies. The object of the whole 'transaction', he said, was as clear as daylight. Carr would not give Gray money, so she had brought a charge against him. 'The law in cases of criminal conviction prevented any of the parties from giving evidence,' Salomons explained, 'and that was the reason this case was carried so far.' He pointed out that, if William Gray ever tried to obtain money from Carr by bringing an action in the supreme court, the evidence to support his case had now been made public. It was all about money. The Grays wanted it, and Carr had it.

Finally, after reading through several depositions, Salomons expressed his confidence that the Bench would fully appreciate the merits of his argument and dismiss the charge.

But David Scott wasn't about to do any such thing. He declared that a serious matter of this kind merited proper consideration. The Bench would need time to read through the testimony, he said. Judgement would be given on Saturday the 3rd, at eleven o'clock in the morning.

Then he and his fellow magistrates addressed the other thirty cases on their summons list, eleven of which concerned hired carriages.

The next day, Thomas Guthrie Carr married Jane Ann Ireland in Scots Church. They can't have had much of a wedding night. She was six months' pregnant and he was facing judgement on a capital case. It's unlikely that she went with him to court; she certainly wasn't mentioned in any of the press coverage. No doubt he had her stashed away somewhere – possibly at Watsons Bay. It would have been a nice, quiet place to keep a pregnant bride.

When Carr finally did appear in the dock again, he wasn't kept there for very long. The proceedings opened when Captain David Scott wondered aloud if it was necessary to ask the defendant a question that had already been put to him earlier in the hearing. There had been some disagreement between Roberts and Salomons as to whether this question had been raised at the proper time. But just to be sure, Scott repeated it.

He asked Carr if he had any kind of statement to make, adding that whatever he did say would be taken down in writing and might be used against him in the future.

Carr's reply was, 'Not guilty.'

Scott then got down to business. He and his fellow magistrates had taken the whole case into consideration, he said. They had read through all the depositions, line for line and word for word. And in light of what they'd read, they felt bound to commit Thomas Guthrie Carr for trial.

In the meantime, the prisoner would be given bail of three hundred pounds, together with two sureties of a hundred and fifty pounds each. Somehow, Carr was able to pay. Possibly he had to borrow the money from well-off friends like John Huxtable.

Scott's judgement must have come as a terrific shock to Carr. The fact that the mesmerist had been 'grinning and waving his hand' at Eliza Gray suggests that he'd felt fairly confident of victory. Now he was one step closer to a death sentence.

But he didn't let it slow him down. An advertisement for his next show appeared in Monday's *Empire*, indicating that he'd gone straight from court to the newspaper office. 'Prior to his Visit to Newcastle and Maitland,' the notice read, 'Dr Carr will deliver an oration on Thursday evening next, on Julius Caesar by Napoleon III, and on Friday evening will give an exhibition of mesmeric phenomena, and preface the same with an exposition of the Science and Modus Operandi of mesmerism.'

Carr wasn't about to slink away and hide under a rock somewhere. On the contrary, he'd undertaken to lecture publicly on two great men, as if hoping that their greatness would rub off on him. The next sitting of the Criminal Court in Sydney wasn't scheduled until mid-November and Carr had a brand-new family to support. He couldn't afford to stop working.

In the end, he was unable to find a venue for his lecture on Julius Caesar. But he did speak about mesmerism at the Masonic Hall on the evening of 10 October. 'Dr Carr has advertised a séance tomorrow, and owing to the recent exposure, a disturbance is expected,' the *Illawarra Mercury* announced. Surprisingly, however, there was no disturbance. The hall was 'tolerably well filled', and apart from a few interruptions by three or four youths in the gallery, the show was described as highly successful.

A large proportion of the audience was female.

Two days later William Maddison wrote a letter to the *Empire*, defending Carr against accusations that he was the infamous ship's surgeon from the *Palm Tree*. 'Will you permit me further to state,' Maddison concluded, 'that, being acquainted with the history of Dr. Carr for many years previous to the commencement of his public career, I can give unqualified contradiction to many other reports concerning him that are quite as untrue.' Like Maddison, Andrew MacLean also rallied round. On 14 October, Carr gave the first of four séances at Newcastle's City Hall – and the following day, MacLean advertised that he himself was visiting Newcastle as a surgeon-dentist, by 'special request'. After announcing that he was a member of London's Royal College of Dentists, he advised his patients that he could be reached at Newcastle's Great Northern Hotel. As it happened, Carr was staying at the same hotel. They must have travelled up together.

Carr's Newcastle shows were quite a hit. There were two hundred people at the second one, and the *Newcastle Chronicle* declared that he was 'by far the cleverest man in this line that we have ever seen'. But his luck didn't hold. In West Maitland he flopped. 'He may do wonderful things,' one correspondent observed, 'but the revelations which took place in a police case, in which he was prominently concerned, have, doubtless, tended to injure him with public, and on that account . . . he has been much less patronised than he would have otherwise been.' Even Prince Tommy, the Aboriginal boy, wasn't enough to boost Carr's takings.

Then, in Singleton, things got even worse. Carr arrived there on Thursday 22 October, having advertised his intention of giving two 'grand seances' at the Mechanics' Institute. But on the first night, half an hour after the scheduled start time, no one had shown up.

So Carr went back to his hotel.

He left Singleton by the morning train, returning to Maitland to do a few more shows. His final performance at the Olympic Theatre was on 31 October. Meanwhile, news of Carr's predicament had spread across the country – spoiling things for people like James Hume, the Melbourne phrenologist. Following Carr's example, Hume had branched out into mesmerism, and by early October was performing in Bendigo. But he wasn't pulling big crowds. 'The general public, since the now notorious exposure of Dr Carr in Sydney, are more unfavourably inclined to the science which was professed by one who has cast disrepute on it by having made it subservient to a very unworthy purpose,' the *Bendigo Advertiser* remarked, 'and that portion of the public who were sceptical are now more so, and even those who were devout believers are somewhat shaken in their belief.'

Carr must have been having a hard time of it. In many people's eyes, he was already a felon; one newspaper condemned him for being 'bumptious' enough to keep showing himself on the streets and in theatres. His barefaced effrontery was considered indecent. Perhaps that's why he was uncharacteristically silent about his whole situation. For a man who'd spent so much time defending himself in print, he had surprisingly little to say about Eliza Gray's charges. Even after judgement had been passed, he never once referred to the case publicly. It may have been that he saw no possible way it could be used to his advantage.

No doubt it was during this period that he began to develop a sympathy for the convicted. Ten years later, in 1878, he would become embroiled in a public dispute about crime prevention in which he proposed that some prisoners were the victims of 'organic conditions', and that a lack of education had condemned them to a life of immorality. 'Many of those prisoners in Darlinghurst and elsewhere have sucked dishonesty and every form of monstrous badness with their mother's milk, been taught it on their father's knee,' he declared, going on to argue that the only cure for such an upbringing was not inexorable hate but goodness of heart. A prison, he said, was only a house of correction; the purpose of punishment was to improve, correct, reform and reclaim. Carr had a complicated relationship with the notion of punishment, to the point where he argued against the existence of Hell. This may, of course, have been a natural consequence of his own behaviour.

Perhaps, when he urged society to help repentant criminals by effacing the guilty brand of their 'broad arrow', he was remembering his own experience as a marked man.

After the 'indifferent success' of his last few shows in Maitland, Carr returned to Sydney. But he didn't advertise any further séances. He may have been worried about the reception he'd face – or too busy arranging his defence to worry about anything else. In the end, however, he didn't need a defence.

Just a few days after replacing Sir James Martin as New South Wales attorney-general, Sir William Manning announced that he wouldn't be filing a bill against Thomas Guthrie Carr. It was a declaration of *nolle prosequi*; the charge against Carr had been dropped. 'The public are greatly dissatisfied in consequence of this decision,' the *Evening Star* observed, 'and expressions of opinion are more free than polite.'

Once again, Carr had dodged a bullet.

III

Sir William Manning, the new attorney-general, had been a key witness in the O'Farrell assassination case. As president of the Sydney Sailors' Home, Manning had actually invited Prince Alfred to the Clontarf picnic. After the first shot was fired, Manning had thrown himself at O'Farrell and had narrowly missed being shot himself. In court he testified that he had ducked to avoid O'Farrell's second bullet, falling over as a consequence.

O'Farrell later said, 'If Sir William Manning had not rushed at me, the Prince would have received a second shot and I should have shot myself.'

A Queen's Counsel and wealthy landowner, fifty-seven-year-old Manning had already thrice served as attorney-general, and had also been elected to parliament. At various times in his life he was a director of the Australian Joint Stock Bank, chancellor of the University of Sydney, vice-president of the Horticultural Society of New South Wales and a steward of the Australian Jockey Club. He was a true pillar of the colonial establishment, enjoying the kind of social position that Thomas Guthrie Carr could only dream about. It's therefore unlikely that Manning's decision was influenced by anything Carr might have said or done. The two men wouldn't have moved in the same circles.

Not that Carr hadn't brushed up against some of the colony's *haut monde*, on occasion. William Charles Windeyer had once chaired a séance for Carr, who'd read his bumps in public. Windeyer had then been chased around the School of Arts by a female subject. At the time, he was a well-known barrister, a member of the Legislative Assembly and a favourite of Sir Henry Parkes.

Later, he would go on to become New South Wales attorney-general. But in 1868, at the age of thirty-three, he was still young enough to enjoy a romp on stage with a mesmerist.

Manning never did anything so undignified, though he may have attended Carr's show. Many people did, and a lot of them were respectable enough. In Sydney, however, Carr hadn't enjoyed the same kind of well-placed support he'd managed to attract in South Australia, where he'd been publicly endorsed by the police commissioner and a justice of the supreme court. In the New South Wales parliament, Sir Henry Parkes had referred to Carr dismissively as someone with 'a sort of reputation for a science or pseudo-science'. The premier, John Robertson, had called Carr a 'showman'. He had attacked Parkes for becoming a hero to 'this class of men', implying that Carr didn't exactly measure up. The official position of Sydney's elite was unfavourable to Carr. He would have been regarded as a grubby figure of doubtful reputation.

So why did Sir William Manning dismiss the charge made against him?

Manning's decision was not unprecedented. A New South Wales attorney-general had the power to overturn any indictment made against anybody committed by a bench of magistrates. Sir James Martin did it all the time. According to one barrister, Martin made a point of dismissing every committal favourable to gamblers who had been bilked of their money, because he believed that 'if men would go gambling, they should suffer the consequences.' In 1865, Attorney-General John Hargrave had refused to file a bill against the politician Thomas Holt, even though Holt had been committed for trial by Police

Magistrate Captain David Scott. Holt had then taken Scott to court for assault and false imprisonment, claiming £5000 in damages – and had lost.

This was the same Captain Scott who'd had his judgement against Carr reversed.

David Charles Frederick Scott was educated at Woolwich Academy, London, and was appointed a captain of the East India Company in 1824. When he arrived in Australia he received a grant of land, resigned his commission and edited the short-lived *New South Wales Sporting Magazine* for a couple of years. In 1860 he became Sydney's police magistrate, a position he held until he died. He was a talented artist, a student of Arabic and Persian and a very charitable man. When news of his death was announced in the Central Police Court, in 1881, William Roberts stood up and saluted Scott as a gentleman in every sense of the word – courteous in his demeanour, humane in his disposition, conciliatory in his manner and 'at all times desirous of administering justice with purity and a strict regard to the rights of suitors'. No one seemed to have a bad word to say about Scott as a person. Even when a select committee was formed to inquire into the running of the Central Police Office, none of the witnesses brought before it would admit to disliking Scott. On the contrary, he was described as being a little too amiable for the job. 'When I say that Captain Scott is a gentleman and impartial, I say what is true,' Rowan Ronald, a justice of the peace, testified, 'but I have seen a want of decision of character.'

Scott's other problem was his lack of legal training. The select committee kept harping on this, asking witness after witness if a lawyer might make a better magistrate. 'I think he may have read himself up better,' Ronald admitted, when questioned about Scott's abilities. Very few police court magistrates had any kind of legal background and sometimes it showed. 'One of the Magistrates ought to be a legal practitioner, to assist the rest of the gentlemen,' said Richard Stubbs, an inspector of licensed vehicles who spent a lot of time hanging around the police court, when questioned by the select committee. 'Why should they be burdened with responsibility, be threatened with prohibitions, and told that they do not know what they are about, by professional gentlemen?'

The committee discovered that many untrained magistrates were treated with contempt by the barristers who appeared before them. Sir William Manning was at the very top of his profession, so he was bound to disagree with some of the judgements made in the colony's police courts. In 1869 Scott committed a woman named Louisa Pilkington, who was charged with throwing vitriol at her husband Frederick. The Pilkingtons' marriage had been on the rocks for some time; eighteen months earlier, the pregnant Louisa had brought an action against Frederick for wife desertion. She had accused him of sleeping with her mother. He had denied that he and Louisa were married at all. After Frederick and Louisa's mother had started living together, Louisa was alleged to have walked into Frederick's Castlereagh Street residence and thrown acid at her husband, hitting one of his friends as well.

But Manning must have felt uneasy about the evidence given in this case, because he declined to file a bill against Louisa. The same thing happened to George Bell, an alleged forger, and to Charles Fawcett, who was charged with manslaughter. Neither of these men had been committed by Scott, so it's unlikely that Manning was engaged in any sort of personal vendetta – despite the fact that his relationship with the magistrate may have been slightly strained. A few years earlier, Manning's daughter Emily had become engaged to Scott's nephew, David Scott Mitchell. But the engagement had ended abruptly. Emily had fled to England for a brief period, before becoming a poet and journalist. Mitchell had gone on to found Sydney's Mitchell Library. No one knows who broke off the engagement, but there must have been a residual awkwardness on both sides.

Still, it would be a stretch to assume that the attorney-general had it in for Captain Scott, just because of an unfortunate love affair.

It's possible, of course, that Sir William Manning simply didn't believe in mesmerism – even though his daughter did. In her article on the British writer Harriet Martineau, Emily related how Martineau had been cured of a chronic illness by a course of mesmerism. 'It seems almost incredible that such bigotry and prejudice should have existed among sensible people, especially the medical profession, as was evinced by their attack on Miss Martineau for her recourse to this new healing agency,' Emily wrote. In her poem 'The Balance of Pain', a dialogue between an invalid husband and his God-fearing wife, Emily demonstrated her knowledge of animal magnetism when she had the husband declare, 'You are a seer/And I have a corresponding power to make you sleep, /And by mesmeric power to cause the state/Well named clairvoyant'.

But Emily's attitude towards animal magnetism wasn't necessarily shared by her father. If he happened to have any doubts on the subject, Eliza Gray's story would have struck him as implausible, since it absolutely hinged on Carr's ability to mesmerise her against her will. And even if he *was* undecided, the efficacy of mesmerism hadn't been legally established in Australian courts. There was no precedent – for good reason. As one columnist said in the *Tasmanian Herald*, when commenting on Henry Louis Bertrand's alleged mesmeric influence over his co-conspirators, 'the best test of this novel, and exceedingly dangerous, doctrine, will be found in the amount of mesmeric power that MR BERTRAND will be able to exercise over his judge and jury'.

The *Herald* blamed Bertrand's influence on his strong will and vicious force of character, and the judiciary tended to draw a similar conclusion when any case involving mesmerism cropped up. In 1881, for example, relatives of the late George Lamont, of Hawthorn, Victoria, applied to set aside a will he'd made in favour of a bunch of spiritualists named McGeorge, Naylor and Punchard. Lamont's family accused these spiritualists of mesmerising Lamont for their own financial gain. 'The ground upon which this will is contested,' the presiding judge declared, 'is the extraordinary power of influencing people which Mrs McGeorge possessed.' Having consulted books on mesmerism, he decided that this woman's agreeable company and general usefulness had been enough to sway Lamont. She may have pretended to have spiritual powers, but they hadn't been proven – and as far as the judge could tell, she had spent most of her time running down Lamont's relatives. 'I discard the idea that he was under any superhuman influences of Mrs McGeorge, or believed that she had any,' he concluded.

Generally speaking, plaintiffs or defendants who cited mesmerism to prove their cases weren't very successful.

In Glen Innes, six years before the Lamont affair, a man was convicted of drunk and disorderly conduct at one of Madame Sibly's séances, even though he tried to excuse himself by claiming that he'd been mesmerised at the time. Frequently, accusations of mesmerism were regarded as proof of mental illness. In 1877 a Queenslander named John White was sent to a mental asylum because he believed himself to be 'under a mesmeric spell'. In 1868 the same thing happened to William Grant (alias McKie) of Bendigo. Occasionally, the courts were more credulous; one police magistrate in Roma, Queensland discharged a prisoner named George Hoops, suspected of being mentally unstable, because a local doctor could find no evidence of delusion. The prisoner, it was stated, 'simply complains of mesmeric influences over him, which are acknowledged facts, and consequently cannot be delusions'.

Like his fellow magistrate in Roma, Captain David Scott must have been undecided about mesmerism. No doubt the unsavoury reputation of this pseudo-science – and the even more unsavoury conduct of Carr's star witness, George James Lees – had further convinced him to give Eliza Gray the benefit of the doubt. But Sir William Manning was made of sterner stuff than the 'too amiable' Scott. And as a result, Thomas Guthrie Carr was cut loose.

Afterwards, Eliza Gray dropped out of sight – except for her brief appearance in the case of Mary Ann Silvey, who stole William Gray's watch. Eliza died on 18 March 1876, in the down-at-heel neighbourhood of Surry Hills, Sydney. Her husband died two years later, in the suburb of Glebe. Her solicitor, William Roberts, died in 1906, after sharing his practice with his son William for several years.

Julian Salomons became solicitor-general, and received a knighthood before dying in 1909.

As for Thomas Guthrie Carr, he escaped as soon as he could. On 12 November he left Sydney on the steamship *Egmont*, bound for New Zealand. 'Dr Carr, electro-biologist, occasional local preacher, medical quack, and something much worse, has left this colony for New Zealand, under the name of Kerr, and companied by his lady,' one newspaper noted. Another was even more damning:

> *Dr Carr, his "lady", his Mesmeric Fluid etc., have left Sydney for New Zealand. The learned gentleman takes a fair store of N.S.Wales lucre with him, and in place thereof, leaves behind him what is of little value, even to its owner – his* carr-*actor.*

He didn't return for nearly a decade.

PART VIII

'TRIUMPHANT CARR'

I

When Thomas Guthrie Carr and his wife arrived in New Zealand, they settled first in Hokitika, where their daughter was born. Then, for nine years, Carr wandered the country like a circus act, from town to town, from show to show, from court case to court case.

Sometimes his family upped stakes and followed him, but for the most part he travelled alone or with a secretary. It was a punishing life, which didn't start off well. Hard on the heels of the new year came his very public battle with John Campbell Kerr, for back pay. This legal stoush was so widely reported that people wrote songs about it; at a charity concert in Auckland, one of the participants sang two comic songs called 'Dr Guthrie Carr' and 'Kerr vs Carr', both of which, according to the *West Coast Times*, 'met with the reception their wit and humour entitle them to'. The case itself led to Carr's fight with John Rutherford

Ryley, the eminent doctor who took exception to some of the statements Carr had made in the witness box. Letters flew back and forth as the two men called each other 'mountebanks'.

Not long afterwards, Carr declared himself bankrupt. This probably wasn't surprising, after all the criticism he'd faced. In an account of his recent failure to mesmerise a group of Maori subjects, the reviewer took him to task for mesmerising a woman. Putting men under the influence was one thing, but the writer strongly disapproved of the way Carr had dragged a woman out of the audience when she was plainly doing everything in her power to resist him. This particular critic may have been reassured by George Sherwood's account of *his* experience as Carr's subject, which was published a few months later. It completely debunked Carr's claims and exposed many of his methods. In Wellington, one correspondent marvelled that Carr continued to draw large audiences despite published accusations that he had tried to 'humbug people'.

Then, in September 1869, Carr was hauled into court again, on two different charges. The first was no more than a claim for a dishonoured cheque; Carr had to pay eight pounds to cover the cheque, as well as fourteen shillings in costs. But the second case was more serious. It was a twenty pound claim for breach of contract. A man called John Anderson had paid £11.5*s* in medical fees to Carr, who had promised to cure him of his sciatica. Instead, Anderson had spent three weeks in bed – a loss of time for which he was also demanding £8.15*s*.

'I went to Dr Carr on the 4th August,' Anderson told the court. '[He] said he could cure me by puncturing the nerves and putting a seton in the back.' A seton was a very traditional 'counter irritant' – a thread drawn through the skin and underlying tissue with a seton needle, then left there to be moved daily, thereby irritating the affected area and causing a discharge. It was a technique already falling out of favour, but Carr wasn't to know that since he wasn't medically qualified. He said he was, though. 'I am a surgeon and a M.R.C.S,' he lied boldly to the court, before admitting that he wasn't registered in New Zealand.

Anderson had already consulted his regular doctor, who had denied that such a treatment would work. But Anderson had gone ahead with it anyway, because Carr had undertaken to cure him in a week. After three operations, one performed by Carr and two by his offsider (a certain Dr Saunders who seemed to have replaced Dr Grant), Anderson's health still hadn't improved. 'I was kept from my work for three weeks,' he declared. 'I had the seton in my back for five weeks, and suffered considerable pain.'

When Anderson's regular doctor took the stand, he poured scorn on the notion that Anderson could have been cured in a week. As for the operation itself, he hadn't thought it a wise one for Anderson to attempt. 'If the nerve were destroyed the cure would be worse than the disease,' he said.

Carr testified that he had promised to give Anderson relief by 'practising Hunter's method' and puncturing the nerves. He had never promised to cure him in a week, but to give him relief and completely cure him in two or three weeks *if he adhered to certain conditions*. But Anderson hadn't done so. He hadn't called on Carr, as promised. So the treatment had failed.

The magistrates weren't impressed. They told Carr to repay the plaintiff's £11.6*s* – as well as three pounds in costs. Anderson didn't mention Carr's choice of anaesthetic, so we don't know if he was mesmerised or not. Carr never brought it up. Even during the weeks that followed, when his mesmeric skills came under fire again and again, Carr didn't refer to Anderson as one of his success stories.

The mesmerist faced a lot of scepticism in Auckland, where his houses were described as 'so-so'. But his attempts to put the blame on the unfavourable notices he'd received there didn't go down well. It was felt that he himself was at fault because he used the same subjects again and again. How could anyone fail to be suspicious? 'If Dr. Carr thinks that the notice the Press has hitherto taken of his seances has not been satisfactory,' the *New Zealand Herald* sourly remarked, 'he should . . . mesmerize the reporters, and make them write his own account of his accumulation of wonders.'

The year concluded with another scandal. This time, Carr was accused of sending someone mad. William Wetherall, of unsound mind, was brought to the Shortland police station by his brother, who allegedly stated that William had never been the same since taking part in one of Carr's seances. William was promptly admitted to the local asylum, where Carr hastened to visit him. According to Carr (who later published an account of this visit), mesmerism was not a factor in Wetherall's admission. The patient's brother had told medical staff at the facility that the cause of Wetherall's madness was a failed love affair. Apparently other witnesses had noticed a 'strange despondency' in Wetherall's manner for months.

Mesmerism, Carr insisted, had nothing to do with the man's derangement.

Carr then went on to claim, in a second letter, that he had never even mesmerised the unhappy Wetherall. 'For a long time I exerted all the power I could command, but it was of no avail,' said Carr. 'I failed to mesmerise him. He told his brother the next morning that Dr Carr had tried to mesmerise him, but that it was all nonsense, he could not do it.' Carr argued that Wetherall, in exercising 'every faculty of resistance' to Carr's powers, had experienced extreme tension and that this tension had probably tipped him into an incipient disease. 'I lament the result deeply,' Carr concluded, arguing that he'd done nothing to drive Wetherall mad.

No one believed him. A few months later, the *Evening Post* announced that Wetherall had recovered from the insanity produced by 'the attempted mesmerism of Dr Carr'. Carr was forced to mount a public defence all over again. In a terse letter, he pointed out that Wetherall had been exhibiting signs of mental illness long before attending his séance, and that Wetherall's brother and uncle had approached Carr with expressions of regret. 'They could not account by what method my name had become associated with the young man's insanity,' Carr revealed. 'Those gentlemen also wrote to the press to contradict the rumour.'

Meanwhile, Carr had gone bankrupt again. But he managed to struggle on and was soon attracting critical acclaim in places like Napier and Hawke's Bay. 'It was one of the most marvellous sights we have beheld,' the *Hawke's Bay Herald* said of his first séance there. In Christchurch, too, he was lauded. Around the middle of 1870, however, he hit a few obstacles. The press at Timaru declared him a humbug – the greatest ever seen in town. It noted his inability to mesmerise any of the local residents, and scoffed at his use of a 'utility' subject who travelled around with him. 'We are astonished to find a man who was recently exposed at Hokitika still presuming to impose on the public,' the *Timaru Herald* remarked.

In Cromwell Carr was labelled an imposter by a local medico. In Dunedin he faced court again after cracking a hotel window by carelessly placing an advertisement board over it; judgement was for the plaintiff, and Carr had to pay £13.10*s*, plus costs. In Roxburgh he was compared unfavourably to Professor Bushell. In Tuapeka his visit was *not* considered a success.

Then he had to skip town, because a warrant was issued against him for an alleged attempt to elude his creditors.

Wherever he went, he had a hard time escaping accusations of fraud. He once attended a meeting of a Mutual Improvement Society, to take part in a discussion about spiritualism. Having lectured on his favourite subject just a few days earlier, he came primed to argue that spiritualism was a scam. But the debate became heated and one local worthy stepped forward (amidst great confusion) to 'lay a charge' against him. This gentleman announced that he had lately attended one of Carr's séances and had been told afterwards, by some of the subjects, that they hadn't been under the mesmeric influence at all. They'd simply done what they'd been paid to do.

Groans and hisses greeted this remark, and the meeting was adjourned when it became impossible to restore order. Once again, Carr's very presence had become a disruptive force. Wherever he went, chaos soon followed.

Matters didn't improve for him in the new year. To boost ticket sales he began to advertise door prizes. A crystal-backed lady's gold watch was one of the articles on offer. 'Is the professor who has just visited us made of the same metal as the eardrops, rings, and chains . . . which he held out to our little public as a glittering bait to his mesmeric trap, finding that his so-called delineations of character would lure no man with even an average good head?' asked someone writing under the pseudonym 'Nemo Me Impune Lacessit'. In the past, Nemo complained, phrenology could command respect; now it was just an excuse for gross remarks and vulgar merriment. 'More brazen and bare-faced libels are seldom placed before an audience who have paid their money to hear a lecture – *a scientific lecture*! – Save the mark!' this critic wrote, almost visibly spluttering. 'Are we to be at the mercy of every charlatan with a bold front and a long tongue . . . and the "cheek" to advertise himself in the local papers as "the real original – none else genuine"?'

Letters like this may or may not have affected Carr's takings, which weren't always good. In one community he netted no more than fifteen pounds during his entire visit, which lasted several days. Prizes weren't helping. Neither was Carr's latest act, which involved criticising the phrenological development of various politicians. It's clear that he must have been under a lot of stress. In September 1871, not long after his most recent attack on spiritualism, he suddenly amazed everyone with a complete change of heart. 'I am now prepared to admit that many of the manifestations I have witnessed have been genuine,' he declared, '. . . and in doing so, I am so far a spiritualist as to believe in the fact of phenomena inexplicable to any known laws, and in the existence of a force I have publicly pronounced as "humbug".' There may have been a carefully thought-out strategy behind this backflip. On the other hand, the fact that he assaulted glove-maker William McLean shortly afterwards suggests that his nerves were a little frayed.

By early 1872 he had shifted his field of operations north. In Taranaki he pulled big crowds. In Wanganui his audiences were far smaller. His first lecture there started late because no one would volunteer to fill the role of chairman; eventually, Carr had to introduce himself. 'The mesmeric portion of the entertainment,' it was reported, 'was hardly so successful as on former occasions.' Towards the end of the show, Carr referred to the 'calamitous statements' made about him after his previous visit, and offered to meet those responsible in public so that he might answer any questions put to him.

Not long afterwards, we find him cutting a pathetic figure on a dockside, having just missed his steamship. In a desperate effort to catch up, he hurriedly hired a small boat to pursue the larger one, but to no avail. The *Auckland Star* painted a vivid picture of him cursing ferociously as the *Royal Alfred* steamed out of sight, leaving him dead in the water.

It wasn't until the middle of the year that he hit upon a device that improved business immeasurably. In June, it was reported that he had given a private exhibition of the effects of 'laughing gas', or nitrous oxide. A chemist on Queen Street had manufactured the gas for Carr and put it in air-tight bags. Carr was the first to inhale it. Then more bags were distributed to the other gentlemen present, who appeared to be in a trance for a few moments after filling their lungs. 'All spoke of the enjoyment and intensely pleasurable feelings in the head whilst under its influence,' the *Auckland Star* related.

Though discovered in the eighteenth century, nitrous oxide wasn't employed as an anaesthetic until the 1840s – and even then, it didn't really take off. In 1878, a Napier newspaper reported that a man named Wilson was about to become the first New Zealand dentist ever to use the gas during his procedures. This happened several years after Thomas Guthrie Carr had started spicing up his séances with nitrous oxide, so in many ways he was a colonial pioneer. And although it was merely a gimmick, the gas proved to be quite a drawcard; Carr was 'besieged' by people who wanted to give it a try. But its effect on many of them was unusual enough to be suspect. 'The nomenclature would be more perfect if it were called "the jumping, dancing, mad-galloping, laughing, singing, and fighting gas,"' one columnist wrote, 'for it makes the inhaler of this subtle vapour do one or other or all.' Carr's subjects would often chase him furiously around the hall, 'regardless of the disparity in size' – suggesting that their reactions may have been carefully engineered beforehand.

On 2 November, the *Waikato Times* noted that Carr had announced his intention of settling in the district for a few months and practising as a 'medical man'. But within weeks he was auctioning off his household furniture, and on 7 December he arrived with his family back on the South Island. Here he began to exhibit a certain high-mindedness. He had already joined the Independent Order of the Rechabites – a temperance organisation – and was soon lecturing on the evils of drink in various temperance halls. 'The worthy doctor is as variable in his mental as in his physical wanderings,' it was noted. 'He is now in Hokitika, and next week may be in Lyttelton or Dunedin. He has passed through theology, psychology, laxology and metaphysics; he has dabbled in mesmerism, electro-biology, and is now a teetotaller. We learn that he is about to venture on the boundary between two worlds, and try his hand at Spiritism.'

In fact, his efforts were being directed more towards organised religion. Returning to his roots, he started preaching lay sermons in schoolrooms and masonic halls – and even at churches like the United Methodist Free Church in Charleston, Nelson. For the most part these attempts were well received, and may have proved to be good advertising for his séances, which were described as 'well attended'. But there can be no doubt that he enjoyed preaching. It was something he did regularly all his life, despite the fact that not everyone appreciated his efforts. 'It does "rile" me,' one South Island detractor complained, 'when I know that Carr is not satisfied with his labours during the weekday, but that on Sunday he pretends to set himself up as a preacher.' Though Carr would state at these affairs that he was delivering a lecture rather than preaching a sermon, he wasn't fooling anybody.

On one occasion, he was heard to say that he preferred Jesus Christ to Buddha, Mohammed, Zoroaster and Confucius because Jesus was more of a gentleman.

In early 1874 Carr joined another temperance organisation, the Independent Order of the Good Templars, and found himself filling halls again. In Canterbury his shows were so popular that he had to extend his visit by several nights. He was a tireless lecturer, traipsing all over the South Island, where he was generally welcomed with politeness and sometimes even with enthusiasm.

But for all his apparent piety, he couldn't seem to keep out of trouble. And it wasn't too long before he ended up in court again.

II

On 20 June 1874, Carr staged a show in Dunedin's Masonic Hall. It was number five in a series, the first of which had received a very complimentary review. Apparently there had been a lot of laughter and applause, and Carr had vouched for the genuineness of his performance. 'The crowd laughs heartily every night,' he promised in his advertisement three days later, adding that his fifth lecture would be on 'True Manhood'.

Unfortunately, this particular show was unlicensed – and Carr soon found himself before the Resident Magistrate's Court.

Carr spoke at length in his own defence. He said that he'd received no official notice that a licence was required. He pointed out that he had never before refused to pay a licence fee, because nowhere in all the other provinces of New Zealand had he ever been asked for one. He believed that the law had been misread in his case, since his entertainments were no more than philosophical lectures and scientific experiments. They didn't really fall into the same category as theatrical or stage shows; there was no scenery and no 'appliances' were used.

He also revealed that, on receiving a summons (out of the blue), he had gone to the town clerk and tried to pay the required fee, but had been rebuffed. It was now a matter for the court, he'd been told.

The magistrate, John Bathgate, remarked that the law could not be stretched – he had to interpret it in its literal sense. Then he asked to see one of Carr's advertisements.

'If you could get this morning's papers you will see it there,' Carr volunteered.

Bathgate called for a copy of the *Otago Daily Times* as Carr went on to relate that he'd gone to visit the mayor, as well as the town clerk. But the mayor had also turned him away. Amidst a ripple of laughter, Inspector Bain was called to the witness stand.

'I may state that Dr Carr did not call and offer to pay for his license till after he was served with a summons,' Bain testified. 'With regard to not knowing that the license was required, I am now prepared to prove that the Doctor called on the 16th of this month at the office, and paid for four nights. He had no license for the 20th, the 22nd or the 23rd inst., the first date being the one complained of.'

Carr interrupted, 'I said that I had received no official notice. I understood from what Mr Hudson told me, that the collector would call on me and receive the fee, but instead of the collector I find this summons is put in my hand!'

There was more laughter. Suddenly the bailiff appeared with a copy of the *Guardian*, which he handed to the magistrate. Bathgate announced that the Licensed Theatres Ordinance applied to a stage play or 'any other entertainment of the stage', including tragedy, comedy, farce, burlesque, burletta, melodrama, pantomime, opera, singing, ballet, dancing, jugglery, tumbling, horsemanship and the exhibition of animals. 'This entertainment by Dr Carr appears to be a lecture upon phrenology or mesmerism,' he said, perusing the paper. 'I am afraid I cannot stretch the Act to meet this case.' He had his doubts that such an entertainment came under the Act. Feeling people's bumps, he said, was not a stage play.

At Bathgate's invitation, Bain then described the show he'd gone to see at the Masonic Hall. The first part, he admitted, had been a lecture on 'True Manhood'. The second part he considered a farce in every sense of the word. A number of men had gone up on stage, but he couldn't say whether or not they'd been mesmerised.

'Were part of the people strangers, or do they belong to the town?' Bathgate inquired.

'One or two of them were townspeople,' Bain answered. 'Mr Sykes played throughout the night as accompanyist [*sic*].'

Bathgate asked if such entertainments were usually licensed. Bain replied, rather obliquely, that his superintendent had the power to waive licensing fees.

'Now with regard to a philosophic lecture,' Bathgate continued, 'would you charge for that?'

His question was met with another burst of laughter, which Bail ignored. 'I would not say that Dr. Carr, strictly speaking, gives a lecture,' the policeman objected.

'Perhaps it affords instruction and is a source of gratification to his audience,' said Bathgate. Then he dismissed the case without prejudice, recommending that Carr decide for himself whether or not he would pay the fee.

Surprisingly, Carr announced that he would.

Reports of this case cast him as a master manipulator. 'The Magistrate seemed spellbound by the doctor's eloquence,' one commentator observed. Another condemned Bathgate's decision with the waspish remark, 'What else can you expect when men without any special training are allowed to dispense law and justice?' Carr himself referred to the case during his next show. After delivering a lecture called 'Man and the Gorilla', in which he attacked the theories of Charles Darwin, he went on to condemn the law that required him to pay a five shilling fee for every performance he gave.

A few days after that he left Dunedin, returning to Christchurch because of an illness in the family. But within weeks he was on the road again. At Invercargill he complained about poor attendances, promising that he would make more people come to his shows even if he had to mesmerise everyone in town. At Tuapeka he was 'only partially successful'. In Lawrence he was robbed. From Carr's room at the Commercial Hotel a man called Fowler stole two diamond studs set in gold, worth five pounds each. Apparently, Fowler was a hotel servant and had helped Carr to pack – at which time the studs were on Carr's dressing table. But when he reached the next town, Carr realised that they were missing.

He continued to have his ups and downs as the years rolled by. In 1875 he enjoyed 'the most successful season that any showman ever had' in Hawke's Bay. Within weeks, however, he was moaning about the small size of his audience and regretting the fact that it was composed entirely of men. The critics kept badgering him. In Auckland someone commenting on his handbills asked what on earth 'soul-splitting' was, and why it had been described as 'extraordinary beyond precedent'. Someone else wrote something so tasteless about Carr that the *Otago Witness* refused to print it. Then came Carr's very public fight with the *Wairarapa Standard* about phrenological charts. This brought even more unsatisfied customers out of the woodwork. 'I paid him two pounds and he was to send me four charts with the phrenological development of my children,' one unhappy customer wrote. 'This he has not yet done.' Even when he had full houses, Carr wasn't satisfied. He complained in Nelson that the local press wasn't actually reporting on them.

By this time Carr had started to lecture on 'public men'. His talk 'Public Men of Napier' triggered several uncomplimentary readings of his own bumps. His 'Public Men of New Zealand' included an adoring sketch of the premier, Sir Julius Vogel. 'Had he lived in the age that produced Severus,' Carr declaimed, 'he might have been an emperor.' It's possible that Carr really did admire New Zealand's only Jewish premier, who championed women's rights. On the other hand, Carr might simply have been trying to ingratiate himself.

By September 1876, he was in Wellington, and seemed to be spending a lot of time hanging around Parliament House. The excuse he gave was a projected course of lectures on the country's greatest men. But he was probably there to schmooze as well. It may be no accident that a few months earlier, he had taken issue with a British MP in a very long letter that was published in the *Taranaki Herald*. The subject of his attack had suggested that Australian explorer Robert O'Hara Burke's expedition had failed because he had 'ignored the Sabbath'. Carr found this claim to be utterly ludicrous:

> *When we remember what Burke endured, his inexorable persistence over worlds of trackless interminable scrub, over*

> *immeasurable plains, foodless, waterless, almost clothesless, back again over the same eternal silence, over the same scorched and blasted desolation, we can forgive him, if he found not even a mud hole to quench his thirst, or a dead dingo to appease his stomach, pursuing his way even on an "English Sunday".*

The mesmerist waxed lyrical on the sufferings of 'lank, lean, ragged' Burke, then went on to defend the notion that Sunday could be a day of rest in nature as well as in church. He was so grandiloquent that he sounded like someone auditioning for parliament.

Perhaps he was nursing a forlorn hope.

The next year, however, brought with it only a series of irritations. In January 1877, an action was taken against him by one Christian Jacob Waeckerle, to recover the £5.12*s* that Carr owed him for the hire of a horse. A default judgement was made against Carr, who didn't appear in court to defend himself; perhaps he was too busy trudging around the country to worry about a five-pound debt. As he hauled his portable gallery of skulls and cartoons from modest settlement to modest settlement – from Kyeburn Diggings to Hill's Creek to Tinker's Gully – he had to contend with the usual annoyances. 'The Doctor found fault on Saturday with a drunken man,' the *Lake County Press* reported, 'who greatly disturbed him and some of his audience, who retired during his performance.' In April came the Sherrin libel case. This minor scandal revolved around journalist Richard Sherrin's attempt to defame the Reverend George McCullogh Reed by comparing him to Thomas Guthrie Carr. Needless to say, Carr didn't let the insult go uncontested.

According to Carr, Sherrin's libel was as 'offensive as an utterly depraved and malignant pen could make it'. But even worse than the libel was Sherrin's ingratitude. Carr described how the journalist had once come to him in tears, begging for a loan of £7.15*s*. As security for the loan he had offered Carr an 'order' on George Bell, the editor of Dunedin's *Evening Star.*

But when Carr presented this document to Bell he was told that Sherrin had never been employed at the paper, and that the money would therefore not be paid. Four years later Carr met Sherrin again and demanded recompense. Sherrin gave him another order, this time directing him to the agent of railway magnate James Brogden for payment. Once again, Carr was stiffed; Sherrin had never worked for Brogden's company. Two years after that another meeting saw Sherrin bombarding Carr 'with promises and moonshine', until – in disgust – Carr returned the worthless order to him.

'Years pass, I never trouble him about the order he dishonoured, I bear with his uncompromising humbug, and in the end present him with £7.15*s*,' Carr concluded. 'The reward is like the ungrateful snake in the fable; he stings me.'

If this was true, it must have rankled. But Carr's campaign against Sherrin wasn't as prolonged as his battles against James Maughan or James Rutherford Ryley. Perhaps age was slowing Carr down. Or perhaps he was preoccupied with an even greater foe – a competitor who seemed louder and more shameless than he had ever been.

Thomas Walker was born to a flour-mill operative in Lancashire, England, in 1858. He was a child preacher on the local Wesleyan circuit before his family emigrated to

Canada, where, at the age of sixteen, he began to perform as a spirit medium. During one of his séances he burned himself with the phosphorus he was using to create 'illuminated writing' and 'spirit lights'. The client who was with him helped extinguish the fire, receiving burns that resulted in his death from tetanus three weeks later. This was blamed on Walker, but by the time a coroner's jury had found him responsible, Walker had left the country.

He worked as a journalist for a while in England and the United States, then finally returned to his old spiritualist activities, joining the entourage of famous American spirit healer, author and minister Dr James Martin Peebles. At the doctor's recommendation, a group of Australian spiritualists invited Walker to visit them – and he arrived in Sydney on 3 March 1877. For a couple of years he successfully toured the colonies, ruffling so many feathers with his racy entertainments that his sponsors finally asked him to leave. But after a brief spell in Britain and South Africa he returned to Australia for good in 1881. A year later he suddenly denounced spiritualism as a fraud and founded the Australian Secular Association; in Sydney he became a writer, publishing poems and several highly successful plays. Then, in 1885, he was convicted for exhibiting obscene pictures while promoting birth control. But he won his appeal, which he conducted himself.

Walker joined the Legislative Assembly in 1887, where he advocated – among other things – easier divorce and the abolition of capital punishment. In 1892 he accidentally shot a clergyman and was convicted of being drunk and disorderly. At that point he became a temperance lecturer. After touring New Zealand again he ended up in Western Australia, where he edited several newspapers, including the *West Australian Sunday Times*. Eventually he gave up newspaper work, dividing his time between farming, the study of law and his parliamentary seat of Kanowna – which he occupied from 1905 until 1932. At one point he was Minister for Justice and Education; later, he was appointed attorney-general. During his time in office he defended Aboriginal rights, legislated against cruelty to animals, promoted the establishment of a central bank and reformed criminal justice. He was Speaker of the Legislative Assembly from 1924 to 1930, and died two years later.

When this complicated, charismatic powerhouse first descended on New Zealand, he was still in his spiritualist phase. The lecture he delivered in Auckland on 10 May 1877, was entitled 'Spiritualism Defined and Defended'. Within a month he was being called an imposter by Carr – whose spiritualist conversion obviously hadn't lasted very long. Carr challenged Walker to prove his claims in front of a committee. 'I am prepared to show to men capable of judging such matters that sounder philosophy can be discoursed on any given subject than that discovered by this trance-medium,' Carr scoffed, adding that the proceeds of such a meeting would be donated to the Benevolent Asylum.

A couple of days later he turned up at one of Walker's shows – which was later described as very rowdy. 'The meeting refused to hear Dr. Carr or the Rev. Mr Fitchett,' it was reported. The press found Carr's outrage most amusing. 'Dr Carr . . . characterises Walker, the trance-medium, as a humbug,' the *Wanganui Chronicle* smirked. 'Surely this is a case of the pot upbraiding the kettle for being black.' The *Thames Star* went even further. 'He has humbugged the public for the last ten or twelve years,' it pointed out, 'and he seems to be as successful now as he was at the beginning of his career. His title of "Dr" is as much a piece of humbug as Mr Walker's pretensions to spirit inspiration. There are humbugs and humbugs, and "Dr" Carr is not the least among the brotherhood.'

It went on to remind its readers that Carr was a liar, having told a Dunedin audience that he'd never mesmerised women. Had he forgotten his shows at the Sydney School of Arts, where several of his regular subjects had been female? Carr had even extracted a young woman's tooth on stage while she was under the influence. 'Dr Carr had better refresh his memory,' the paper concluded, 'and then perhaps he will be more careful in making rash assertions, or accusing a fellow adventurer with being a humbug.'

But Carr refused to back down. When Walker failed to answer his challenge, he published an enormous screed in the *Otago Daily Times*, lambasting the medium's cowardice. 'I offered to do all he could, and do it better, without spiritual aid,' Carr wrote. 'Why did he shrink from such a test?' Carr knew why – because spiritualism was a fraud. He went on to argue the point, raising the subject of his old friends the Davenport Brothers. In 1864, Carr said, he had attended one of their séances. Since then, the 'utter falsehood' of their pretensions had been displayed in nearly every country around the world – including New Zealand.

'Deserted by their ghosts in Auckland a few days ago,' he continued, 'one of the Brothers had to be released from his wretched dilemma – this only after he acknowledged before a large and respectable audience that he was unable to extricate himself. Were not these men imposters?'

It was true; the Davenport Brothers had arrived in New Zealand at around the same time as Thomas Walker. What's more, they had been sorely embarrassed during an Auckland performance in May, when they'd condemned a knot tied by a volunteer as being too 'brutal'. It must have warmed the cockles of Carr's heart to hear that the Davenports' audience had been in an uproar, and that the brothers themselves had retired from the stage most ungracefully, amidst 'tremendous howls'.

But even so, it would have been obvious to Carr that the competition in New Zealand was growing too fierce. As well as Thomas Walker and the Davenport Brothers, Carr was up against illusionist Professor Hennikie, whose Arabian box mystery was said to have put the Davenports 'entirely in the shade'. For this reason, perhaps, Carr finally acknowledged defeat. In July he left for Sydney on the SS *Rotorua*. With him went his wife, his daughter and his agent, whose name was McLure.

A week or so before his departure, the *Evening Post* saluted him with a double-edged send-off:

> *For years he has traversed this colony from extreme north to extreme south, and from south to north again . . . He has appeared separately and conjointly as mesmerist, phrenologist, electro-biologist, exhibitor of the effects produced by laughing gas, doctor, and preacher. His lectures have comprised the whole of the above subjects, spiritualism, clairvoyancy [sic], on trance mediums, and the Immortality of the Soul . . . He has, in turn, been vilified, called the Prince of Humbugs and admired by Press writers, has been prosecuted as an imposter by paid "subjects", and has had actions taken against him for practising as a doctor,*

and receiving fees for drawing teeth and extracting tumours without being possessed of a diploma. But through all trials and vicissitudes the doctor has emerged, Phoenix-like, as fresh as ever . . .

By early August, he was in Queensland.

III

'The success of Dr Carr last evening was a still greater and MOST BRILLIANT ACHIEVEMENT! A larger fashionable audience assembled, demonstrating its approval by incessant and uproarious applause. . .'

Carr's advertising in Brisbane suggested that his 'royal séance' was a huge hit, but this was an exaggeration. The earliest reviews were only cautiously positive. One referred to Carr's imperfect articulation and poor delivery.

By the end of August, it was generally agreed that his shows had not been attracting large crowds.

As a result he turned his attention away from the cities, and for a couple of years wandered all over regional Queensland and New South Wales. He started off in Charters Towers and Rockhampton, where he was very well received. In 1878 he visited Maryborough, then Gympie, before moving south into New South Wales. He popped up in Grafton, Wollongong and Kiama. In Araluen the local paper gave him a lukewarm review, describing his show as 'not very successful', and complaining about his mispronunciations. 'Without diving fully into the matter, we may state that the lecture was brimful of assertions, but barren of proof,' it declared. In Wagga Wagga Carr compelled the mesmerised president of the local Band of Hope (a temperance organisation) to announce that he liked 'a drop of good beer'.

Finally, towards the end of 1878, Carr ended up in Queanbeyan. Though historically quite a prosperous little town – thanks to its successful wheat-farming heritage and its brief flirtation with gold – Queanbeyan was at that time experiencing an economic slump. The poor turnouts that Carr attracted there were blamed by the local press on 'the impecuniosity of the district', as well as on a recent over-supply of public entertainments. One of Carr's shows in nearby Bungendore was patronised by only twenty people; in Cootamundra the press all but apologised for the 'meagre attendance' at his seances. But something about Queanbeyan must have appealed to Carr, because he made it his base for the next year. Though he ranged as far as Braidwood, Goulburn and even Sydney, he always returned to Queanbeyan, where his wife and daughter were living. Perhaps his attachment to the district had something to do with his burgeoning medical practice there. In Cootamundra his surgical skills were in such great demand that he had to delay his planned departure for a while. In Bungendore he cut a tumour from the neck of a resident named Riley, after 'the most popular surgeon of Goulburn' had failed to do so. In Yass it was reported that Carr's treatment of someone called Medway, the victim of a dangerous accident, had been 'eminently successful'.

Or perhaps Queanbeyan's chief attraction was William Gregg O'Neill, Carr's new friend. O'Neill was a local auctioneer and former chief constable, whose daughters were particular favourites of Carr's wife. It was O'Neill who testified on behalf of Carr's employee, Charles Kessler, after Kessler had fired a gun at the local police station. In fact, once Kessler had been fined by the court, O'Neill was promptly tried for 'making use of language calculated to incite a breach of the peace'. Apparently, during the altercation that had followed Kessler's offence, O'Neill had called one constable a liar and a pup, adding, 'Go to hell out of this, with your nose up!' He had been whirling a stick around at the time.

Thomas Guthrie Carr staunchly defended his friend, denying that O'Neill had ever called the constable a 'pup' or a 'dog'. Carr maintained that the same constable had thrust his face into O'Neill's, and had accused him of having no character to lose. The constable's manner, Carr insisted, had been both insulting and offensive.

But in the end, despite Carr's support, O'Neill was fined one pound and costs. It's easy to see why Carr and O'Neill were friends; they clearly shared the same short fuse. Even Carr admitted that O'Neill was 'a passionate tempered man, impulsive and injudicious at times with his tongue'. But he was also 'brimful of kindness', as Carr pointed out in a letter defending O'Neill against a charge of slander brought against him by a fellow auctioneer. This letter was eventually published in the *Queanbeyan Age*, which happened to be edited by O'Neill's brother, John Allan O'Neill. Carr would later claim that John Allan had been so impressed by the piece that he'd commissioned several more articles from Carr. But though the mesmerist had written these articles, he'd never been paid for them – or so he said.

That was why, in November 1879, he sued his 'kind friend's' brother for the £4.7*s* he was allegedly owed.

There was some sort of history behind this dispute. John O'Neill had already taken Carr to court over an eight pound debt, probably for unpaid advertising. According to John, Carr's written work had arrived at his office without any prompting. 'I will swear that I never asked Dr Carr to write articles for my paper,' John declared, 'but he said that owing to the friendship existing between my nieces and Mrs Carr and my brother and himself, he had written the letters for me.'

Carr had a different story to tell. He stated that on 21 July he had gone to John O'Neill's office, where he'd been asked to sit down and write something for the paper. The article he'd produced had been called 'The Stage and M. Creswick' and he'd signed it 'Amicus'. The second article, though commissioned by John O'Neill, had never been published owing to a 'difference of opinion'. The third and fourth articles had been about William O'Neill's run-in with a fellow member of the Mechanics' Institute, whom he'd called a 'low scoundrel' in public. 'These were written at the special request of Mr. J. A. O'Neill,' Carr testified, 'and so pleased was he with them that he came to my house at about 2 o'clock in the morning and told me that several people had spoken to him about them and that they were well pleased.' At the same time, according to Carr, John O'Neill had offered him the editorship of a new journal John was planning to launch in Cooma. 'I afterwards mentioned this conversation to his brother, who treated it with contempt,' Carr added.

Under John O'Neill's cross-examination, the mesmerist refused to comment on whether he had paid his printer's bills or the rent for the Mechanics' Hall in Goulburn. The plaintiff seemed to be suggesting that Carr was so desperate for money he'd decided to lie about unpaid fees. Certainly the magistrates weren't convinced. They declared the case a 'non-suit' – much to Carr's disgust. He wrote an angry rebuttal that was published in the *Queanbeyan Age* three days later. 'If the decision of the Bench was not a miscarriage,' he complained, 'it presents features very like one.' Though the letter was signed 'Northumberland', it's obvious that Carr must have been responsible for it; he'd signed his first letter to the *Age* 'Northumberland' too.

Northumberland was the English county of his birth.

William O'Neill's spell in the witness box had been marked by a distinct lack of enthusiasm. 'I do not recollect saying that if you liked you could write for my brother,' he'd stated, in response to one of Carr's more pointed questions. It's possible that their friendship failed to survive Carr's disagreement with John O'Neill, because the mesmerist didn't stay in Queanbeyan for very long afterwards. In December he was on his way to the north coast, where he was wrecked in the *Agnes Irving.* In January 1880 he was fighting a house fire in Port Macquarie. In May he was entertaining the inhabitants of Dungog. And by June he had settled in Morpeth, New South Wales – where he would live for the rest of his life.

Named after a town near Newcastle-on-Tyne, Morpeth was a pretty little settlement on the Hunter River. Birthplace of the iconic Arnott baking company, it was a busy steamship port with a handsome court house, a stately School of Arts and a lavish assortment of hotels. Carr stayed at the Crown and Anchor when he first arrived; on 5 June he announced in the local paper that he intended to become a resident of Morpeth, where he would 'practice his profession'. By the end of the month he was living at a house called Tyneside Cottage, suggesting that his wife and daughter had joined him. And for the next five years, though he set off on various lecture tours that took him as far as Sydney, he appears to have put down roots in an electoral district that was named Northumberland, after his own home county.

His aim was to establish a proper medical practice. 'DR CARR may be seen at his residence daily. Night calls promptly attended to,' he advertised. In September 1880 he performed an operation on a seventy-year-old resident of Morpeth called William Hicks, removing a tumour from his lower lip 'without pain' – or so it was claimed in the newspaper report for which Carr himself was probably responsible. The mesmerist also started appearing at various local events: a school prize-giving night, a clergyman's talk on 'Diligence Rewarded', a half-yearly meeting of the Morpeth School of Arts – during which Carr was thanked for donating the proceeds of a lecture he'd given. These School of Arts lectures became quite a feature of Morpeth's social calendar. In 1883, after discoursing on phrenology in May, he gave a 'winter course of lectures' in July, presumably to the same group of people every night. These lectures were all slavishly transcribed and published by the local press, including one in which Carr – the father of a teenage daughter – tackled the vexed subject of modern fashion:

> *There are great numbers of girls here going and returning from academies and schools, their shops and their homes, most of them just into their teens, dressed like ladies, and verily they are called "young ladies". Did you not see in last Saturday's Mercury that one of those doll girls was so trussed up, so corseted, panniered, improved and malformed,*

> *that when she dropped her parachute in the street in broad daylight, she could not stoop to pick it up – could not stoop for fear of splitting the monstrous machinery which fashion has invented to make God's work better than He designed it should be. Who does this? Your mothers do it. Your fathers are content to think it right because the wife says it is the fashion. I have a daughter going on fifteen, but it shall never be said that fashion malformed her.*

Poor little Monica Carr must have been dressed like a Quaker.

Meanwhile, Carr didn't neglect other towns in the region. His Woodville lecture was described as 'clever and interesting'. In Copeland he drew a large and admiring audience – though in Clarence Town attendance was so thin that he refused to mesmerise anyone and instead proceeded to examine heads without, apparently, finding a single redeeming feature among them. In Maitland the hall 'was crowded each night, the admission being free'. In Newcastle his condemnation of free thought and free-thinkers was noted with interest. 'It is expected that the Morpeth doctor and his opponents will have a hot time of it, the hotter perhaps the better,' a local commentator observed.

He also went further afield in New South Wales – to Tamworth, Armidale, Cootamundra and Yass. 'Dr Carr . . . is Consulting Surgeon and Physician to the Oddfellows, Druids, Sons of Temperance, and People's Sick Club,' his advertisements ran. The *Cootamundra Herald* observed that Carr looked well, and that age appeared to have 'touched him very gently'. 'He still has much of his old fire, energy and eloquence' was the final conclusion.

Some of this energy and eloquence surfaced in Sydney around the middle of 1884. Carr had been touring the central west, lecturing at places like Wellington, and may very well have visited Sydney to catch a steamship back to Morpeth. But instead of conducting a séance in one of the many halls around town, he decided to address the unemployed in Hyde Park.

At least one observer found this unaccountable. 'Wondering what Dr. Carr could have to say to the unemployed,' he observed, 'I determined to go to that meeting and find out.' There can be no question that this anonymous correspondent was male, because on reaching the park, he began to converse freely with one of the 'Park sleepers' – who told such a disturbing tale of hardship that the writer was quite moved. 'Passing by the statue,' he concluded, 'I heard Dr. Carr telling a crowd that they should have been more careful in the time of their prosperity. Somehow I wasn't in the humour to listen to that line of argument just then; so I left the doctor to it.'

This was Carr's final visit to Sydney. It's curious that he hadn't settled there, even though his wife's family was based nearby. Possibly none of the Irelands wanted a bar of him, but it's also likely that Sydney held painful memories. Even in the Hunter Valley, people hadn't quite forgotten. One resident, responding in print to Carr's criticism that he lacked education, said simply, 'I may state that as late as the years 1868-69, I was able to read newspapers.'

Despite his murky past, however, Carr was elected to the Morpeth municipal council in February 1884. This must have been a very important moment for him. After years of struggling on the peripheries, he'd finally become respectable. At last he was a real doctor, with a real practice and a real constituency.

But he wasn't able to enjoy his achievement for very long – because in 1885, his health began to fail.

His slow decline began after a burst of activity that had seen him lecturing tirelessly around Newcastle, mostly on religious topics. 'We regret that we cannot allow a theological controversy to take up space in our correspondence columns,' the *Newcastle Morning Herald* informed him at one point. Though he'd always been fond of preaching, his preoccupation with the evils of free thought may very well have had something to do with his new position of authority. Or there may have been another, more ominous reason behind his outbreak of religious fervour.

In September he was suddenly struck down while on a visit to the little mining town of Tumbarumba, at the foot of the Snowy Mountains. For weeks he lay bed-ridden, his condition so serious that his wife was sent for. 'We have not been informed of the exact nature of his illness,' the *Morpeth Times* admitted, 'but it is well known here that when the doctor left town he was suffering from a severe cold, from which, it seems, he has never been able to free himself thoroughly.' Carr was no stranger to colds so bad that they made it into the papers, but one later report mentioned that Carr had suffered a bout of rheumatism in Tumbarumba, while another described his affliction as an attack of paralysis. Whether this so-called paralysis was physical or mental, we don't know – but thanks to his wife's careful nursing, he was back in Morpeth within a fortnight. Here the residents were gratified to see his 'gigantic figure' once again pacing the streets.

From some reason, however, Carr decided that his health would benefit from the bracing effects of mountain air. In December he travelled to the northern tablelands town of Glen Innes, leaving his wife and daughter behind. It wasn't a rest cure, by any means; he gave at least three performances at Glen Innes to 'small but appreciative' audiences. 'Several subjects were made to cut fantastic figures and perform extraordinary tricks,' the local paper dutifully reported, adding with a certain lack of enthusiasm, 'This latter part of the programme could, we think, be very well excised . . . for the reason that it is not in harmony with what must be considered as highly interesting entertainment.'

During his visit, Carr opened a consulting room in the Commercial Hotel. He also wrote a critique of a sermon he heard at the local Anglican church, giving the clergyman responsible one or two tips on public speaking. (It was important to meet people's eyes, he pointed out.) According to the *Morpeth Times*, Carr wrote home just before Christmas with the news that he was enjoying 'splendid health' and had established a large practice. But he was lying. Business wasn't good at all.

Later, it was determined that the failure of his tour must have preyed on his mind.

Carr's letters home became more and more peculiar. There was a 'remarkable want of cohesion' in his sentence structure, and his thoughts seemed wrapped in the deepest melancholy. On the morning of 15 January 1886, he bought ten grains of morphia from a local chemist. Morphia was the Victorian name for morphine and ten grains was easily a fatal dose. Later, in the reading room of the Commercial Hotel, Carr commented that he would probably be dead in a few hours. This must have been taken for a joke, since no one tried to intercede. At about eleven o'clock he retired to his room, leaving behind him several letters and a twist of paper that had contained the drug. Nothing more was heard from him for the rest of the night.

On Sunday morning, at around eight o'clock, a waiter saw that Carr's door was standing slightly ajar. On entering the room he found the mesmerist lying face up on the bed, fully dressed except for his coat. One hand was draped across his chest. He had been killed by a narcotic overdose.

'From a book found in his possession, it appeared that he was 48,' the *Glen Innes Examiner* noted, 'but appearances indicate he was much older.' Either Carr had aged rapidly during the last few months of his life, or he had been lying about his birth date on official documents for years. The letters he'd left behind in the reading room were addressed to his wife Jane, his daughter Monica, two gentlemen in Morpeth, and the adopted daughter whose name seems to have been expunged from the records. Most of them were written in a manner described as 'irrational'. Only the note to Monica made any sense:

> *Glen Innes. Saturday evening. Monica – I am that ill I do not know how to write to you. What queer distressing feeling is bothering me! I feel very bad, my love; I kiss and embrace you, ma, and Queen Mab (I mean 'slops'.) I am truly ill. The storm I think, is just about to fall – the sooner the better. I am, your affectionate papa, T. GUTHRIE CARR. Monica Carr, from pa.*

News of Carr's death reached Morpeth in a telegram on Monday morning. A police sergeant by the name of Gordon had to break the news to Jane Carr, who was 'very much affected'. She arrived at Glen Innes that night. Her husband was buried two days later, on 20 January, in the Anglican churchyard. The same day a coroner's inquest concluded that, although Carr had died from an overdose, there was no evidence to show whether it had been an accident or not. The tone of his letter to Monica was regarded as suspicious, but Jane Carr did everything in her power to disprove the suicide theory. She argued that Carr often wrote 'strangely concocted' letters, so there was nothing unusual about Monica's. To prove it, she gave the *Glen Innes Guardian* a whole stack of old correspondence. After examining this material, the *Guardian* agreed cautiously that the letter to Monica 'shed no light whatever' on the case.

Carr's will, which had been drawn up and witnessed in Narrabri, New South Wales, years earlier, left everything to his wife Jane. It made no mention of his daughter, his adopted daughter, or an illegitimate son in Adelaide. His estate was valued at just over one thousand pounds. Five years later, Jane also died. At the age of forty-seven she suffered a stroke in the Sydney office of her sister's brother-in-law, solicitor Andrew Hardie McCulloch. The following year, Monica Carr wed Isaac Broad, a watchmaker from Hay. They were married at St Paul's Anglican church, Burwood, and Jane's brother William served as a witness. Monica had no children, and died in 1949. What happened to Carr's adopted daughter is impossible to discover without a name. But Jane's siblings were blessed with numerous children and a number of their descendants still live in Sydney.

Carr's death was reported in a good many newspapers across Australia and New Zealand. Suicide was mentioned by every single one of them. Most were noncommittal in tone, referring to Carr's 'remarkably chequered' career, but some assessed him more warmly. 'There are thousands who remember Dr Carr in the zenith of his fame 15 years ago,' the *Morpeth Times* mused, 'and we doubt if a more popular man ever travelled the colonies. We vividly recollect the giant doctor in the prime of life lecturing to packed audiences, receiving thunderous applause, and excellent critiques from the Press. And now the same doctor is dead! And we can truly say his like we'll see no more.'

Carr himself had nursed very particular views on the afterlife. A lecture that he'd often delivered was 'The Soul After the Grave' or 'The Grave and After.' In it, he had repudiated the doctrine of Hell. 'A man who believes in the Dr's theories must feel greatly relieved after listening to his discourse,' one journalist had commented, on hearing these views. It seems that, for many years, Carr had cherished a profound faith in God's unstinting forgiveness – a faith that, at one point, he expressed in verse. 'Behind the Veil' was published in the *North Otago Times* on 20 February 1877, and included the following stanzas:

What is this life? This light? This soul?
This great percipient, this whole –
This spark, great God! Of Thee?
So crowned with reason, and with sense
To comprehend this world immense;
Yet not its destiny.
Behind the veil we fain would look –
Behind the veil, Thy priv'leged book –
But this – it must not be.

Like creatures born to live a day
We grope our way, we grope our way,
And for thy light we cry,
To guide us to Thy altar stairs
Where we would lay our hearts and cares
And on thy love rely.
Life is so cold, so sad withal,
We fain would on Thy mercy fall
And lay us down to die.

But, while we in our darkness grope,
Love gives us Faith, Faith gives us Hope,
E'en while to thee we call.
Yet lab'ring tow'rds the higher life,
Amidst life's sorrows and its strife,
We still should faint and fall
But that we know, behind the Veil,
Thy love immortal will prevail
For all, kind God, for all.

Was Carr fully convinced that God's immortal love *would* prevail, even for him? Or was he trying to reassure himself? For much of his life he'd behaved as if he were a stranger to doubt, displaying an aggressive confidence that had left many victims in its wake. Towards the end, however, his mask had slipped. The fragile core of his grandiose, self-important, narcissistic personality had somehow been damaged. Perhaps illness had been a contributing factor. Perhaps guilt destroyed him, or self-pity. It's impossible to say.

His legacy wasn't an enduring one, though he was remembered for the next twenty or thirty years. Somehow news of his demise drifted across the Pacific to America, where Frank Chester Fowler mentioned it in his book. Carr's reputation remained dubious; his achievements, such as they were, went largely unremarked. But the *Morpeth Times* mentioned 'a dozen instances of his kindness to strolling players and others in Morpeth', none of whom, apparently, had left Carr's presence empty-handed. And as an example of the consummate, archetypal Victorian showman, Carr was fondly recalled by a great number of people who'd enjoyed his unbridled, uproarious shows. One of these admirers even wrote a short poem in his honour, which sums up his life as well as any solemn eulogy, even as it slyly refers to the Eliza Gray case:

Alas he's passed away from aye
Pale Death has drawn his stumps
Who used to mesmerise us and
Manipulate our bumps.
Let's hope that when he goes aloft
He'll see the gate ajar,
And hear the joyful cherubs sing
"Roll in, triumphant Carr!
We'd also like our bumps described.
Nay, do not look so red.
We cannot compromise you for
We're limited to head."

A wink and a nod and he was gone forever, leaving nothing but a generous number of newspaper clippings, a single phrenological chart and a few unanswered questions. Was he guilty? Did he do it? What *really* happened to Eliza Gray?

As Carr himself would have said, 'Behind the veil we feign would look . . . but this – it must not be'.

NOTES

Preface

p. 1 'Dr Rudolphe's Specific Remedy', Medical Office of Professor F C Fowler. *Dr Rudolphe's Specific Remedy. Good News for Debilitated Men*, Abe Books, Moodus, Connecticut, 1884 (Drug Ephemera).

p. 1 'By 1894 Fowler was calling himself', *The Pharmaceutical Era*, 15 August 1893, p. 92.

p. 1 'Fowler was just thirty-seven years old', *all-biographies.com/business/frank_chester_fowler.htm.*

p. 1 'prompted by a benevolent desire', Fowler, F C, *Life: How To Enjoy It and How To Prolong It*, Moodus, Connecticut, 1896, pp. 1–2.

p. 2 'the case of Walter Montgomery', ibid., p. 149.

p. 2 'Dr. Carr, who recently died', ibid., p. 149.

p. 2 'consulted in perfect confidence', ibid., p. 210.

Part I: The Incident

I

p. 5 'George Street was the main artery', Mundy, Godfrey Charles, *Our Antipodes or Residence and Rambles in the Australasian Colonies, with a glimpse of the gold fields*, 3rd edn, Richard Bentley, London, 1855, p. 9.

p. 5 'tragical posters', Wilson, F, 'A Day at the Central Police Court', *The Australian Journal*, vol. 2, no. 98, 13 July 1867, p. 733.

p. 6 'William Roberts', *sydneyaldermen.com.au/alderman/william-roberts.*

p. 6 'among his past clients', *Sydney Morning Herald*, 3 July 1900, p. 5.

p. 6 'Salomons, aged thirty-three', Edgar, Suzanne, and Bede Nairn, 'Salomons, Sir Julian Emanuel (1835–1909)', *Australian Dictionary of Biography*, vol. 6, Melbourne University Press, Melbourne, 1976.

p. 7 'he would face a possible death penalty', Lennan, Joe, and George Williams, 'Death Penalty in Australian Law', *Sydney Law Review*, vol. 34:659, p. 666; *Sydney Morning Herald*, 31 May 1877, p. 3.

p. 7 'Eliza Gray, was thirty years old', 'Lilias Wallace and Frederick Louis Veniard', *Genealogy*, http://genealogy.northern-skies.net/gray.php?number=306.

p. 7 'Monster Clothing Hall', *Sydney Morning Herald*, 22 February 1868, p. 7.

p. 7 'the best and most varied stock', ibid., 7 December 1868, p. 6.

p. 8 'According to Gray', ibid., 15 September 1868, p. 2; *Empire*, 16 September 1868, p. 3; *Sydney Morning Herald*, 22 September 1868, p. 2; *Empire*, 25 September 1868, p. 3.

p. 8 'stocking feet', *Wairarapa Standard*, vol. 7, no. 446, 1 July 1876, p. 2.

p. 8 'gave Carr's alias', NSW *Police Gazette*, October 7 1868, p. 204.

p. 8 'coarse and sensual', *Evening News* (Sydney), 21 January 1899, p. 2.

p. 8 'giant doctor', *Waikato Times*, 27 February 1886, p. 2.

p. 8 'during an assault trial', *Evening Post*, vol. VII, no. 214, 16 October 1871, p. 2.

p. 8 'he wasn't a big man', *Otago Daily Times*, 29 January 1896, p. 3.

p. 8 'fine voice', *Maitland Mercury and Hunter River General Advertiser*, 30 August 1883, p. 7.

p. 8 'the art of saying just enough', *Empire*, 17 April 1868, p. 2.

p. 8 'As a lecturer', *Star*, 27 April 1870, p. 2.
p. 9 'his familiar off-hand style', *South Australian Register*, 17 May 1867, p. 2.
p. 9 'an impersonator gave an impression', *Cromwell Argus*, 2 July 1872, p. 5.
p. 9 'was a very fast talker', *Star*, 26 April 1870, p. 2.
p. 9 'perhaps it was his vocabulary', *Manawatu Times*, 30 June 1877, p. 2.
p. 9 'One Melbourne commentator', *Ovens and Murray Advertiser* (Beechworth), 17 December 1867, p. 2.
p. 9 'Another infuriated columnist', *Geelong Advertiser*, 31 August 1866, p. 3.
p. 9 'One detractor described him', *Oamaru Times*, 21 July 1871, p. 2.
p. 9 'the gift of the gab', *Manuatu Times* 21 July 1871, p. 2.
p. 10 'phreno-mesmeric, electro-biological', *Sydney Morning Herald*, 7 March 1868, p. 6.
p. 11 'as was his habit', *Wellington Independent*, vol. 24, Issue 2845, 5 June 1869, p. 3.
p. 11 'the School of Arts', Dictionary of Sydney staff writer, Sydney Mechanics School of Arts, *Dictionary of Sydney*, 2008, http://dictionaryof Sydney.org/entry/Sydney_mechanics_school_of_arts.
p. 11 'While many of the "splendid establishments"', Askew, John, *A Voyage to Australia and New Zealand by a Steerage Passenger*, Simpkin, Marshall & Co, London, 1857, p. 185.
pp. 11–12 'young lady somnambulist', *Newcastle Chronicle*, 8 April 1868, p.1.
p. 12 'a dozen young men', *Sydney Morning Herald*, 12 March 1868, p. 4.
p. 14 'the most "comfortable" address', Macpherson, Mrs Allan (A Lady), *My Experiences in Australia, Being Recollections of a Visit to the Australian Colonies in 1856-7*, J.F. Hope, London, 1860, pp. 16–65.
p. 14 'the older woman's lodgings', *Sydney Morning Herald*, 25 September 1868, p. 2.

II

p. 15 'There were balls. There were concerts', ibid., 8 February 1868, p. 7.

p. 16 'As soon as they were about sixty yards', Emily Nuttall Thorne, 'Clontarf', an account of the attempted assassination of Prince Alfred, Duke of Edinburgh, at Clontarf on 12 March 1868, manuscript, State Library of NSW.

p. 17 'The Duke fell on his hands', *South Australian Advertiser,* 28 March 1868, p. 2.

pp. 17–18 'his clothes were in ribbons', *Sydney Morning Herald,* 13 March 1868, p. 5.

p. 18 'it was evident that', *South Australian Advertiser,* 20 March 1868, p. 2.

p. 18 'Come, come, it is not fair', *South Australian Advertiser,* 20 March 1868, p. 2.

p. 18 'he was cancelling his show', *South Australian Advertiser,* 20 March 1868, p. 2.

p. 19 'bandied around the New South Wales Legislative Assembly', *Sydney Morning Herald,* 22 April 1868, p. 2.

p. 19 'we have amongst us', Travers, Robert, *The Phantom Fenians of New South Wales*, Kangaroo Press, 1986, p. 95.

p. 19 'In a letter that O'Farrell wrote', *West Coast Times,* 9 May 1868, p. 4.

p. 20 'Parkes had already warned', Travers, *The Phantom Fenians,* p. 65.

p. 20 'Carr was quick to retaliate', *Sydney Morning Herald,* April 24, p. 5.

p. 22 'Somehow, on 21 April', *Evening Post,* 7 May 1868, p. 2.

p. 22 'was read before parliament', *Sydney Morning Herald,* 15 February 1869, p. 2.

p. 23 'Carr had concluded that', *South Australian Chronicle and Weekly Mail,* 2 May 1868, p. 9.

p. 24 'In one advertisement', *Lachlan/Grenfell Mining Record and Grenfell Advertiser,* 18 July 1868, p. 1.

III

p. 24 'Gray herself wasn't sure', *Sydney Morning Herald*, 15, 22 and 25 September 1868, p.2; *Empire*, 15, 22 and 25 September 1868, p.3.

pp. 25–6 'his advertisement for mutton', ibid., 18 March 1868, p. 10.

p. 26 'ten shillings and sixpence', *Empire*, 6 May 1868, p. 1.

p. 29 'a letter appeared in the *Herald*', *Sydney Morning Herald*, 16 September 1868, p. 5.

p. 29 'It may be thought by some', *Newcastle Chronicle*, 17 September 1868, p. 3.

Part II: Before the Incident

I

p. 30 'Some time in 1839', New South Wales Marriage Certificate 916/1868; New South Wales Death Certificate 9607/1886.

p. 30 'Ira Erastus and William Henry Davenport', Nichols, T L, *A Biography of the Brothers Davenport*, Saunders, Otley & Co., London, 1864, p. 213.

p. 30 'were greeted by riots in Liverpool', Broadbent, R J, *Annals of the Liverpool Stage, from the Earliest Period to the Present*, Benjamin Blom, New York, 1908, p. 277.

p. 30 '*Modern Spiritualism an Imposture*', Carr, Thomas, *Modern Spiritualism an Imposture; or the Davenport Fraternity Unmasked*, Religious Tract Society, London, 1864, p. 4.

p. 35 'he was performing nightly', *Glasgow Herald*, 5 November 1864, p. 7.

p. 35 'in a letter to', *Otago Daily Times*, 23 June 1877, p. 1.

p. 35 'he remembered taking part in *three*', ibid., 20 June 1870, p. 2.

p. 35 'laws of nature', ibid., 22 June 1870, p. 2.

p. 35 'East End Phrenological Society', *Age*, 13 October 1866, p. 1; *Sydney Morning Herald*, 9 March 1868, p. 8; *Ballarat Star*, 24 January 1867, p. 3.

p. 35 'he'd authored several books', *The Press* (NZ), 5 March 1870, p. 8; *Queanbeyan Age*, 16 August 1879, p. 3; *Age*, 25 August 1866, p. 1, and 3 September 1866, p. 8.

p. 36 'Guy's Hospital', *The Press*, 20 January 1870, p. 4.

p. 36 'William Murray', The National Archives, William Murray, 1839–1920, discovery.nationalarchives.gov.uk/details/rd/8314c9cb-4054-b20c-6f3089db9de1.

p. 36 'start using the honorific "Dr"', *West Coast Times*, 8 January 1869, p. 2.

p. 36 'I decline to answer', ibid.

p. 37 'Eichler could only say', *Empire*, 29 September 1868, p. 3.

p. 37 'a fraud and a humbug', *Thames Star*, 16 June 1877, p. 3.

p. 37 'a committee of Adelaide worthies', *South Australian Register*, 30 July 1867, p. 2.

p. 37 'John Rutherford Ryley', *The Press*, March, 16 1869, p. 2; *West Coast Times*, 12 January 1869, p. 3.

p. 37 'Ryley poured scorn', *West Coast Times*, 20 January 1869, p. 3.

p. 38 'Carr's response', ibid., 20 January 1869, p. 3.

p. 38 'The dispenser at the local hospital', ibid., 21 January 1869, p. 2.

p. 38 'her husband brought an action', *Sydney Morning Herald*, 10 January 1870, p. 5.

p. 38 'John James Hill', *Age*, 15 August 1866, p. 5; *Sydney Morning Herald*, 24 August 1866, p. 2.

p. 39 'in a published letter', *Empire*, 12 October 1866, p. 3.

p. 39 'the only ship from England', *Ballarat Star*, 26 July 1866, p. 2.

II

p. 39 'an English newspaper', *Age*, 3 November 1868, p. 2.

p. 40 'One account of his talk', *Newcastle Daily Journal*, 19 November 1864, p. 2.

p. 40 'During a concert', *Newcastle Guardian and Tyne Mercury*, 19 November 1864, p. 5.

p. 40 'When the Newcastle doctor', *Thames Star*, 11 April 1877, p. 3.

p. 41 'Modern Spiritualism', *Age*, September 3 1866, p. 8.

p. 41 'the Apocalyptic Gospel', *Argus*, 8 Sept 1866, p. 8.

p. 41 'St John the Mystic', ibid., 25 August 1866, p. 1.

p. 41 'Baxter in the Crucible', *Argus*, 4 September 1866, p. 4; *Age*, 4 September 1866, p. 5.

p. 41 'The Reverend H Higginson', *Argus*, 4 August 1866, p. 8.

p. 42 'a review complained', *Geelong Advertiser*, 31 August 1866, p. 3.

p. 42 'One South Australian correspondent', *Bunyip* (Gawler), 22 June 1867, p. 3.

p. 42 'all the mistakes he'd made', *South Australian Register*, 26 December 1867, p. 3.

p. 43 'Another critic once described', *Thames Advertiser*, 6 October 1877, p. 2.

p. 43 'The Sohiers' notorious collection', Catherine Bishop, *Minding Her Own Business: Colonial Businesswomen in Sydney*, NewSouth Publishing, Sydney, 2015, chapter 6 'Entertaining Women'.

p. 43 'An account of Carr's show', *Launceston Examiner*, 27 November 1866, p. 2.

p. 44 'Carr was advertising', *Argus*, Friday 26 October 1866, p. 8.

p. 44 'Soon he was lecturing', ibid., 22 November 1866, p. 8.

p. 44 'The Mayor of Melbourne', *Argus* 3 December 1866, p. 8.

p. 44 'his phrenological analysis of Robert Closky', Geelong Advertiser, 5 December 1866, p. 4.

p. 44 'Closky's execution', *Victorian Government Gazette*, 7 December 1866, p. 2708.

p. 44 'once publicly condemned', *Age*, 24 July 1869, p. 2.

p. 44 'A General Difficulty', ibid. 19 May 1866, p. 8.

p. 45 'We, the undersigned', *Argus*, 28 November 1866, p. 8.

p. 46 'Huxtable had business interests', Skinner, Graeme, Huxtable, John Alfred', *A Biographical Register of Australian Colonial Musical personnel—H,* http://Sydney.edu.au/paradisec/australharmony/register-H.php.

p. 46 'first lecture in Ballarat', *Ballarat Star,* 17 January 1867, p. 3.

p. 46 'settlement of their little bills', *Age,* 22 February 1867, p. 5.

p. 46 'Carr's response', ibid., 26 February 1867, p. 7.

p. 47 'overdue advertising fees', *Ovens and Murray Advertiser,* 4 January 1868, p. 2.

p. 47 'Alexandra Lodge', *Timaru Herald,* 19 August 1874, p. 4.

p. 47 'Organ Fund', *South Australian Register,* 21 August 1867, p. 2.

p. 47 'hospital at Copeland', *Maitland Mercury and Hunter River Advertiser,* April 29 1880, p. 7.

p. 47 'a Hill End widow', *Australian Town and Country Journal,* 21 June 1879, p. 38.

p. 47 Benevolent asylum governorship, *Bendigo Advertiser,* 16 April 1867, p. 2.

p. 47 'Anglican church at Sebastopol', *Ballarat Star,* 23 February 1867 p. 1.

p. 47 'still hadn't been placed', ibid., 13 March 1867, p. 2.

p. 47 'the fault of church administrators', ibid., 2 July 1867, p. 3.

p. 47 'erect public baths', *North Otago Times,* 21 July 1871, p. 2.

p. 48 'Dunedin's citizens were still waiting', *Otago Daily Times,* 6 August 1907, p. 2.

p. 48 'another local widow,' *South Australian Advertiser,* 27 May 1867, p. 2.

p. 48 'his lecture on Sunday evening', ibid., 31 May 1867, p. 2.

p. 48 'Carr had abandoned', *South Australian Weekly Chronicle,* 23 November 1867, p. 5.

p. 48 'he would bombard', *Nelson Evening Mail*, 22 March 1878, p. 2.

p. 48 'a local recalled', *Bendigo Advertiser*, 9 January 1909, p. 3.

p. 49 'Prince Tommy', *Lachlan/Grenfell Mining Record and Grenfell Advertiser*, 18 July 1868, p. 1.

p. 49 'a mesmerised shoemaker', *Evening Post*, 30 October 1871, p. 2.

p. 49 'On turning up', *Nelson Evening Mail*, 17 April 1869, p. 2.

p. 49 'a Maori mailman', *Taranaki Herald*, 7 February 1872, p. 2.

p. 49 'On our way home', *Hawke's Bay Herald*, 21 January 1870, p. 3.

p. 50 'According to the *Herald*', *Sydney Morning Herald*, 28 March 1868, p. 6.

p. 51 'filled almost to overflowing', *South Australian Register*, 17 May 1867, p. 2; *South Australian Weekly Chronicle*, 18 May 1867, p. 1.

p. 51 'His second lecture', *South Australian Register*, 18 May 1867, p. 2.

p. 51 'his third on "Modern Mystery"', *South Australian Advertiser*, 20 May 1867, p. 2; *South Australian Register*, 20 May 1867, p. 3.

p. 52 'the *Register* related', *South Australian Register*, 22 May 1867, p. 2.

p. 52 'a £50 prize', ibid., 23 May 1867, p. 2.

p. 52 'he proceeded to ignore', *South Australian Weekly Chronicle*, 22 June 1867, p. 2.

p. 52 'he was back in town', *South Australian Register*, 28 May 1867, p. 2.

p. 52 'His next lecture', ibid., 31 May 1872, p. 2.

p. 53 'The Chairman was careful', *South Australian Advertiser*, 27 May 1867, p. 2.

p. 53 'publicly but anonymously', ibid., 5 June 1867, p. 2.

p. 53 'The feeble visual organs', ibid., 8 June 1867, p. 3.

p. 53 'Scepticism continued to mount', ibid., 20 May 1867, p. 3.

p. 53 'He had to cancel his show', ibid., 7 June 1867, p. 2.

p. 54 'convenience of schools', ibid., 1 June 1867, p. 2.

p. 54 'Carr shared his stage', ibid., 13 June 1867, p. 2.

p. 54 'White's Assembly Rooms', *Treasures of the State Library*, http:/www.samemory.sa.gov.au/site/page.cfm?u=967&c=7395; *The Chronicle* (Adelaide), 5 February 1916, p. 31.

p. 54 'Osbaldeston freed himself', South Australian Advertiser, 29 June 1867, p. 2.

p. 55 'at a Turkish bathhouse', Shifrin, Malcolm, 'Burton's Turkish Baths', *The Victorian Turkish Bath: Its Origin, Development, and Gradual Decline*, http/www.victorianturkishbath.org.

p. 55 'he was on a ship', Register of passengers on immigrant ships arriving in Queensland, pp. 226–8, archiver.rootsweb.ancestry.com/th/read/AUS-QLD/2004-07/1089621022

p. 55 'was in Melbourne, advertising', *Argus*, 19 July 1866, p. 8.

p. 55 'Mr Osbaldeston then gave', *South Australian Register*, 19 October 1867, p. 2.

p. 56 'to treat the boy's deafness', *The Register* (Adelaide), 16 May 1927, p. 3.

p. 56 'Turkish baths in Lonsdale Street', *Age*, 7 December 1866, p. 5.

p. 56 'Ballarat's Turkish baths', *Ballarat Star*, 21 December 1866, p. 3.

p. 56 'a new bathhouse in Adelaide', *Sydney Morning Herald*, 26 November 1867, p. 2.

III

p. 56 'James Maughan', Cooke, William, *The Man of All Work. A Memoir of the Life and Labours of Reverend James Maughan*, Hodder & Stoughton, London, 1872, pp. 2, 10, 13.

p. 57 'He once read a paper', Hambly, F, 'Maughan, James (1826–1871), *Australian Dictionary of Biography*, National Centre of Biography, Australian National University, http://adb.anu.edu.au/biography/maughan-james-4173/text6701.

p. 57 'rashness and folly', Cooke, *Man of All Work*, p. 95.

p. 57 'The Great Events', *South Australian Advertiser*, 16 December 1870, p. 3.

p. 57 'Wonders', ibid., 26 August 1864, p. 6.

p. 57 'Beefsteaks and Apple Dumplings', *South Australian Register*, 16 March 1867, p. 2.

p. 57 'The Swindling Aspects', ibid., 19 July 1867, p. 2.

p. 57 'assessed by a medical committee', ibid., 28 June 1867, p. 4.

p. 57 'the audience had baulked', *South Australian Advertiser*, 2 July 1867, p. 3.

pp. 58–9 'As far away as Victoria', *Hamilton Spectator*, 10 July 1867, p. 3.

p. 59 'He pointed out', *South Australian Advertiser*, 9 July 1867, p. 3.

p. 59 'He turned up at Maughan's lecture', *South Australian Register* 19 July 1867, p. 2.

p. 61 'huge public demand', *South Australian Weekly Chronicle*, 15 June 1867, p. 2.

p. 61 'a committee had been established', *South Australian Register*, 22 July 1867, p. 3.

p. 61 'It met on the evening', ibid., 30 July 1867, p. 2; *South Australian Weekly Chronicle*, 17 August 1867, p. 2.

p. 63 'all ended in smoke', *Geelong Advertiser*, 16 August 1867, p. 2.

p. 63 'Carr advertised his next two', *South Australian Advertiser*, 13 August 1867, p. 1.

p. 63 'the committee promptly reconvened', *South Australian Register*, 20 August 1867, p. 3.

p. 64 'a letter from James Maughan', *South Australian Advertiser*, 22 August 1867, p. 3.

p. 65 'Carr hit back', ibid., 22 August 1867, p. 3.
p. 66 'In a letter to the *Advertiser*', ibid., 2 August 1867, p. 2.
p. 68 'I consider Dr Carr has behaved', *South Australian Register*, 26 August 1867, p.3.
p. 68 'two more letters at Carr's request', *South Australian Register*, 24 August 1867, p. 2.
p. 69 'defended his phrenological skills', ibid., 21 August 1867, p. 2.
p. 69 'declared the winner', *Adelaide Observer*, 11 May 1867, p. 1.
p. 69 'a barrage of criticism', *South Australian Weekly Chronicle*, 6 July 1867, p. 3, and 3 August 1867, p. 2.
p. 70 'I beg, with great respect', *South Australian Weekly Chronicle*, 6 July 1867, p. 5.
p. 70 'anything but an untroubled reception', *Hamilton Spectator*, 24 August 1867, p. 3.
p. 70 'Your correspondent', ibid., 18 September 1867, p. 3.
p. 70 'A Melbourne Correspondent', *South Australian Weekly Chronicle*, 23 November 1867, p. 5.
p. 70 'Carr began his first lecture', *Bendigo Advertiser*, 11 October 1867, p. 2.
p. 70 'In Clare, for example', ibid., 2 October 1867, p. 2.
p. 71 'His father's name', South Australian Births, 1842–1906 Book 55 Page 202. District Adelaide.

IV

p. 71 'passed through Moonta', *South Australian Advertiser*, 21 September 1867, p. 2.
p. 71 'and Castlemaine', *Mount Alexander Mail*, 4 November 1867, p. 2.
p. 71 'In Eaglehawk', *Bendigo Advertiser*, 23 October 1867, p. 2.
p. 71 'popped back down to Melbourne', *Argus*, 4 August 1868, p. 6.
p. 71 'In Heathcote', *McIvor Times and Rodney Advertiser*, 1 November 1867, p. 2.

p. 72 'Next came Beechworth', *Ovens and Murray Advertiser*, 17 December 1867, p. 2.

p. 72 'In the same issue', ibid., p. 3.

p. 72 'After Beechworth came Albury', *Nelson Evening Mail*, 20 March 1868, p. 2.

p. 72 'Yass', *Gundagai Times and Tumit, Adelong and Murrumbidgee District Advertiser*, 15 February 1868, p. 2.

p. 72 'the cheque bounced', *Bendigo Advertiser*, 3 March 1868, p. 3.

p. 73 'Joseph Thompson', NSW *Police Gazette*, 4 March 1868, p. 75.

p. 73 'This wasn't his first arrest', GRG Correspondence Files 5/2 Police Commissioners Office (Attorney General SA) 1868 336 Commissioner 'Arrest of Dr Carr at Wagga Wagga'; 1868 332 Confession of E. T. Osbaldeston.

p. 73 'a series of petty thefts', *South Australian Register*, 19 November 1867, p. 3; *Sydney Morning Herald*, 26 November 1867, p. 2.

p. 77 'Three flags which were missing', *Launceston Examiner*, 17 December 1867, p. 2.

p. 77 'Osbaldeston tried to hang himself', *Maitland Mercury and Hunter River General Advertiser*, 26 November 1867, p. 2.

p. 77 'stealing a horse', *Sydney Morning Herald*, 29 March 1926, p. 11; *National Advocate* (Bathurst), 29 March 1926, p. 2.

p. 78 'he'd lectured on "hydropathy"', *Marlborough Express*, 26 August 1876, p. 5.

p. 78 'he'd served a brief term', *Timaru Herald*, 23 August 1876, p. 3.

p. 78 'breaking out of prison', *The Star* 2 September 1876, p. 2.

p. 78 'believed gone to San Francisco', GRG 5/2 = Correspondence Files Police Commissioner's Office 1876 File 1217 p. 55.

p. 78 'returned to Melbourne then travelled to England', National Register of Archives and Manuscripts, NZ, Osbaldeston, Dr Edwin Turner, Ref # Archive 55.

p. 78 'had repeatedly assaulted', *World*, 6 June 1893, p. 9.
p. 78 'Mrs Frank Lugas', *Malone Farmer*, 19 August 1903, p. 1.
p. 79 'In fact, Louisa Lugas', ibid., 26 August 1903, p. 1.
p. 79 'one newspaper wondering how deep', *Bunyip*, 23 November 1867, p. 2.
p. 79 'South Australia's Governor sent', *Border Watch* (Mount Gambier), 14 December 1867, p. 2.
p. 80 'He was joined there', *Sydney Morning Herald*, 5 September 1868, p. 1.
p. 80 'described in the press', *Empire*, 17 April 1868, p. 2.
p. 80 'as Carr's "buttoner"', ibid., 2 October 1868, p. 3.

Part III: After the Incident

I

p. 81 'she had begun to feel ill', *Sydney Morning Herald*, 15 September 1868, p. 2.
p. 81 'always been very healthy', ibid., 22 September 1868, p. 2.
p. 81 'liable to faints', *Sydney Morning Herald*, 25 September 1867, p. 2.
p. 82 'although Carr later claimed', ibid., 2 October 1868, p. 3.
p. 82 From 'She went straight to Carr' to 'But his cheque for 30 shillings certainly had', ibid., 22 September 1868, p. 2; *Empire*, 22 September 1868, p. 3; ibid., 25 September 1868, p. 2; *Empire*, 25 September 1868, p. 3.
p. 83 'He was forty-two years old', 'Lilias Wallace and Frederick Louis Veniard', *Genealogy*, http://genealogy.northern-skies.net/gray.php?number=36.
p. 83 'in 1853 he married', NSW Marriage V1853179 99/1853.
p. 84 'on the night of the 22nd of March', *Empire* 29 September 1868, p. 3.
p. 85 'he advertised himself', *Bell's Life in Sydney and Sporting Chronicle*, 1 December 1866, p. 1.
p. 85 'yet another on "infantile education"', *Empire*, 13 February 1867, p. 2.

p. 85 'After many years spent knocking around', Sabine, Lois, 'Dr William Bell (1815–71): Experiences of a 19th-century doctor on either side of the Blue Mountains', *Blue Mountains History Journal*, vol. 1, 2010, pp. 22–35.

pp. 86–7 'unpleasantly crowded', *Empire*, 26 March 1868, p. 2.

p. 87 'Hunter Street', Macpherson, Mrs Allan (A Lady), *My Experiences in Australia, Being Recollections of a Visit to the Australian Colonies in 1856-7*, J.F. Hope, London, 1860, pp. 16–65.

p. 87 'birdstuffers' shops', *Empire*, 21 December 1866, p. 3.

p. 87 'Carr's Prince of Wales engagement', *Empire*, 6 May 1868, p. 1.

p. 88 'farewell performance', *Sydney Morning Herald*, 23 May 1868, p. 7.

p. 88 'he was at Newton', ibid.

p. 88 'he was in Woollahra', *Empire*, 17 May 1868, p. 1.

p. 88 'Early application is necessary', ibid., 13 May 1868, p. 1.

p. 89 'Dr Eichler, who later testified', ibid., 29 September 1868, p. 3.

II

p. 90 'Carr was in Bathurst', *Empire*, 16 June 1868, p. 2; *Kiama Independent and Shoalhaven Advertiser*, 2 July 1868, p. 1.

p. 90 'his show in Grenfell', *Lachlan/Grenfell Mining Record and Grenfell Advertiser*, 18 July 1868, p. 1.

p. 91 'a man named Ingram', *South Australian Register*, 14 September 1868, p. 3; *Maitland Mercury and Hunter River General Advertiser*, 27 August 1868, p. 3.

p. 94 'another court case to worry about', *Argus*, 4 August 1868, pp. 4, 6, and 21 August 1868, p. 7.

p. 94 'a recent, scathing review', ibid., 22 November 1867, p. 4.

p. 95 'Carr's new rooms', *Sydney Morning Herald*, 9 October 1868, p. 12; State Record NSW Photo Investigator—Digital ID 725_a019_a019000003.jpg.

p. 95 'shared his premises with Arthur Cubitt', *Grey River Argus* (NZ) 4 July 1868, p. 4; *Sydney Morning Herald*, 14 February 1868, p. 8.
p. 96 'Dalton, at the time', *Empire*, 2 October 1868, p. 3.
p. 98 'a thirty-five-year-old man', Weaver, Rachael, 'The Kinder Tragedy', *Meanjin*, vol. 70, no. 4.
p. 98 'Eichler held out', *A complete report of the examination in the alleged murder case of the late Henry Kinder: with all the correspondence, the diary, and four photographs, by Milligan Brothers*, 84 King Street, 1865, p. 7.
p. 98 'According to Maria', ibid., p. 5.
p. 98 'Bertrand also testified', ibid., p. 5.
p. 99 'Bertrand was then twenty-five years old', ibid., p. 8.
p. 99 'number 7, Wynyard Square', ibid., p. 13.
p. 99 'armed himself with a hatchet', ibid., pp. 15–16.
p. 99 'numerous attempts to poison', ibid., p. 18.
p. 99 'disguised himself as a woman', ibid., p. 17.
p. 99 'He told her that his wife', ibid., pp. 24–6.
p. 100 'said he was a powerful mesmerist', ibid., p. 23.
p. 100 'Robertson had heard Bertrand confess', ibid., p. 36.
p. 100 'she had reported his confession', *Sydney Morning Herald*, 16 February 1866, p. 2.
p. 101 'a defence of mental derangement', *Maitland Mercury and Hunter River General Advertiser*, 7 December 1865, p. 3.
p. 101 'In the course of the investigation', *Sydney Morning Herald*, 9 December 1865, p. 6.
p. 101 'Bertrand himself is an insignificant common-place fellow', *Empire*, 21 December 1865, p. 3.

II

pp. 102–107 *Sydney Morning Herald*, 22 September 1868, p. 2;ibid., 25 September 1868, p. 2; ibid., 2 October 1868, p.3; ibid., 29 September 1868, p. 2.
pp. 102–107 *Empire*, 22 September 1868, p. 3; ibid., 25 September 1868, p. 3; ibid., 2 October 1868, p.3.

Part IV: Animal Magnetism

I

p. 108 'Mesmerism has scarcely advanced', *Queanbeyan Age*, 9 May 1868, p. 4.

p. 109 'A French Royal Commission', *Report of the Experiments on Animal Magnetism made by a Committee of the Medical Section of the French Royal Academy of Sciences Read at the Meetings of the 21st and 28th of June 1831. Translated and Now for the First Time Published with an Historical and Explanatory Introduction and an Appendix by J.C. Colquhoun*, Robert Cadell, Edinburgh, 1833, p. 192.

p. 110 'Professor John Elliotson', Stanbury, P, 'Reflections of Mesmerism in Literature', *Anaesthetic Intensive Care*, vol. 40, supp. 1, 2012, p. 13.

p. 110 'The placid look of his countenance', Todd, Elizabeth, 'Numerous Cases of Surgical Operations without Pain in the Mesmeric State', John Elliotson, London, H. Bailliere, 1843, p. 18.

p. 110 'the Okey sisters', Thornton, E M, *Hypnotism, Hysteria and Epilepsy: An Historical Synthesis*, Butterworth-Heinemann, London, 2016, pp. 84–92.

p. 111 'Scottish surgeon James Braid', Crabtree, Adam, *Animal Magnetism, Early Hypnotism, and Psychical Research 1766–1925, An Annotated Bibliography*, Kraus International, White Plains, New York, 1988, p. 158.

p. 111 'Electro-biology, Electro-psychology', Gregory, William, MD FRSE, *Letters to a Candid Inquirer on Animal Magnetism*, Taylor, Walton & Maberley, London, 1851, p. 203.

p. 112 'whiff of fraudulence', Leighton, Mary Elizabeth, 'Under the Influence: Crime and Hypnotic Fiction in the Fin de Siecle', in *Victorian Literary Mesmerism*, ed. Martin Willis and Catherine Wynne, Rodopi, Amsterdam, 2006, p. 207.

p. 113 'Joseph P F Deleuze', Deleuze, J P F, *Animal Magnetism*, Fowler & Wells Co. Publishing, New York, 1879 (1843), pp. 143, 215.

p. 113 'Caroline Harper Dexter', Stanbury, 'Reflections of Mesmerism in Literature', p. 15; Donnelly, Tiffany, 'Mesmerism, Clairvoyance and Literary Culture in Mid-Century Australia', in *Victorian Literary Mesmerism*, ed. Martin Willis and Catherine Wynne, Rodopi, Amsterdam, 2006, p. 113.

p. 113 'very lively affection' Deleuze, *Animal Magnetism*, p. 143.

p. 113 'He claimed that the affection', Sandby, George, *Mesmerism and Its Opponents*, Longman Brown Green, London, 1844, pp. 192–3.

p. 114 'the morality of mesmerism', Leighton, 'Under the Influence', p. 208.

p. 114 'the *Gazette Médicale de Paris* reported', Modi, Rai Bahadur Jaising P, *A Textbook of Medical Jurisprudence and Toxicology*, Elsevier, Amsterdam, 2013, p. 347.

p. 114 'a woman named Madeleine Grille', Leighton, 'Under the Influence' in 'Victorian Literary Mesmerism', p. 203.

p. 114 'So far, hypnotism', Binet, Alfred, and Charles Féré, Animal Magnetism, D. Appleton, New York, 1888, pp. 362–3.

p. 115 'Eichler gave his views', *Empire*, 29 September 1868, p. 3.

p. 116 'most rare cases of extreme sensibility', Sandby, *Mesmerism*, pp. 192–3.

p. 117 'They may be taken by surprise', Binet and Féré, *Animal Magnetism*, p. 103.

II

p. 118 'Kerr had brought an action against him', *West Coast Times*, 8 January 1869, p. 2.

p. 118 'the qualities of a smart check-taker', *Age* 19 January 1869, p. 2.

p. 120 'I was mesmerised at Ross', *Evening Post*, 4 June 1869, p. 2.

p. 126 'Five months later he was in court again', *West Coast Times*, 24 June 1869, p. 2.

p. 127 'he wrote to the local paper about it', ibid., 5 January 1869, p. 2.

p. 127 'suffering from a disease of the hip', *Wellington Independent*, 5 June 1869, p. 3.

p. 127 'he was working for the mesmerist in Bendigo', *Bendigo Advertiser*, 16 October 1867, p. 2.

p. 129 'as Melbourne's *Age* pointed out', *Age*, 19 January 1869, p. 2.

III

p. 130 'The *Geelong Advertiser* broke the story', *Argus*, 17 May 1870, p. 6.

p. 130 'a newspaper in Nelson', *Nelson Evening Mail*, 23 April 1869, p. 2.

p. 131 'Years earlier, in Bendigo', *Bendigo Advertiser*, 9 January 1909, p. 3.

p. 132 'The general public are apt', *Wellington Independent*, 5 June 1869, p. 3.

p. 132 'one Edward Wrixton', *The Daily Southern Cross*, 2 September 1870, p. 2.

p. 132 'James Cowley Morgan Fisher', Metcalf, William J, and Guy Featherstone, 'A Messiah for the West: J.C.M. Fisher and the Church of the Firstborn in Western Australia', *Journal of Australian Colonial History*, vol. 8, 2007, pp. 118–19.

p. 133 'Fisher, however, wasn't the only one', *Argus*, 15 July 1871, p. 1.

p. 133 'According to Wilson', *Southern Argus* (SA), 14 July 1871, p. 4.

p. 134 'Later, a theory arose', *Queanbeyan Age*, 27 July 1871, p. 4.

p. 134 'Many people believed that Fisher deprived', *Launceston Examiner*, 15 July 1871, p. 3.

p. 135 'the magistrate declared', *Queanbeyan Age*, 27 July 1871, p. 4.

p. 135 'a certain "Professor Nash"', *West Coast Times*, 11 September 1872, p. 2.

pp. 136–7 'Professor Nash, who is about as much a professor', *Age*, 2 January 1868, p. 4.

Part V: Marriage Problems

I

p. 138 'The first witness called', *Empire*, 29 September 1868, p. 3; *Sydney Morning Herald*, 29 September 1868, p. 2.

p. 142 'George James Lees was born', *Australian Royalty: A Family Tree of Colonial Australians, Their Forbears and Descendants*, australianroyalty.net.au; NSW Births Deaths and Marriages.

p. 142 'arrested for forgery', NSW *Police Gazette*, 26 June 1867, p. 204.

p. 142 'he was arrested again', ibid., 16 October 1867 p. 365; *Sydney Morning Herald*, 28 June 1867, p. 5.

p. 142 'Lees was released', NSW *Police Gazette*, 1 April 1868, p. 101.

p. 142 'Charlotte had been born', *geni.com/people/Charlotte/6000000012559736680.*

p. 143 'Elizabeth Greenfield's funeral notice', *Sydney Morning Herald*, 5 January 1897, p. 8.

p. 143 'Botany Road', Jevons, William Stanley, 'Remarks upon the social map of Sydney, 1858', B864, Mitchell Library manuscript, pp. 26–8.

p. 143 'Margaret Thomas, who lived near Gray', 'Mary Ann Silvey', *The Newcastle Industrial School for Girls*, http://nis.wikidot.com/silvey.

p. 143 'Mary had already been sent', *Sydney Morning Herald*, 15 January 1869, p. 2.

p. 144 'her husband's watch and chain were missing', ibid., 11 June 1870, p. 4; *Evening News*, 10 January 1870, p. 2.

p. 148 'five "in memoriams"', *Sydney Morning Herald*, 17 July 1908, p. 6.

II

p. 149 'Jane Ann Ireland', New South Wales Marriage Certificate 916/1868; Australian Royalty, *australianroyalty.net.au/individual.php?pid=12965&ged=purnellmccord.ged.*

p. 149 'John Ireland', *Australian Royalty*, australianroyalty.net.au/individual.php?pid=129165&ged=purnellmccord.ged.

p. 149 'Dr David Ramsey', McMartin, Arthur 'Ramsay, David (1794–1860), *Australian Dictionary of Biography*, National Centre of Biography, Australian National University, http://adb.anu.edu.au/biography/ramsay-david-2571/text3513.

p. 149 'This mansion is now Yasmar', NSW Department of Environment and Heritage, Heritage Office, Database 5045179, file number: 10/4693; S90/05565.

p. 149 'one of the finest places', *Sydney Gazette*, 7 December 1816, p. 1.

p. 150 'it was leased to John Ireland', Coupe, Sheena, and Robert Coupe, *Speed the Plough*, Council of the Municipality of Ashfield, Sydney, 1988 pp. 39–41.

p. 150 'they had five children', Australian Royalty, *australianroyalty.net.au/individual.php?pid=12965&ged=purnellmccord.ged.*

p. 152 'a mail contract', Dunlop, Eric, *Harvest of the Years: The Story of Burwood*, Council of the Municipality of Burwood, Sydney, 1974, pp. 19–20.

p. 152 'except that of bullock drivers', ibid., p. 21.

p. 154 'William took over this establishment', ibid., pp. 19-20.

p. 153 'opened another inn directly opposite', *Sydney Morning Herald*, 17 April 1852, p. 2.

p. 153 'the "Woodman's Purse"', *Bell's Life in Sydney and Sporting Review*, 15 November 1856, p. 4.

p. 153 'forty-eight square miles of land', research by Bev Giveen, descendent of John Ireland through his son William.

p. 154 'Mrs Carr had given birth', *West Coast Times*, 15 December 1868, p. 2.

p. 155 'her mother's death certificate', New South Wales Death Certificate 34/1891.

p. 155 'her daughter Monica's marriage', New South Wales Marriage Certificate 2974/1892.

p. 156 'William took out a coaching licence', *Sydney Morning Herald*, 26 October 1870, p. 2; *Evening News*, 26 October 1870, p. 3.

p. 156 'her name was published', *West Coast Times*, 24 November 1868, p. 2.

p. 156 'small parcel of nuggets', *Lake Wakatip Mail*, 17 May 1871, p. 3.

p. 156 'Mrs Carr had suffered a severe injury', *Waikato Times*, 18 December 1875, p. 2.

p. 156 'Carr had his own views', *Southland Times*, 15 July 1874, p. 2.

p. 157 'In 1882 a local paper related', *Maitland Mercury and Hunter River General Advertiser*, 14 October 1882, p. 3.

p. 157 'A meeting was organised', *Newcastle Morning Herald and Miners' Advocate*, 4 August 1886, p. 7.

p. 159 'money to a ten-year-old beggar', *Star* (NZ), 30 March 1874, p. 2.

pp. 159–60 'a young boy was thrown from a horse', *Lake Wakatip Mail*, 19 April 1871, p. 2.

p. 160 'In 1876, he remitted a telegraph money order', *Evening Post*, 21 July 1876, p. 2.

p. 160 'Some two weeks later, he published a letter', *Wanganui Herald*,17 August 1876, p. 2.

p. 160 'one local observer, who accused', *Wanganui Chronicle*, 19 August 1876, p. 2.

p. 160 'he sent a telegram', ibid., 25 August 1876, p. 2.

p. 161 'came to the aid of a policeman', *Evening Post*, 24 April 1876, p. 2.

p. 161 'personally ejected a drunken audience member', *Grey River Argus*, 16 July 1875, p. 2.

p. 161 'Carr entered a burning building', *Hawke's Bay Times*, 24 January 1870, p. 2.

p. 161 'did exactly the same thing', *Australian Town and Country Journal*, 10 January 1880, p. 39.

p. 161 '*Agnes Irving* ran aground', *Argus*, 30 December 1879, p. 5.

p. 162 'had been racing against another steamer', *Clarence and Richmond Examiner and New England Advertiser* (Grafton), 10 January 1880, p. 3.

Part VI: Organ of Destructiveness

I

p. 165 'principally phrenological', Southland Times, 20 April 1877, p. 3.

p. 166 'When lecturing on the subject', *Maitland Mercury and Hunter River Advertiser*, 22 May 1883, p. 6.

p. 166 'Every degree and character of crime', Phillips, Peter J, *Kill or Cure: Lotions, Potions, Characters and Quacks of Early Australia*, Rigby, Adelaide, 1978, pp. 141–2.

p. 167 'Every degree and character', Peter J Phillips, 'Kill or Cure – Lotions, Potions, Characters and Quacks of Early Australia', Rigby, 1978, pp. 141–2.

p. 167 'A bit of an expert', Hamilton Roginski, Alexandra, *The Hanged Man and the Body Thief: Finding Lives in a Museum Mystery*, Monash University Publishing, Melbourne, 2015.

p. 167 'forced to borrow his skulls', *Hawkes Bay Herald*, 21 January 1870, p. 3.

p. 167 'skulls and casts', *Mount Ida Chronicle*, 1 March 1877, p. 2; *Oamaru Mail*, 9 February 1877, p. 3.

p. 167 'he lost his box of skulls', *Oamaru Mail*, 5 June 1877, p. 3.

p. 167 'marked and sometimes violent manifestation', Sandby, George, *Mesmerism and Its Opponents*, Longman Brown Green, London, 1844, p. 228.

p. 168 'Is the science of Phrenology', Neal, George, *New Zealand Herald*, 3 November 1869, p. 5.

p. 168 'We would remind Mr Hamilton', *Brisbane Courier*, 17 January 1862, p. 4.

p. 169 'Thomas Buddle', Buddle, Thomas, papers relating to Phrenology, 1875, Auckland War Memorial Museum Library MS–43.

p. 169 'he was advertising freshly printed', *The Press*, 11 November 1874, p. 4.

p. 171 'Early in 1876, a journalist', *Wairarapa Standard*, 1 July 1876, p. 2; *Grey River Argus*, 21 November 1876, p. 2.

p. 171 'Hume had publicly accused Carr', *Age*, 24 July 1869, p. 2.

p. 172 'Some twenty inhabitants of Alexandra', *Bruce Herald*, 19 October 1870, p. 5.

p. 172 'To the editor of the *Standard*', *Evening Post*, 29 June 1876, p. 2.

p. 173 'a rash and presuming young man', *Bendigo Advertiser*, 16 October 1867, p. 2.

p. 173 'That became obvious to William McLean', *Evening Post*, 16 October 1871, p. 2; *Wellington Independent*, 17 October 1871, p. 2.

II

p. 176 'Is this the same Dr. Carr', *Australian Medical Journal*, November 1871, p. 371.

p. 176 'a man called King', *Empire*, 21 December 1870, p. 3; *Southland Times*, 22 November 1870, p. 2.

p. 176 'A man named Francis Porter', *Queensland Times, Ipswich Herald and General Advertiser*, 18 August 1877, p. 5.

p. 178 'would cheat all the week', *Clutha Leader*, 9 February 1883, p. 5.

p. 178 'obtuse, very obtuse', *Wellington Independent*, 8 June 1869, p. 2.

p. 178 'indolent brain', *Wairarapa Standard*, 20 July 1875, p. 2.

p. 178 'not to be trusted', *Colonist* (NZ), 13 July 1876, p. 3.

p. 178 'a mere pimple', *McIvor Times and Rodney Advertiser*, 1 November 1867, p. 2.

p. 178 'Dr Carr, in trying to prove', *Evening Star*, 30 June 1877, p. 2.

p. 179 'revelled too much', *Hawke's Bay Herald*, 4 February 1870, p. 2.

p. 179 'When a phrenologist', *Maitland Mercury and Hunter River General Advertiser*, 30 October 1883, p. .

p. 179 'under the pseudonym "Stella"', *Thames Star*, 10 August 1875, p. 2.

p. 179 '"Vera" was even less complimentary', *Mount Ida Chronicle*, 6 November 1875, p. 2.

p. 180 'The doctor said that Mr Stevens', *Ovens and Murray Advertiser*, 14 December 1867, p. 2.

p. 180 'the audience fairly screamed', *Southland Times*, 7 October 1870, p. 2.

p. 181 'Then he sat down and let a local', *Wellington Independent*, 16 October 1871, p. 2.

p. 181 'Carr wrote to *Bell's Life*', *Leader* (Melbourne), 6 June 1868, p. 10.

p. 182 'presented with a disguised pumpkin', *Rockhampton Bulletin*, 10 September 1877, p. 2.

p. 182 'a spectator writing twenty-five years later', *Evening News*, 21 June 1899, p. 2.

III

p. 183 'In her book', Winter, Alison, *Mesmerized: The Power of Mind in Victorian Britain*, University of Chicago Press, Chicago, Illinois, 2000, pp. 126–8.

p. 183 'An American electro-biologist', *Argus*, 7 June 1864, p. 7.

p. 183 'the electro-biologist Madame Sibley', Catherine Bishop, *Minding Her Own Business: Colonial Businesswomen in Sydney,* NewSouth Publishing, Sydney, 2015; *North Otago Times*, 4 October 1870, p. 3.

p. 184 'Sometimes his subjects would chase him', *Evening Star*, 17 July 1872, p. 4.

p. 184 'Sometimes he would cast one', *Auckland Star*, 11 July 1872, p. 2.

p. 184 'Sometimes a subject who had previously declared', *Wairarapa Standard*, 11 April 1876, p. 2.

p. 184 'a reluctant subject of this kind', *Auckland Star*, 8 July 1872, p. 3.

p. 184 'For instance, we may mention', *The Queenslander* (Brisbane), 4 August 1877, p. 13.

p. 185 'Carr was reported to have told', *Auckland Star*, 8 July 1872, p. 3.

p. 185 'This was certainly true', *West Coast Times*, 7 December 1868, p. 2.

p. 185 'where a cry of "Snake!"', *Southern Argus*, 3 August 1867, p. 3.

p. 185 'Some of Carr's subjects rode chairs', *Hawke's Bay Times*, 27 January 1870, p. 2.

p. 185 'Some of them *behaved* like horses', *Nelson Examiner and New Zealand Chronicle*, 10 April 1869, p. 6.

p. 185 'compelled them to climb the scenery', *Evening Post*, 26 June 1869, p. 2.

p. 185 'During a particularly frantic "police" chase', *Nelson Examiner and New Zealand Chronicle*, 18 December 1872, p. 2; *Nelson Evening Mail*, 17 December 1872, p. 2.

p. 186 'knocking his legs about', *Queenslander*, 4 August 1877, p. 13.

p. 186 'one even used an awl', *Southern Argus*, 3 August 1867, p. 3.

p. 186 'people were put out', *Otago Daily Times*, 16 June 1870, p. 2; *Star*, 9 January 1874, p. 3; *Grey River Argus*, 16 July 1875, p. 2.

p. 186 'Audiences would often roar', *Star*, 10 November 1876, p. 2.

p. 186 'Carr's fake funerals', *Mercury*, 24 May 1879, p. 2.

p. 186–7 'Dr. Carr . . . was never, even in his best days', *Timaru Herald*, 29 June 1873, p. 2, and 18 May 1891, p. 3.

p. 187 'The Bob Sawyers', *Empire*, 17 April 1868, p. 2.

p. 187 'medical man', *Waikato Times*, 2 November 1872, p. 2.

p. 187 'he was reported to have amputated', *Waikato Times*, 19 October 1872, p. 2.

p. 187 'We have been requested to state', *New Zealand Herald*, 24 November 1869, p. 6.

p. 187 'the same young woman', *Daily Southern Cross*, 10 November 1869, p. 5.

p. 187 'on a youth named Sheather', *Newcastle Morning Herald and Miners' Advocate*, 7 July 1885, p. 6.

p. 188 'set a boy's broken limb', *Waikato Times*, 18 December 1875, p. 2.

p. 188 'tending to several of the victims', *Tuapeka Times*, 19 May 1875, p. 5.

p. 188 'to have removed a tumour', *Queanbeyan Age*, 29 February 1868, p. 3.

p. 188 'but there was no blood', *Wairarapa Standard*, 11 April 1876, p. 2.

p. 189 'Dr Carr may perform valuable surgical operations', *Wairarapa Standard*, 12 August 1869, p. 2.

p. 189 'Sherwood was local watchmaker', *Cyclopedia of New Zealand*, vol. 6, *Taranaki, Hawke's Bay and Wellington Provincial Districts*, Cyclopedia Company, Wellington, 1897, p. 256.

p. 191 'Bloodless surgeon', *Register* (Adelaide), 8 December 1909, p. 5.

p. 192 'He had to defend himself', *Daily Southern Cross*, 4 November 1869, p. 3.

p. 192 'The crippled "Cooper"', *Wellington Independent*, 5 June 1869, p. 3.

p. 192 'When a mesmerist called Bruce', *Mount Ida Chronicle*, 31 July 1875, p. 3.

p. 193 'wicked hoax', *New Zealand Herald*, 29 June 1874, p. 2.

p. 193 'The public are cautioned', *North Otago Times*, 9 September 1870, p. 3.

p. 193 'This was a few months', *Otago Daily Times*, 26 May 1870, p. 3.

p. 193 'In Queanbeyan, NSW', *Queanbeyan Age*, 8 January 1879, p. 2.

Part VII: The Verdict

I

p. 195 'Robert Lucas was the first witness', *Empire*, 2 October 1868, p. 3; *Sydney Morning Herald*, 2 October 1868, p. 3.

p. 198 'Benjamin, who had become Henry's business partner', *New South Wales Government Gazette*, 1862, p. 749.

p. 198 'committee of inspection', *Evening News*, 15 April 1880, p. 2.

pp. 198–9 'Henry dissolved his partnership', *New South Wales Government Gazette*, 25 June 1881, p. 498.

p. 199 'Ellen Batts', *Sydney Morning Herald*, 14 October 1889, p. 4; *Evening News*, 23 October 1889, p. 6.

p. 199 'her mother was finally married off', ibid., 17 October 1889, p. 1.

p. 199 'Benjamin died of a narcotic overdose', ibid., 21 October 1889, p. 3.

p. 201 'On his father's death', ibid., 21 May 1862, p. 5.

p. 201 'which was the only wharf', ibid., 3 August 1868, p. 4.

p. 201 'commodious and excellent', *Empire*, 2 January 1866, p. 5.

p. 201 'A typical weekend offering', *Sydney Mail*, 29 December 1860, p. 4.

p. 201 'zebras, harnessed to a "park phaeton"', *Golden Age* (Queanbeyan), 23 March 1861, p. 3.

p. 201 'The two dead cubs', *Sydney Morning Herald*, 13 February 1862, p. 8.

p. 201 'Madame Sohier's waxwork collection', *Bell's Life in Sydney*, 22 May 1869, p. 3.

p. 201 'his St Andrew's Day festivities', *Sydney Morning Herald*, 30 November 1865, p. 8.

p. 201 'a very handsomely deformed dog', *Bell's Life in Sydney*, 8 March 1862, p. 2.

p. 202 'Carr was living in Watsons Bay', *Leader*, 6 June 1868, p. 10.

II

p. 209 'When Carr finally did appear in the dock again', *Empire*, 5 October 1868, p. 3.

p. 209 'An advertisement for his next show', *Empire*, 5 October 1868, p. 1.

p. 209 'he was unable to find a venue', *Sydney Morning Herald*, 8 October 1868, p. 8.

p. 209 'Dr Carr has advertised', *Illawarra Mercury*, 9 October 1868, p. 2.

p. 209 'William Maddison wrote a letter', *Empire*, 12 October 1868, p. 3.

p. 210 'MacLean advertised that', *Newcastle Chronicle*, 15 October 1868, p. 1.

p. 210 'at Newcastle's Great Northern Hotel', ibid., 15 October 1868, p. 1.

p. 210 'by far the cleverest man', ibid., 17 October 1868, p. 3.

p. 210 'In West Maitland he flopped', ibid., 24 October 1868, p. 3; *Maitland Mercury and Hunter River General Advertiser*, 29 October 1868, p. 3.

p. 211 'He left Singleton', *Newcastle Chronicle*, 27 October 1868, p. 2; *Empire*, 24 October 1868, p. 4.

p. 211 'His final performance', *Maitland Mercury and Hunter River General Advertiser*, 31 October 1868, p. 1.

p. 211 'The general public, since the now notorious exposure', *Bendigo Advertiser*, 7 October 1868, p. 2.

p. 211 'condemned him for being "bumptious"', *Wagga Wagga Advertiser and Riverine Reporter*, 14 November 1868, p. 2.

p. 211 'a public dispute about crime prevention', *Sydney Morning Herald*, 9 July 1878, p. 5, and 10 July 1878, p. 5.

p. 212 'the charge against Carr', *Bendigo Advertiser*, 7 November 1868, p. 2.

III

p. 213 'Manning had thrown himself at O'Farrell', *Age*, 23 March 1868, p. 4.

p. 213 'A Queen's Counsel and wealthy landowner', Rutledge, Martha, 'Manning, Sir William Montagu (1811–1895'), *Australian Dictionary of Biography*, National Centre of Biography, Australian National University, http://adb.anu.edu.au/biography/manning-sir-william-montagu-4150/text6657.

p. 213 'William Charles Windeyer had once chaired', *Sydney Morning Herald*, 20 April 1868, p. 5; *Empire*, 20 April 1868, p. 3.

p. 213 'he was a well-known barrister' 'Windeyer, Sir William Charles (1834-1897)', *Australian Dictionary of Biography*, National Centre of Biography, Australian National University, http://adb.anu.edu.au/biography/windeyer-sir-william-charles-1062/text8145.

p. 214 'In the New South Wales parliament', *Maitland Mercury and Hunter River General Advertiser*, 25 April 1868, p. 2.

p. 214 'A NSW Attorney-General had the power', *Empire*, 3 November 1868, p. 2.

p. 214 'According to one barrister', ibid., 9 August 1873, p. 4.

p. 214 'Holt had been committed for trial', *Sydney Morning Herald*, 1 November 1865, p. 2.

p. 215 'David Charles Frederick Scott', Grey, Nancy, 'Scott, Helenus (1802–1879), *Australian Dictionary of Biography*, National Centre of Biography, Australian National University, http://adb.anu.edu.au/biography/scott-helenus-2851/text3673.

p. 215 'a little too amiable for the job', 'Minutes of Evidence Taken Before the Select Committee on the Central Police Office', 25 July 1862, in *Votes and Proceedings of the Legislative Assembly During the Session of 1862, with the Various Documents connected Therewith*, vol. 2, 1862, p. 63.

p. 215 'Rowan Ronald, a justice of the peace', ibid., p. 60.

p. 215 'a lawyer might make a better magistrate', ibid., p. 106.

p. 215 'I think he may have read himself', ibid., p. 65.

p. 216 'One of the Magistrates', ibid., p. 107.

p. 216 'a woman named Louisa Pilkington', *Sydney Morning Herald*, 23 August 1869, p. 2; *Empire*, 3 January 1868, p. 4, and 19 August 1869, p. 3.

p. 216 'The same thing happened to George Bell', *Sydney Mail*, 28 August 1869, p. 3.

p. 216 'Charles Fawcett, who was charged', *Australian Town and Country Journal*, 2 April 1870, p. 8.

p. 217 'Manning's daughter Emily had become engaged', *A Grand Obsession: The D.S. Mitchell Story*, Paul Brunton and Elizabeth Ellis, State Library of NSW, June 2007 p. 6.

p. 217 'In her article on the British writer', *Sydney Morning Herald*, 16 February 1878, p. 3.

p. 217 'In her poem "The Balance of Pain"', *Sydney Mail and NSW Advertiser*, 6 May 1876, p. 602.

p. 218 'As one columnist said', *Tasmanian Morning Herald*, 16 December 1865, p. 2.

p. 218 'relatives of the late George Lamont', *Burrowa News*, 28 October 1881, p. 4.

p. 219 'In Glen Innes, six years before', *Glen Innes Examiner and General Advertiser*, 4 August 1875, p. 2.

p. 219 'a Queenslander named John White', *Maryborough Chronicle Wide Bay and Burnett Advertiser*, 30 June 1877, p. 2.

p. 219 'the same thing happened to William Grant', *Bendigo Advertiser*, 12 February 1868, p. 3.

p. 219 'discharged a prisoner named George Hoops', *Western Star and Roma Advertiser*, 17 April 1875, p. 3.

p. 219 'Eliza died', *http://genealogy.northern-skies.net/gray.php?numbers306*.

p. 220 'Dr Carr, electro-biologist, occasional local preacher', *Gundagai Times and Tumut, Adelong and Murrumbidgee District Advertiser*, 28 November 1868, p. 2.

p. 220 'Dr Carr, his "lady", his Mesmeric Fluid, etc.,', *Wagga Wagga Advertiser and Riveine Register*, 21 November 1868, p. 2.

Part VIII: 'Triumphant Carr'

I

p. 222 'Kerr vs Carr', *West Coast Times*, 18 January 1869, p. 2.

p. 222 'Carr declared himself bankrupt', *Empire*, 13 April 1869, p. 3.

p. 222 'the reviewer took him to task', *Nelson Evening Mail*, 23 April 1869, p. 2 .

p. 222 'humbug people', *Wellington Independent*, 19 August 1869, p. 2.

p. 222 'The first was no more than a claim', *Nelson Evening Mail*, 22 September 1869, p. 2.

p. 222 'A man called John Anderson', *Wanganui Herald*, 21 September 1869, p. 2; *Wairarapa Standard*, 6 October 1869, p. 2.

p. 223 'A seton was a very traditional', Museum of Health Care at Kingston, artefact.museumofhealthcare.ca/?p=574.

p. 224 'his houses were described as "so-so"', *New Zealand Herald*, 3 November 1869, p. 5; *Daily Southern Cross*, 10 November 1869, p. 5.

p. 224 'the unfavourable notices he'd received', *Daily Southern Cross*, 4 November 1869, p. 3.

p. 224 'If Dr. Carr thinks', *New Zealand Herald*, 5 November 1869, p. 3.

p. 224 'accused of sending someone mad', *New Zealand Herald*, 1 December 1869, p. 4; *Westport Times*, 1 December 1869, p. 2; *Argus*, 14 January 1870, p. 5; *Evening Post*, 11 April 1870, p. 2; *The Press*, 19 April 1870, p. 3.

p. 225 'Carr had gone bankrupt again', *Evening Post*, 12 January 1870, p. 2.

p. 225 'It was one of the most marvellous sights', *Hawke's Bay Herald*, 21 January 1870, p. 3.

p. 226 'The press at Timaru', *Timaru Herald*, 21 May 1870, p. 2.

p. 226 'In Dunedin he faced court again', *Evening Star*, 13 June 1870, p. 2.

p. 226 'In Tuapeka his visit', *Tuapeka Times*, 11 August 1870, p. 7.

p. 226 'Then he had to skip town', *Wellington Independent*, 11 August 1870, p. 4.

p. 226 'He once attended a meeting', *Otago Daily Times*, 22 June 1870, p. 2.

p. 226 'Having lectured on his favourite subject', ibid., 20 June 1870, p. 2.

p. 227 'he began to advertise door prizes', *Mount Ida Chronicle*, 7 July 1871, p. 4; *Otago Daily Times*, 24 June 1871, p. 3.

p. 227 'Is the professor who has just visited us', *North Otago Times*, 21 July 1871, p. 2.

p. 227 'he netted no more than £15', *Otago Witness*, 29 July 1871, p. 9.

p. 227 'criticising the phrenological development of various politicians', *Otago Daily Times*, 17 June 1871, p. 2; *Wellington Independent*, 16 October 1871, p. 2.

p. 228 'In Taranaki he pulled big crowds', *Taranaki Herald*, 7 February 1872, p. 2.

p. 228 'his audiences were far smaller', *Wanganui Herald*, 5 January 1872, p. 2.

p. 230 'Not long afterwards', *Auckland Star*, 27 July 1872, p. 2.

p. 228 'it was reported that he had been given a private exhibition', ibid., 15 June 1872, p. 2.

p. 229 'wasn't employed as an anaesthetic', Eger, Edmond I, Lawrence J. Saidman and Rod N. Westhorpe (eds), *The Wondrous Story of Anaesthesia*, New York, Springer, 2013, pp. 307, 308.

p. 229 'Carr was "besieged"', *Auckland Star*, 8 July 1872, p. 3.

p. 229 'The nomenclature would be more perfect', *Daily Southern Cross*, 4 July 1872, p. 3.

p. 229 'Carr's subjects would often chase', *Evening Star*, 17 July 1872, p. 4; *New Zealand Herald*, 9 November 1875, p. 2.

p. 229 'On 2 November', *Waikato Times*, 2 November 1872, p. 2.

p. 229 'But within weeks he was auctioning', *Taranaki Herald*, 30 November 1872, p. 2.

p. 229 'on 7 December he arrived', *Nelson Evening Mail*, 7 December 1872, p. 2.

p. 229 'He had already joined the Independent Order', *Wellington Independent*, 22 April 1873, p. 2.

p. 230 'He is now in Hokitika', *Taranaki Herald*, 18 June 1873, p. 2.

p. 230 'Returning to his roots', *Westport Times*, 7 November 1873, p. 2, and 17 October 1873, p. 2; *Otago Daily Times*, 16 October 1873, p. 5; *Southland Times*, 7 November 1873, p. 2.

p. 230 'It does "rile" me,' *Bruce Herald*, 20 February 1877, p. 5.

p. 230 'he was heard to say that he preferred', *Southland Times*, 14 May 1877, p. 2.

p. 230 'In early 1874 Carr joined another', *The Press*, 10 January 1874, p. 2.

p. 230 'filling halls again', *Star*, 2 January 1874, p. 2, and 7 January 1874, p. 2; *The Press*, 6 April 1874, p. 2.

p. 230 'In Canterbury his shows were so popular', *Star*, 9 January 1874, p. 2.

II

p. 231 'received a very complimentary review', *Evening Star*, 17 June 1874, p. 2.

p. 231 'The crowd laughs heartily', ibid., 20 June 1874, p. 3.

p. 231 'before the Resident Magistrate's Court', ibid., 25 June 1874, p. 2; *Otago Daily Times*, 26 June 1874, p. 3.

p. 233 'The Magistrate seemed spellbound', *Cromwell Argus*, 30 June 1874, p. 6.

p. 234 'What else can you expect', *Evening Star*, 26 June 1874, p. 2.

p. 234 'he went on to condemn', *Otago Daily Times*, 24 June 1874, p. 2.

p. 234 'A few days after that', *Evening Star*, 27 July 1874, p. 2.

p. 234 'At Invercargill he complained', *Thames Star*, 29 July 1874, p. 2.

p. 234 'only partially successful', *Tuapeka Times*, 26 September 1874, p. 2.

p. 234 'Fowler stole two diamond studs', *Otago Daily Times*, 21 December 1874, p. 3; *Evening Star*, 19 December 1874, p. 2, and 12 December 1874, p. 2.

p. 234 'the most successful season', *Auckland Star*, 6 September 1875, p. 3.

p. 234 'composed entirely of men', *Bay of Plenty Times*, 13 October 1875, p. 2.

p. 234 'what on earth "soul-splitting" was', *Auckland Star*, 30 October 1875, p. 2.

p. 234 'refused to print it', *Otago Witness*, 11 September 1875, p. 13.

p. 235 'I paid him two pounds', *Wairarapa Standard*, 13 July 1876, p. 2.

p. 235 'Even when he had full houses', *Colonist*, 13 July 1876, p. 3.

p. 235 'adoring sketch of the premier', *Timaru Herald*, 11 March 1876, p. 7.

p. 235 'hanging around Parliament House', *Evening Post*, 21 September 1876, p. 2.

p. 235 'When we remember what Burke endured', *Taranaki Herald*, 24 June 1876, p. 2.

p. 236 'In January 1877, an action', *Akaroa Mail and Banks Peninsula Advertiser*, 19 January 1877, p. 2; *The Press*, 19 January 1877, p. 3.

p. 236 'from Kyeburn Diggings to Hill's Creek to Tinker's Gully', *North Otago Times*, 10 February 1877, p. 3; *Mount Ida Chronicle*, 1 March 1877, p. 2.

p. 236 'The Doctor found fault on Sunday', *Lake County Press*, 29 March 1877, p. 2.

p. 236 'According to Carr', *Otago Daily Times*, 14 April 1877, p. 5.

p. 237 'Thomas Walker was born', Smith, F B, 'Walker, Thomas (1858–1932)', *Australian Dictionary of Biography*, National Centre of Biography, Australian National University, http://adb.anu.edu.au/biography/walker-thomas-4789/text7975.

p. 239 'Spiritualism defined and defended', *New Zealand Herald*, 10 May 1877, p. 4.

p. 239 'I am prepared to show', *Otago Daily Times*, 12 June 1877, p. 3.

p. 239 'described as very rowdy', *Oamaru Mail*, 14 June 1877, p. 2.

p. 239 'Surely this is a case of the pot', *Wanganui Chronicle*, 15 June 1877, p. 2; *Thames Star*, 16 June 1877, p. 3.

p. 240 'he published an enormous screed', *Otago Daily Times*, 23 June 1877, p. 1.

p. 241 'What's more, they had been sorely embarrassed', ibid., 31 May 1877, p. 1.

p. 241 'illusionist Professor Hennikie', *Auckland Star*, 14 June 1877, p. 2.

p. 241 'In July he left for Sydney', *Thames Advertiser*, 4 July 1877, p. 3.

p. 241 'For years he has traversed', *Manawatu Times*, 30 June 1877, p. 2.

III

p. 242 'The success of Dr Carr last evening', *Brisbane Courier*, 3 August 1877, p. 1.

p. 242 'The earliest reviews', *Queenslander*, 4 August 1877, p. 13.

p. 242 'By the end of August', *Sydney Mail*, 25 August 1877, p. 6.

p. 242 'Charters Towers and Rockhampton', *Northern Miner*, 3 October 1878, p. 3; *Rockhampton Bulletin*, 10 December 1877, p. 2.

p. 242 'then Gympie', *Gympie Times and Mary River Mining Gazette*, 19 January 1878, p. 3.

p. 242 'Grafton, Wollongong and Kiama', *Clarence and Richmond Examiner*, 23 March 1878, p. 2; *Illawarra Mercury*, 19 July 1878, p. 2; *Kiama Independent and Shoalhaven Advertiser*, 30 July 1878, p. 2.

p. 242 'In Araluen the local paper', *Freeman's Journal*, 5 October 1878, p. 9.

p. 243 'a drop of good beer', *Wagga Wagga Advertiser*, 26 June 1878, p. 3.

p. 243 'the impecuniosity of the district', *Queanbeyan Age*, 18 December 1878, p. 2.

p. 243 'in nearby Bungendore', ibid., 22 January 1879, p. 3.

p. 243 'meagre attendance', *Cootamundra Herald*, 15 February 1879, p. 2.

p. 243 'In Cootamundra his surgical skills', *ibid.*, 15 February 1879, p. 2.

p. 243 'the most popular surgeon of Goulburn', *Queanbeyan Age*, 15 October 1879, p. 3.

p. 243 'had been "eminently successful"', ibid., 1 February 1879, p. 3.

p. 244 'making use of language calculated', ibid., 8 January 1879, p. 2.

p. 244 'a passionate tempered man', ibid., 28 May 1879, p. 2.

p. 244 'Carr pointed out in a letter', ibid., 11 June 1879, p. 2.

p. 244 'he sued his "kind friend's" brother', ibid., 5 November 1879, p. 2.

p. 245 'The third and fourth articles had been about', ibid., 19 July 1879, p. 2.

p. 246 'If the decision of the Bench', ibid., 8 November 1879, p. 2.

p. 246 'In May he was entertaining', *Newcastle Morning Herald and Miners' Advocate*, 28 May 1880, p. 8.

p. 246 'Carr stayed at the Crown and Anchor', *Maitland Mercury and Hunter River General Advertiser*, 12 June 1880, p. 6.

p. 246 'on 5 June he announced', ibid., 5 June 1880, p. 4.
pp. 246–7 'living at "Tyneside Cottage', ibid., 26 June 1880, p. 2.
p. 247 'DR CARR may be seen', ibid., 20 October 1883, p. 1.
p. 247 'from his lower lip "without pain"', ibid., 4 September 1880, p. 4.
p. 247 'a school prize-giving night', ibid., 25 December 1880, p. 4.
p. 247 'a clergyman's talk', ibid., 26 August 1880, p. 3.
p. 247 'half-yearly meeting of the Morpeth School of Arts', ibid., 5 July 1883, p. 2.
p. 248 'His Woodville lecture', ibid., 30 August 1883, p. 7.
p. 248 'In Copeland he drew', ibid., 29 April 1880, p. 7.
p. 248 'though in Clarence Town', ibid., 30 October 1883, p. 4.
p. 248 'was crowded each night', ibid., 3 May 1884, p. 4.
p. 248 'It is expected that the Morpeth doctor', *Newcastle Morning Herald and Miners' Advocate*, 13 December 1884, p. 4.
p. 248 'to Tamworth, Armidale, Cootamundra and Yass', ibid., 28 May 1881, p. 8; *Australian Town and Country Journal*, 17 March 1883, p. 14; *Cootamundra Herald*, 4 March 1885, p. 4; *Riverine Grazier*, 13 June 1885, p. 2.
p. 249 'lecturing at places like Wellington', *Evening News*, 25 June 1884, p. 6.
p. 249 'Wondering what Dr. Carr could have to say', *Evening Post*, 31 July 1884, p. 2.
p. 249 'I may state that as late', *Maitland Mercury and Hunter River General Advertiser*, 19 January 1884, p. 14.
p. 249 'Carr was elected', ibid., 12 February 1884, p. 2.
p. 250 'lecturing tirelessly around Newcastle', *Newcastle Morning Herald and Miners' Advocate*, 18 and 22 December 1884, p. 2.
p. 250 'We regret that we cannot allow', ibid., 6 December 1884, p. 4.

p. 250 'We have not been informed', ibid., 24 September 1885, p. 6.

p. 250 'has suffered a bout of rheumatism', ibid., 21 January 1886, p. 4.

p. 250 'an attack of paralysis', *Waikato Times*, 27 February 1886, p. 2.

p. 250 'gigantic figure', *Newcastle Morning Herald and Miners' Advocate*, 10 October 1885, p. 4.

p. 251 'Several subjects were made to cut', *Glenn Innes Examiner and General Advertiser*, 8 December 1885, p. 2.

p. 251 'He also wrote a critique', *Newcastle Morning Herald and Miners' Advocate*, 20 February 1886, p. 7.

p. 251 'Business wasn't good', *Waikato Times*, 27 February 1886, p. 2.

p. 251 'Carr's letters home', *Maitland Mercury and Hunter River Advertiser*, 9 February 1886, p. 4.

p. 251 'On the morning of 15 January', *Newcastle Morning Herald and Miner Advocate*, 20 January 1886, p. 3.

p. 251 'easily a fatal dose', Modi, Rai Bahadur Jaising P, *A Textbook of Medical Jurisprudence and Toxicology*, Elsevier, Amsterdam, 2013, p. 620.

p. 252 'From a book found in his possession', *Glen Innes Examiner*, 19 January 1886, p. 2.

p. 252 'News of Carr's death', *Evening News*, 20 January 1886, p. 6.

p. 252 'She arrived at Glen Innes', *ibid.*, 20 January 1886, p. 6.

p. 253 'Her husband was buried', *ibid.*, 20 January 1886, p. 6.

p. 253 'Carr often wrote "strangely concocted" letters', *Maitland Mercury and Hunter River Advertiser*, 9 February 1886, p. 4.

p. 253 'Jane also died', New South Wales Death Certificate 34/1891.

p. 253 'suffered a stroke', research by George Bev Giveen, descendent of John Ireland through his son William.

p. 253 'Monica Carr wed', New South Wales Marriage Certificate 2974/1892.

p. 253 'Monica had no children', *records.nsw.gov.au/item/768075.*

p. 253 'Carr's "remarkably chequered" career', *Queanbeyan Age*, 21 January 1886, p. 2.

p. 253 'There are thousands who remember', *Waikato Times*, 27 February 1886, p. 2.

p. 253 'A lecture that he'd often delivered', *Wanganui Chronicle*, 16 March 1876, p. 2.

p. 253 'What is this life?', *North Otago Times*, 20 February 1877, p. 2.

p. 256 'Alas he's passed away from aye', Phillips, Peter J, *Kill or Cure: Lotions, Potions, Characters and Quacks of Early Australia*, Rigby, Adelaide, 1978, p. 142.

ACKNOWLEDGMENTS

With extra special thanks to Bev Giveen and Maureen Robinson (John Ireland's descendents) and to Dr Peter Stanbury, librarian at the Australian Society of Anaesthetists' Richard Baily Library.

ABOUT THE AUTHOR

Catherine Jinks (born 1963) is an Australian writer of fiction books for all age groups. She has won many awards including the Children's Book Council of Australia Book of the Year Award four times, the Victorian Premier's Literary Award, the Aurealis Award for science fiction, the IBBY Australia Ena Noël Encouragement Award, the Adelaide Festival Award, and the Davitt Award for crime fiction. In 2000 she received the Prime Minister's Medal for her contribution to Australian Children's Literature.